Critical discourse analysis

LANGUAGE IN SOCIAL LIFE SERIES

Series Editor: Professor Christopher N. Candlin

Critical discourse analysis: the critical study of language

Norman Fairclough

An imprint of **Pearson Education**

Harlow, England · London · New York · Reading, Massachusetts · San Francisco
Toronto · Don Mills, Ontario · Sydney · Tokyo · Singapore · Hong Kong · Seoul
Taipei · Cape Town · Madrid · Mexico City · Amsterdam · Munich · Paris · Milan

Pearson Education Limited
Edinburgh Gate
Harlow
Essex CM20 2JE
England

and Associated Companies throughout the world

Visit us on the World Wide Web at:
http://www.pearsoned.co.uk

First published 1995

ISBN 0 582 21980 9 Csd
ISBN 0 582 21984 1 Ppr

British Library Cataloguing-in-Publication Data

A catalogue record for this book is
available from the British Library

Library of Congress Cataloging-in-Publication Data

Fairclough, Norman, 1941–
      Critical discourse analysis : papers in the critical study of
   language / Norman Fairclough.
         p. cm. — (Language in social life series)
      Chiefly a collection of previously published articles and essays,
   1980-1993.
      Includes bibliographical references and index.
      Contents: Critical and descriptive goals in discourse analysis —
   Register, power, and sociosemantic change — Discourse
   representation in media discourse — Language and ideology —
   Discourse, change, and hegemony — What might we mean by "enterprise
   discourse?" — Critical discourse analysis and the marketization of
   public discourse : the universities — Ideology and identity change
   in political television — Discourse and text : linguistic and
   intertextual analysis within discourse analysis — Critical language
   awareness and self-identity in education — The appropriacy of
   "appropriateness."
      ISBN 0-582-21980-9. — ISBN 0-582-21984-1 (pbk.)
      1. Discourse analysis. 2. Sociolinguistics. I. Title.
   II. Series.
   P302.F34   1995
   306.4′4-dc20
                                                              94-23292
                                                                 CIP

12 11
07 06 05

Set by 15 in 10/12pt Monophoto Palatino
Printed in Malaysia (LSP)

Contents

General Editor's Preface

One of the powerful affirmations of interest in the underlying themes of the *Language in Social Life Series* has been the success accorded to Norman Fairclough's introductory book in the Series: *Language and Power*. Although itself well rooted in an existing tradition at that time of what has since come to be termed, not unproblematically, Critical Discourse Analysis, *Language and Power* has proved to offer a wide range of students of linguistics, language studies and professional education a framework and a means of exploring the inbrications between language and social-institutional practices and between these, taken together, with broader social and political structures. Its innovation for students of linguistics in particular, was to critique some of the premises and the constructs underlying mainstream studies in sociolinguistics, conversational analysis and pragmatics, to demonstrate the need of these sub-disciplines to engage with social and political issues of power and hegemony in a dynamic and historically informed manner, and yet as a fundamental part of this process of linking the micro to the macro to reaffirm the traditional disciplinary centre and basis of the subject, the detailed and polysystemic description of language variation. For students of professional disciplines, of law, medicine, health care, social work, language and literacy education, Fairclough's formulations in that book have proved especially productive, allowing the practitioners of such disciplines whose professional practices are most obviously languaged, a means of describing, interpreting and explaining how their practices are discursively accomplished and thus offering a way of clarifying the ideological bases of the purposes, and methods of the professions themselves.

Readers of *Language and Power* will recall the presence there of other themes which have subsequently found expression in Norman Fairclough's other writings since that publication, the relationship between the study of discourse and sociocultural change in post-industrial market economies, notably dealt with in depth in his 1992 publication for Polity Press, *Discourse and Social Change*, the importance he has always accorded to the analysis of the *texture* of texts in undertaking social institutional research, as evidenced in his publications in the *Journal of Pragmatics* and *Discourse & Society*, and perhaps of greatest potential significance because of its engagement with schooling, the writings with his colleagues from Lancaster and elsewhere in defining the framework for and extensively illustrating the practice of critical language awareness in the curriculum, collected in his 1992 edited publication under that title in Longman's *Real Language Series*.

Notwithstanding however this productive interest from such a variety of audiences, and in part because of it, it is clear that to some commentators and practitioner-researchers the very scope and attraction of critical discourse analysis has placed it at some risk of theoretical blurring. This is a concern shared by Norman Fairclough himself as he makes plain in his Introduction to this collection of his papers. For some there is an urgent need to re-engage with central constructs of power and knowledge, and above all, ideology, to question what is this 'real world' of social relations in institutional practices that is represented linguistically, for others this has led to calls to re-examine the apparent determinism of the relationship between the macro and the micro, for others again to expand our focus to encompass not only what is discoursed but what is not, for some whose definition of discourse is centrally bound to the organization of meanings, to balance what they see as too great a the critical study of *production* with an equally critical study of *consumption.*. Methodologically also, despite some quite notable recent achievements in the critical analysis of spoken discourse in workplace settings and professional encounters, as well as more extensively in the more tractable fields of written texts, there is continuing practical concern about the doability in the*full* descriptive, interpretive and explanatory sense, of critical linguistic research. There is a good deal of so-called critical analysis going on which removes texts (usually portable and written) from their conditions of production and reception in particular sites and on the basis of rather superficial linguistic and content analysis makes too large a leap to the macro. Fairclough has warned about that before, and rightly so. Not that we should underestimate how the impeccably grounded polysystemic approach of Firth and Halliday poses considerable descriptive demands, suggesting as it does and as Fairclough reformulates here, that discourse analysis is not a 'level' of analysis as, say, phonology or lexico-grammar, but an exploration of how 'texts' at *all* levels work within sociocultural practices. This, taken with the acknowledged difficulty of undertaking collaborative interdisciplinary research, suggests that Norman Fairclough's consistent emphasis on the need for critical discourse analysis to establish a viable research methodology is both cautionary and well-judged.

These are not intended as arguments *contra*, ; what they point up is that Fairclough's papers have not only opened a rich and for many like myself a determining avenue for linguistic research, they have also set an agenda for linguists' education and practice which requires a close connection between descriptive ability, an engagement with issues of social and individual concern, an involvement with and from the points of view and experiences of those with whom we research, an informed-ness about institutional practices in the context of a dynamic and struggling social order and a grounding in those social theorists, amply referred to in these pages, whose engagement in different ways has been with the production of the social through discourse. Above all, as van Dijk made plain in a recent Editorial for *Discourse & Society*, critical discourse analysis needs always to keep its audience in view, asking '*to whom its results with be relevant and useful*'. Norman Fairclough's work by any account has kept all these concerns in view, as these papers amply demonstrate.

There was no doubt, then, that the opportunity to publish a collection of Norman Fairclough's key papers from the period of 1983 to 1993, some published and some written for this collection, would offers readers of the *Language in Social Life Series* a means themselves of engaging with these concerns. Four themes structure the collection:

- the relationship between language, ideology and power
- the relationship between discourse and sociocultural change
- the centrality of textual analysis to social research
- the principles and practice of critical language awareness

Crossing these governing themes of Fairclough's research we can identify three central constructs of critical discourse analysis:

- text and the study of 'texture'
- discoursal practices and the concept 'orders of discourse'
- sociocultural practices and the concept of 'culture'

The dynamic interplay between these themes and these constructs enables the reader to engage with what for me is the overriding metaphor uniting these papers, highlighted by Norman Fairclough in his discussion of the contributions of Bakhtin and Gramsci, that of the tension and struggle between the creativity potential of Bakhtin's heteroglossia, the centripetal-centrifugal intertextuality of texts, and Gramsci's hegemony, that 'stabilized configuration of discursive practices' as Fairclough puts it, which acts to control and constrain creativity in discourse.

What is there for the reader's action, apart, that is from a vicarious and vigorous engagement with these issues? Here, I believe, will be the merit in this book. What critical discourse analysis needs most now is practical but informed, reasoned and above all collaborative action; expanding the universe of inquiry to Gumperz's crucial sites, identifying with those most chiefly engaged, and collaborating in an explanatory analysis of the production and reception of the discoursed and the non-discoursed communication at critical moments in those sites. Such work is not application of some pre-set code of principles, it is *praxis* and as such constantly reengages theory and practice in a continuously self-informing process of inquiry. What it does do is to challenge our capacities, both technical and conceptual, as linguists and discourse analysts to handle variation in a multi-level mode as boundaries between discourses constantly change symbiotically with social change; in its emphasis on the conditions of reception of texts it compels engagement with cognitive processes and requires them to be socially and critically grounded, and to be augmented by understanding of the organizational routines governing such reception; it invites ethnographic research not as some convenient and occasional adjunct but as central to the process of linguistic inquiry; it directs attention to the historicity of discursive events and to the archaeology of knowledge and experience, and as such, crucially privileges the life experiences of those with whom we both collaborate as researchers and as co-providers of data and thus restores in part the inherent imbalances between those who study and those who act.

Seen in this way, Norman Fairclough's *Critical Discourse Analysis* is not just a reflective study of those issues canvassed above. It takes on a rather different role. It suggests rather plainly, if you read it that way, how we might construct a linguistics for the next century which in addition to its pervasively critical and explanatory focus would require interdisciplinarity as a central principle, without however compromising in any way on the central capacity to describe. Consider only Fairclough's discussions on Halliday and Foucault on the engagement of textual analysis with the analysis of discursive practices and socio-cultural practices as one such example. The issue becomes rapidly clear; whether the academy and its constricting siloisation could stand the strain. The answer, in my experience and that of my co-workers, is that while we agitate and wait inside the walls, we simultaneously engage our maximum efforts with those who work with language in the community, where talk is work and where the issues so clearly presented and critiqued here are the very matter of everyday existence and activity.

Professor Christopher N Candlin
Centre for Language in Social Life
Department of Linguistics
Macquarie University, Sydney
Australia

Acknowledgements

We are grateful to the following for permission to reproduce copyright material:

Department of Trade and Industry for the extract 'The Design Initiative' taken from a brochure about The Enterprise Initiative Consultancy Scheme (EICS) produced in 1989; Elsevier Science B.V., Amsterdam, The Netherlands, for the paper 'Critical and Descriptive Goals in Discourse Analysis' by Norman Fairclough originally published in *Journal of Pragmatics*, 9, 1985, 739–763; Foris Publications for the paper 'Discourse Representation in Media Discourse' by Norman Fairclough from *Sociolinguistics*, 17, 1988, 125–39; The Guardian for the article 'MPs urge harsher heroin penalties' by David Hencke in *The Guardian* (c) 24.5.85; Lancaster University for extracts from their University Prospectuses 1967–8, 1986–7, and 1993; Longman Group Ltd for the paper 'The appropriacy of 'appropriateness'' by Norman Fairclough from *Critical Language Awareness*, Norman Fairclough (ed.) (c) Longman 1992; Mirror Syndication International for the article 'War on Drug Pushers' by John Desborough in *The Daily Mirror* 24.5.85; News Group Newspapers Ltd for the article 'Call up forces in drug battle' by David Kemp in *The Sun* 24.5.85; International Thomson Publishing Services Ltd for the paper 'What Might We Mean by 'Enterprise Discourse'?' by Norman Fairclough from *Enterprise Discourse*, R. Keat and N Abercrombie (eds) (Routledge, Chapman & Hall, 1980); Sage Publications Ltd for the papers 'Discourse and text: linguistic and intertextual analysis within discourse analysis' by Norman Fairclough from *Discourse and Society*, 3, 1992, 193–217 and 'Critical discourse analysis and the maketisation of public discourse: the universities' by Norman Fairclough from *Discourse and Society* 4, 1993, 133–68; Sheffield Hallam University, University of Newcastle and University of Nottingham for their advertisements that appeared in the *Times Higher*

Education Supplement 22.5.92; The University of Birmingham for the paper 'Language and Ideology' by Norman Fairclough from the *English Language Research Journal* 3, 1989, 9–27.

General introduction

This book is a collection of papers on critical discourse analysis which were written between 1983 and 1992 and (except for papers 5, 8 and 10 which have not been previously published) appeared between 1985 and 1993 (see Acknowledgements for publication details).[1] I have grouped the ten papers into four sections which correspond to major concerns of my work over this period; Language, ideology and power, Discourse and sociocultural change, Textual analysis in social research, and Critical language awareness. Although this grouping reflects a diversity of concerns, there are substantial thematic overlaps between sections and papers, all of which are orientated towards a single broad objective; to develop ways of analysing language which address its involvement in the workings of contemporary capitalist society.

Each section has an introduction which summarizes the papers and identifies salient themes. But I shall begin this general introduction with a broad characterization of the concerns of the four sections. This will provide a basis for the main business of the introduction: to identify a range of issues and problems which are, I believe, on the current agenda of critical discourse analysis.

The three papers in the first section (Language, ideology and power) reflect my early (roughly 1983–87) concerns in this field with the development of an analytical framework – a theory and method – for studying language in its relation to power and ideology. This framework is seen here and throughout as a resource for people who are struggling against domination and oppression in its linguistic forms. I call this framework, which in various versions informs the whole book as well as other publications (Fairclough 1989, 1992a, 1992b, forthcoming), critical discourse analysis. Power is conceptualized both in terms of asymmetries between participants in discourse events, and in terms of unequal capacity to control how texts are produced, distributed and consumed (and hence the shapes of texts) in particular sociocultural contexts. A range of properties of texts is regarded as potentially ideological, including features of vocabulary and metaphors, grammar, presuppositions and implicatures, politeness conventions, speech-exchange (turn-taking) systems, generic structure, and style. The first paper emphasizes the ideological importance of the implicit, taken-for-granted assumptions (presuppositions) upon which the orderliness and coherence of texts depend. The power to control discourse is seen as the power to sustain particular discursive practices with particular ideological investments in dominance over other alternative (including oppositional) practices.

The second section (Discourse and sociocultural change) also includes four papers, which were written between 1989 and 1992. The concern in this section is to integrate discourse analysis with social analysis of sociocultural change, developing the thematization of change which is already a feature of paper 3 in Section A. The role of discourse within the society and culture is seen as historically variable, and I argue that in modern and contemporary ('late modern') society discourse has taken on a major role in sociocultural reproduction and change. CDA is consolidated here as a 'three-dimensional' framework where the aim is to map three separate forms of analysis onto one another: analysis of (spoken or written) language texts, analysis of discourse practice (processes of text production, distribution and consumption) and analysis of discursive events as instances of sociocultural practice. A characteristic of the framework is that it combines a Bakhtinian theory of genre (in analysis of discourse practice) and a Gramscian theory of hegemony (in analysis of sociocultural practice). The former highlights the productivity and creativity of discourse practice and its realization in texts which are heterogeneous in their forms and meanings, the heterogeneity emanating from their intertextuality; texts are constituted from other already produced texts and from potentially diverse text types (genres, discourses). The theory of hegemony highlights both how power relations constrain and control productivity and creativity in discourse practice, and how a particular relatively stabilized configuration of discourse practices ('order of discourse') constitutes one domain of hegemony. Change is investigated in terms of the mapping onto one another of shifting, unstable sociocultural practices (e.g. where new domains are in the process of being 'marketized'), a complex and creative discourse practice involving new combinations of genres and discourses, and texts which are heterogeneous in forms and meanings. The heterogeneities of texts are a sensitive indicator of sociocultural contradictions, and a sensitive barometer of their evolution. A particular focus is what I call 'technologization of discourse' – calculated intervention to shift discursive practices as part of the engineering of social change.

The third and fourth sections are shorter than the first two, consisting of one and two papers respectively. The paper in Section C (Textual analysis in social research) is addressed mainly to discourse analysts based outside language studies, and is an argument for the inclusion of a substantial element of textual analysis within discourse analysis as a method of social research in various disciplines. As well as linguistic analysis, textual analysis here includes intertextual analysis of how available genres and discourses are drawn upon and combined in texts. Section D (Critical language awareness) is concerned with educational applications of critical work in discourse analysis and more generally in language studies, in programmes for stimulating a critical awareness of language. Such programmes are on the one hand supportive of the general case for language awareness work in schools which has been made in recent years (Hawkins 1984, NCLE 1985, DES 1988, DES 1989), but on the other hand critical of the views of language and language education which are built into such work. In particular, the papers in this section include a detailed critique of the concept of 'appropriateness' which grounds theories of language variation which are prevalent in language education, and sketch out a view of learning which stresses the integration of critical language awareness both with past language experience and with the developing capacities of learners, individually and collectively, to engage not only in conventional but also innovative and unconventional language practice. Another concern is the possibility and danger of CDA partially shifting its focus in the context of educational applications from critique to involvement in the production of alternative practices.

The discussion of issues and problems in critical discourse analysis which will occupy the rest of this introduction will be organized around the three dimensions of the analytical framework sketched out above: text, discourse practice, sociocultural practice. I discuss in turn issues relating to text and language, genre and orders of discourse, and society and culture. Part of my objective here is to point to and engage in controversies which have arisen from the project of critical discourse analysis, differences between critical discourse analysts and scholars in adjacent fields, and differences amongst critical discourse analysts. I shall also identify some limitations of the work represented in this book, and indicate directions for the future.

TEXT AND LANGUAGE

A text is traditionally understood to be a piece of written language – a whole 'work' such as a poem or a novel, or a relatively discrete part of a work such as a chapter. A rather broader conception has become common within discourse analysis, where a text may be either written or spoken discourse, so that, for example, the words used in a conversation (or their written transcription) constitute a text. In cultural analysis, by contrast, texts do not need to be linguistic at all; any cultural artefact – a picture, a building, a piece of music – can be seen as a text. This view of text has its dangers; it can obscure important distinctions between different types of cultural artefact, and make the concept of a text rather nebulous by extending it too far. Nevertheless, I think it is necessary to move further towards this view than I have done in these papers, where a text is mainly understood as written or spoken language. A strong argument for doing so is that texts in contemporary society are increasingly multi-semiotic; texts whose primary semiotic form is language increasingly combine language with other semiotic forms. Television is the most obvious example, combining language with visual images, music and sound effects. But written (printed) texts are also increasingly becoming multisemiotic texts, not only because they incorporate photographs and diagrams, but also because the graphic design of the page is becoming an ever more salient factor in evaluation of written texts. We can continue regarding a text as a primarily linguistic cultural artefact, but develop ways of analysing other semiotic forms which are co-present with language, and especially how different semiotic forms interact in the multisemiotic text. This poses a challenge to critical discourse analysis which is already being taken up in the development of a 'social semiotics' (Hodge and Kress 1988, Kress and van Leeuwen 1990).

Another challenge is to convince the increasing number of discourse analysts whose disciplinary base is outside linguistics or language studies that textual analysis should mean analysis of the *texture* of texts, their form and organization, and not just commentaries on the 'content' of texts which ignore texture. The premise of this argument is that the sorts of social and cultural phenomena that such analysts are orientated towards are realized in textural properties of texts in ways which make them extraordinarily sensitive indicators of sociocultural processes, relations, and change. Social and cultural analyses can only be enriched by this textural evidence, which is partly linguistic and partly intertextual – partly a matter of how links between one text and other texts and text types are inscribed in the surface of the text. At issue here is the classical problem of the relationship between form and content. My contention is that no analysis of text content and meaning can be satisfactory which fails to attend to what one might call the *content of texture* (or, the content of its form). (See chapter 8 for supporting examples.)

There are problems and challenges for discourse analysis in this position. Considerations of texture may always in principle be an important element in discoursally orientated sociocultural research, but existing models for textural analysis are not always very effective in providing ways of analysing texture which are relevant to the sociocultural agenda. A great deal more work is needed on the development of socially relevant models for text analysis. Take the case of *absences* from texts. Textual analysis can often give excellent insights about what is 'in' a text, but what is absent from a text is often just as significant from the perspective of sociocultural analysis (see paper 8 for examples). For instance, political analysts of media may be particularly concerned to know whether reports on the Gulf War did or did not include the topic of civilian casualties, as well as how that topic was handled texturally where it was included, in terms of thematization, foregrounding or backgrounding – see Fairclough (forthcoming, chapter 6) for analysis of a particular example. A framework for textual analysis which allows for a systematic focus upon absences through more sustained comparative analysis of texts is described in Van Leeuwen (1993). This depends upon a systemicist view of text as choice, operationalized as networks of systems of options which are selected amongst in the production of texts.

Surprisingly, on the face of it, the contrast between presence in and absence from texts is not a sharp one. In addition to (significant) absences from a text, what is 'in' a text may be explicit or implicit. Two categories of implicit content which have received extensive discussion are presupposition and implicature (Levinson 1983). The implicit content of a text is a sort of halfway house between presence and absence. In the case of a standard example such as *The Soviet threat cost the West dear*, the presupposition – that there is a Soviet threat – is absent from the text in this sense that it is not actually asserted there, and is commonly seen as supplied by the listener or reader in interpreting the text. On the other hand, the expression *the Soviet threat* and in particular the definite article (the) 'triggers' (Levinson) the presupposition, so the latter is in that sense present in the text. The distinction between what is explicit and what is implicit in a text is of considerable importance in sociocultural analysis. Analysis of implicit content can provide valuable insights into what is taken as given, as common sense. It also gives a way into ideological analysis of texts, for ideologies are generally implicit assumptions (see paper 3). One might also include on the presence–absence scale the relative foregrounding or backgrounding of explicit textual content (see Fairclough forthcoming chapter 6). The ideological importance of implicit textual content has received attention in French critical discourse analysis, but not enough attention so far within work published in English. The concept of 'preconstructed' has been used to give an intertextual understanding of implicit content (presupposition); the unsaid of a text, what it takes as given, is taken as the already-said-elsewhere, the form in which a text is shaped and penetrated by (ideological) elements from domains of prior textual practice (see Pêcheux 1982, Williams forthcoming).

Texts are social spaces in which two fundamental social processes simultaneously occur: cognition and representation of the world, and social interaction. A multifunctional view of text is therefore essential. I have followed systemic linguistics (Halliday 1978) in assuming that language in texts always simultaneously functions ideationally in the representation of experience and the world, interpersonally in constituting social interaction between participants in discourse, and textually in tying parts of a text together into a coherent whole (a text, precisely) and tying texts to situational contexts (e.g. through situational deixis). This multifunctionality of language in texts can be used to operationalize theoretical claims about the socially constitutive properties of discourse and text (Foucault 1972). Texts in their ideational functioning constitute systems of knowledge and belief (including what Foucault refers to as 'objects'), and in their interpersonal functioning they constitute social subjects (or in different terminologies, identities, forms of self) and social relations between (categories of) subjects. Any part of any text can fruitfully be examined in terms of the co-presence and interaction of these constitutive processes. Approaches to (critical) discourse analysis which have an ideational bias (e.g. Potter and Wetherell 1987, Pêcheux 1982, van Dijk 1988) are ill-equipped to capture the interplay between cognition and interaction which is a crucial feature of textual practice. Nor is an ideational bias justified, as it may appear to be on the face of it, by a focus on ideology. Interpersonal aspects of texts may be ideologically invested; indeed, naturalized properties of genres such as the turn-taking system or the pragmatic politeness conventions of medical interviews are perhaps more ideologically potent in modern societies than features of ideational meaning, as a Foucaultian emphasis on the salience of 'technologies' in modern forms of power would suggest (Foucault 1979).

Textual analysis demands diversity of focus not only with respect to functions but also with respect to levels of analysis. Let me stress that discourse analysis itself is not here taken to be a particular level of analysis. For some linguists, it is: 'discourse analysis is analysis of text structure above the sentence' (Sinclair and Coulthard 1975). My view is that 'discourse' is use of language seen as a form of social practice, and discourse analysis is analysis of how texts work within sociocultural practice. Such analysis requires attention to textual form, structure and organization at all levels; phonological, grammatical, lexical (vocabu-lary) and higher levels of textual organization in terms of exchange systems (the distribution of speaking turns), structures of argumenta-tion, and generic (activity type) structures. A working assumption is that any level of organization may be relevant to critical and ideological analysis. Some approaches to critical discourse analysis by contrast have tended to focus just on particular levels (e.g. grammar and lexis in critical linguistics, lexical semantics in earlier French discourse analysis).

It is important to avoid a one-sided emphasis on either repetitive or creative properties of texts. Any text is part repetition, part creation, and texts are sites of tension between centripetal and centrifugal pressures (Bakhtin 1981, 1986). Texts vary in the relative weight of these pressures depending upon their social conditions, so that some texts will be relatively normative whereas others are relatively creative. Centripetal pressures follow from the need in producing a text to draw upon given conventions, of two main classes; a language, and an order of discourse – that is, a historically particular structuring of discursive (text-producing) practices (see further below). More concretely, one obviously has to use English words and sentence structures in produc-ing a text in English, and one has to select amongst the genres and discourses available in the order of discourse. Centrifugal pressures come from the specificity of particular situations of text-production, the fact that situations do not endlessly repeat one another, but are, on the contrary, endlessly novel and problematic in new ways. Texts negotiate the sociocultural contradictions and more loosely 'differences' (Kress 1988) which are thrown up in social situations, and indeed they constitute a form in which social struggles are acted out. For instance, with respect to the ideational function, people deal textually with contradictions or differences in beliefs, knowledges and representations. With respect to the interpersonal function, texts negotiate social relations between people in circumstances of doubt or contestation, and people attempt to work out textually, in their use of language, the dilemmas they face in defining their own identities (Billig *et al.* 1988). Text producers have nothing except given conventions of language and orders of discourse as resources for dealing with centrifugal pressures, but they are able to use these resources in new ways, generating, for instance, new configurations of genres and discourses (see below).

The tension between repetition and creation, centripetal and centrifugal pressures, manifests itself in varying degrees of homogeneity or heterogeneity of textual forms and meanings. A relatively homogeneous text is relatively consistent semantically and formally – a consistent construction of relations between text producer and audience through the text for instance may be partly realized through consistencies of modality. A relatively heterogeneous text may by contrast construct text producer–audience relations in diverse and contradictory ways, partly realized in inconsistent and clashing modalities. The heterogeneities of texts code social contradictions. It is this property of texts that makes them the sensitive indicators of sociocultural processes and change I referred to above in discussing texture. Social contradictions may even be condensed into particular collocations in texts, particular patterns of co-occurrence and mutual predictability between words, for instance, the collocation *enterprise culture* (see paper 5). The homogeneities/heterogeneities of texts can be shown through intertextual analysis of the links between a text and other texts and text types, which is (as I argue in paper 8) a necessary complement to linguistic analysis within the analysis of texts (see also Talbot 1990, Slembrouck 1992). I suggest in paper 7 that ambivalence and disfluency may be consequences of a high level of heterogeneity in texts.

Much work in discourse analysis including critical discourse analysis has focused upon a more or less idealized version of the homogeneous text, and virtually ignored heterogeneous texts, and more generally what Bakhtin (1981) called 'heteroglossia'. This is true of the Birmingham school (Sinclair and Coulthard 1975), earlier work in conversation analysis and in French discourse analysis, and critical linguistics (Fowler *et al.* 1979). Other work has attended to heterogeneity but in limited forms which do not, I think, come to terms with the profound theoretical and methodological implications of heterogeneous texts (see further in below). I would include here more recent work in conversation analysis (for instance, Drew and Heritage 1992 – see also Fairclough 1992c), and the work of Labov and Fanshel on therapeutic discourse (1977).

In the three-dimensional framework for CDA I referred to earlier (text, discourse practice, sociocultural practice), the analysis of discourse practice involves attention to processes of text production, distribution and consumption. This feature of the framework encapsulates what I think is an important principle for critical discourse analysis; that analysis of texts should not be artificially isolated from analysis of institutional and discoursal practices within which texts are embedded. This principle has been recognized in some but not all approaches to CDA (e.g. in van Dijk 1988 but not in Fowler *et al.* 1979). This principle would mean for instance that in analysing the text of a TV programme one should also have regard to the routines and processes of programme production, and the circumstances and practices of audience reception. Text analysis in isolation from audience reception has been widely criticized in media studies, and there has been a shift in attention from the former to the latter (Morley 1980). This argument is very relevant to CDA, for part of the critique is directed at analysts who postulate ideological effects solely on the basis of analysis of texts without considering the diverse ways in which such texts may be interpreted and responded to. But there is a danger here of throwing the baby out with the bathwater, by abandoning textual analysis in favour of analysis of audience reception. The interpretation of texts is a dialectical process resulting from the interface of the variable interpretative resources people bring to bear on the text, *and* properties of the text itself. Textual analysis is therefore an important part, if only a part, of the picture, and must be defended against its critics (Brunsdon 1990).

The principle that textual analysis should be combined with analysis of practices of production and consumption has not been adequately operationalized in the papers collected here. I have referred to text production but rarely to text consumption, and focused only upon the question of how text producers draw upon and restructure orders of discourse, producing new configurations of genres and discourses. There is still a need to bring close textual analysis together with social analysis of organizational routines for producing and consuming texts, and with analysis of specifically discoursal processes within the processes of production and consumption, such as the analysis of how news articles are transformed in the process of their production in Bell (1991), or analysis of how media texts are transformed in audience talk about media (briefly discussed in paper 8, see also Thompson 1990). There is also a need to bring together critical discourse analysis of discursive events with ethnographic analysis of social structures and settings, in the search for what some have called a critical ethnography (Bourne 1992).

Textual analysis presupposes a theory of language and a grammatical theory, and one problem for critical discourse analysis is to select from amongst those available. I have referred at various points to systemic linguistics, which has a number of strengths from the perspective of CDA. It is a functional theory of language orientated to the question of how language is structured to tackle its primary social functions. Thus grammar is seen as structured by the three (macro) functions of language I referred to earlier, the ideational, interpersonal and textual functions. It is also a textually orientated theory concerned with producing grammatical descriptions which are useable in textual analysis. The view of language as social semiotic (Halliday 1978) incorporates an orientation to mapping relations between language (texts) and social structures and relations. While systemic linguistics is thus a congenial theory to work with, in the longer term critical discourse analysis should, as Kress has argued (1993), be informing the development of a new social theory of language which may include a new grammatical theory.

GENRE AND ORDERS OF DISCOURSE

The discourse practice dimension of the three-dimensional analytical framework introduced above shows, for any discursive event, how text producers and interpreters draw upon the socially available resources that constitute the order of discourse. As I indicated above, the two major centripetal forces in any discursive event are the language and the order of discourse. Discursive events are, on the one hand, dependent upon and shaped by them, but on the other hand cumulatively restructure them. Intertextual analysis links the text and discourse practice dimensions of the framework, and shows where a text is located with respect to the social network of orders of discourse – how a text actualizes and extends the potential within orders of discourse.

Discourse practice, orders of discourse, and intertextual analysis have a crucial mediating role in this framework; they mediate the relationship between texts on the one hand and (nontextual parts of) society and culture on the other. What I mean is that (a) the order of discourse is the social order in its discoursal facet – or, the historical impress of sociocultural practice on discourse; (b) any discursive event necessarily positions itself in relation to this historical legacy, selectively reproducing or transforming it; (c) the specificity of the particular sociocultural practice which a discursive event is a part of is realized first in *how* the discursive event draws upon and works upon the order of discourse, which is in turn realized in features of texts, so that the text–sociocultural practice link is mediated by discourse practice. As this formulation implies, discourse practice ensures attention to the historicity of discursive events by showing both their continuity with the past (their dependence upon given orders of discourse) and their involvement in making history (their remaking of orders of discourse).

Other approaches to (critical) discourse analysis neglect or play down the discourse practice dimension and intertextuality. A case in point is recent work within conversation analysis which focuses upon institutional discourse and upon relationships between 'talk-in-interaction' and social structure (Boden and Zimmerman 1991, Drew and Heritage 1992). This work shows continuity with earlier conversation analysis in its concern to minimize appeal to the traditional categories of social structure in analysing talk, and to find ways of excluding such categories from the analysis. Schegloff (1992) for instance, formulates principles of 'relevance' and 'procedural consequentiality'; a social category should enter the analysis only if it is manifestly orientated to by (relevant for) participants, and consequential for the way in which the text is structured or organized. I would argue that social categories which do not have such manifest consequences may nevertheless be necessary to the analysis of a text in the dimension of discourse practice – they may be relevant to the field of practices within which the text is located even if they are not manifestly consequential for the text itself. For instance, in a mixed-gender job interview the category of participant gender may apparently be neither relevant nor procedurally consequential on Schegloff's criteria, yet analysis of discourse practice may show its absence to be a marked and significant absence when this job interview is located with respect to the extant range of practices of job interview – perhaps, for instance, because a feminist political position is being taken up.

Certain categories which have been of key importance in the analysis of social structure will of course do badly on Schegloff's criteria for analytical relevance, including social class, power (in a social structural rather than a situational sense) and ideology. Analysis of discourse practice by contrast requires such categories. We can best see this in relation to what I want to call hidden variability. Various approaches to discourse analysis, including not only conversation analysis but also, for instance, the Birmingham school (Sinclair and

Coulthard 1975), ignore an important type of variability in language use (discourse), through an often implicit reliance upon what I call in paper 11 an appropriateness theory of language variability – a theory which assumes a rather straightforward matching between types of social situation and language varieties, such that each social situation is associated with a single, unitary variety. The hidden variability is the variability of practice within particular social situations – within the lesson, within the medical consultation, within the media interview. My contention is that a social situation is better regarded as having its own order of discourse within the social network of orders of discourse, in which different discourse types are ordered in relation to each other. Such alternative practices are characteristically ordered in dominance in the sense that there may be a dominant ('normal', naturalized) practice and dominated (marginalized, 'alternative') practices. The category of power in a structural sense (and perhaps the category of social class) is needed to make sense of the ordering and dominance relations between practices *and* how people select from amongst available practices on specific occasions. The category of ideology is needed to make sense of the differences between practices; practices may be ideologically invested, and diversity of practices may be part of ideological struggles (see paper 1 and *passim*).

I have adapted the concept of order of discourse from Foucault (1981) to refer to the ordered set of discursive practices associated with a particular social domain or institution (e.g. the lecture, the seminar, counselling, and informal conversation, in an academic institution), and boundaries and relationships between them. Discursive practices may be relatively strongly or relatively weakly demarcated – the boundaries may be rigid or permeable, and discursive practices may be in various sorts of relationship. They may be in the complementary sort of relationship assumed in theories of appropriateness (discussed in paper 10) such that different discursive practices are used in different social situations, but they may also be alternatives in the same social situation, and may be in relationships of opposition. For instance, doctors or teachers may select or reject available discursive practices for modelling their medical consultations or classes on the basis of theoretical or ideological position (see above). In addition to the 'local' orders of discourse of particular social domains, it is useful to refer to a societal order of discourse to chart the relationships and boundaries between 'local' orders of discourse (e.g. between orders of discourse of the classroom, peer group, and family). Boundaries between and within orders of discourse are constantly shifting, and change in orders of discourse is itself part of sociocultural change.

I described the discourse practice dimension of the framework as concerned with the production, consumption and *distribution* of texts. Distribution, how texts circulate within orders of discourse, can be investigated in terms of 'chain' relationships (as opposed to paradigmatic or 'choice' relationships) within orders of discourse. There are more or less settled chains of discursive practices within and between orders of discourse across which texts are shifted and transformed in systematic ways (Fairclough 1992a). For instance, in the mass media there are chains connecting various public orders of discourse (politics, law, science, etc.), media orders of discourse, and orders of discourse in the private domain (the domain of reception). Texts are transformed in systematic ways across these boundaries, and even within media orders of discourse the text production process may involve complex chains of discursive practices and transformations (described in Bell 1991). Distribution is a relatively neglected issue which merits more attention.

One area of controversy concerns the constitution of what I have referred to above as the constituent discursive practices of an order of discourse. In particular, there has been a great deal of debate recently over conflicting views of genre, which has been made sharper through policy implications for the teaching of genre in schools (see, for example, Martin 1989, Threadgold 1989, van Leeuwen 1987). In my view, the debate has not been helped by a common failure to distinguish different levels of abstraction. The primary distinction is between actual texts, and the conventions which people draw upon in producing and interpreting them. A secondary distinction within conventions is between what I shall call text types, and the more abstract constituents of text types (genre and discourse in particular). When people produce or interpret texts, they orientate towards conventions as ideal types, by which I mean that texts are produced and interpreted by reference to them but certainly do not simply instantiate them. In saying that conventions have the status of ideal types I am not suggesting they are purely imaginary; there are texts which closely match ideal types (as well as others which do not), so that people learn them from concrete textual experience. Let us work from the most abstract to the most concrete (textual) level.

One issue in the controversy over genre is whether a genre should be understood as a rigid schema made up of stages, all or some obligatory, in a fixed order (see for instance the analysis of narrative in Labov and Waletsky 1967), or whether genres are more flexible, unpredictable, and heterogeneous (Threadgold 1989). If one assumes that texts directly instantiate genres, the former ('schematic') view cannot be sustained as a general view of genre, because many texts manifest complex mixed genres. Nevertheless, the schematic view does have some reality as an ideal type and a convention – and some textual reality, in that some texts do adhere tightly to generic schemata. Even so, even at the level of greatest abstraction, only some genres have a tight schematic structure. One might compare for instance the relatively predictable structuring of a canonical instance of a job interview or the sort of oral narrative Labov and Weletsky are concerned with, and a family conversation over dinner.

Even at this level of abstraction, it is not helpful to conceive of a genre simply in terms of structuring with respect to stages. I regard a genre as a socially ratified way of using language in connection with a particular type of social activity (e.g. interview, narrative, exposition). Such a way of using language is not just a way of staging a text, it also involves particularities of (in the terms of Halliday 1978) 'field' – what social practices are referred to and how they are signified (van Leeuwen 1993), of 'voice' – who the participants are, and how they are constructed, of 'style' – how participant relations are constructed, and of 'mode' – what forms of textualization (not just staging) and of text–context relations apply. We can use the terms voice, style, and mode to refer to these particular facets of genre, and the term 'activity type' (Levinson 1979) to refer specifically to the schematic structuring of a genre in terms of stages. Rather than using field we can use 'discourse'; a discourse is a way of signifying a particular domain of social practice from a particular perspective, and a genre may predictably draw upon a particular range of discourses, though a given discourse may be drawn upon in various genres.

At a lower level of abstraction, text types are those *configurations* of genres (and so of discourses, voices, styles, modes, activity types) which have developed and become conventionalized for particular categories of activity in particular types of social situation. A text type is situationally and historically quite particular, a genre is more abstract, though particular text types may be more or less generically complex, closer to or more distant from genres. One can specify text types at various levels of particularity – for example, news interview, TV news interview, Channel 4 news interview, and so forth. Actual texts may be more or less closely modelled upon text types. In the intertextual analysis of a text, the objective is to describe its 'intertextual configuration', showing for instance how several text types may be simultaneously drawn upon and combined. It follows from what I have said that actual texts can have extremely complex intertextual configurations, though they can also be relatively simple.

This account of genre is rather different from, and I hope more satisfactory than, what readers will find in the papers in this volume. On the one hand, it reflects the critique of a simple schematic view of genre which arises from the work of Bakhtin (1981, 1986) and has more recently been formulated by Kress and Threadgold (1988), and Threadgold (1989). On the other hand, it claims that the schematic view does have force and validity, provided we distinguish between different levels of abstraction. [The framework can accommodate various types of complex intertextuality in texts: sequential intertextuality (see for instance the account of media genres in van Leeuwen (1987)), embedded intertextuality (see the account of therapeutic discourse in Labov and Fanshel 1977), mixed intertextuality (Fairclough 1992a, 1993).] In sequential intertextuality, different stages of generic schema are modelled in different genres, in embedded intertextuality one genre is embedded within another, but in mixed intertextuality it is impossible to ascribe different parts of a text to different genres – even a single clause may be multi-generic. Kress and Threadgold use the term 'genre' across the three levels of abstraction I have distinguished, for what I have called intertextual configuration, and text type, as well as genre. This may capture the dialectical relationship between convention and action, but it strikes me as confusing.

SOCIETY AND CULTURE

I shall raise two major issues under this heading; the need to defend and sustain critical analysis at a time when it is under attack, and the case for focusing upon change within CDA – change in discursive practices as part of wider processes of social and cultural change.

Critical theory[2] and critical analysis are currently under attack from various theoretical quarters, and many analysts are becoming increasingly hesitant in their use of basic theoretical concepts such as power, ideology, class, and even truth/falsity. I see these developments in theory as linked to the defeats and retreats of the left in many countries over the past decade or more, and the emergence of an aggressive 'new right'. This is not to attribute allegiance to the new right to the theorists concerned or indeed to postmodernism as an intellectual movement, but to suggest that they are part of a common social and political climate. In practical terms in contemporary Britain for instance, the attack on critical concepts and positions often appears to be two-pronged, coming from certain social theorists on the one hand and right wing 'think tanks' or government ministers on the other, even granted that the two prongs have little sympathy or contact with each other. I see the situation as one of political and ideological struggle, in which the issues are by no means new. My view is that the abuses and contradictions of capitalist society which gave rise to critical theory have not diminished, nor have the characteristics of discursive practice within capitalist society which gave rise to critical discourse analysis. There is therefore every reason to sustain the critical enterprise against its critics. I shall focus my arguments here upon ideology and critique of ideology.

The concepts of ideology and ideological analysis have recently been criticized from various perspectives. Abercrombie, Hill and Turner (1980) is a critique of the 'dominant ideology thesis' according to which social order is sustained largely through the effects of dominant ideologies in winning the consent or acquiescence of the majority. They question to what extent unitary dominant ideologies exist, argue that people are often capable of resisting and rejecting them in so far as they do, and suggest that a variety of non-ideological (e.g. economic) mechanisms are instrumental in securing the (limited) level of social cohesion that is achieved. As Eagleton (1991) points out, this book was a useful corrective to the tendency of culturalist versions of Marxism to overstate the role of ideology in social reproduction, but it considerably underestimates the contemporary potency of ideology.

A more fundamental attack on ideology comes from post-structuralist and post-modernist theory. One line of argument here is that any form of ideological critique presupposes that the critic has privileged access to the truth, whereas any such claim to truth or knowledge is (as Nietzsche (1886/1990) argued) really just a coded 'will to power' (Foucault 1979). This position is associated with a relativist and nominalist theory of discourse, according to which different discourses are in Wittgenstein's terminology so many 'language games' which are incommensurate, so that one cannot privilege one discourse as a space for evaluating others (Lyotard 1988, Norris 1992). Another line of attack comes from a different quarter. Baudrillard has argued that in postmodernity the distinction between image and reality has collapsed, so that we are living in a hyperreality where it is impossible for instance to separate the images of war on TV and the actual thing (Poster 1988, Norris 1992). Social life has emptied of meaning. Correspondingly, the concept of ideology, which presupposes a distinction between appearance and reality, is superseded. There is an element of truth in Baudrillard's analysis, but he has unjustifiably generalized tendencies in certain domains of social life as absolutes for social life as a whole (Eagleton 1991). The critique of ideology in terms of its truth claims is, I think, a more serious one which I discuss below.

A more indirect way of attacking ideological critique is to use the concept of ideology in a neutral way, without its critical edge (Thompson 1990), as virtually synonymous with 'worldview', so that any group has its particular ideology corresponding to its interests and position in social life. What makes a theory critical is that it takes a 'pejorative' view of ideology as a means through which social relations of power are reproduced. Some critical theories also stress ideology as falsification (or 'false consciousness', Marx and Engels 1976). In my view, particular representations and constructions of the world *are* instrumental (partly in discourse) and important in reproducing domination, they do call for investigation and critique, and the force and specificity of the concept of ideology has come from its deployment in the critique of these particular processes. If the concept of ideology is to be used, it should be used critically.

In tying ideology to social relations of power, I am alluding to asymmetrical relations of power, to domination. Foucault's work in particular has popularized a different understanding of power as a ubiquitous property of the technologies which structure modern institutions, not possessed by or attached to any particular social class, stratum or group (Foucault 1979). My concern is that this sense of power has displaced the former, more traditional one, and more importantly has helped divert attention from the analysis of power asymmetries and relations of domination. An important objective for critical analysis is the elision of power/domination in theory and analysis.

If ideology is tied to power and domination, it has within the Marxist tradition more specifically been tied to class power and domination, including power exercised by the state on behalf of a dominant social class. Recent forms of Marxism which have emphasized (and in some cases over-emphasized) the ideological moment in social reproduction have conceptualized power in terms of Gramsci's concept of hegemony, which foregrounds the winning of consent in the exercise of power. There has also been a relative backgrounding of social class as the focus has shifted to the role of ideology in securing domination especially in gender relations, and in relations between cultural/ethnic groups. It is necessary to extend one's understanding of the role of ideology in this way, but I would stress that the concern in most analysis is with social relations of domination *within a social system* which is capitalist, and dominated by − but not reducible to − relations of class. I believe it is misleading to focus upon, for instance, gender relations (or for that matter class relations) without attention to their functioning within the social system (and therefore to how gender intersects with class, ethnicity, etc.).

There is a danger here in over-emphasizing reproduction. There is nothing mechanical or deterministic about the workings of ideology (see paper 3). It is a domain and focus of struggle, and critique of ideology is itself a theorized form of struggle which dominated social classes, as well as feminists, ethnic minorities, gay people and so forth, have engaged in as part of their struggles. Ideological critique as a part of academic and intellectual activity, including CDA and its educational application as 'critical language awareness' (see papers 9 and 10), should be seen in terms of the relationship between sections of the intellectuals as a social stratum, and these struggles on the part of social classes and other primary social groups. For instance, academic critique of patriarchal ideology has not been sealed off from critique in the wider feminist movement − on the contrary, they have informed each other. A major focus of social struggle is over the shifting alliances and allegiances of intellectuals in the struggles of classes and other primary groups.

In claiming that a discursive event works ideologically, one is not in the first instance claiming that it is false, or claiming a privileged position from which judgements of truth or falsity can be made. One is claiming that it contributes to the reproduction of relations of power. On this view of ideological analysis, attacks on ideological critique because of its supposed privileged truth claims (referred to above) miss their target. But critical (discourse) analysis cannot remain indifferent to questions of truth, be it a matter of omissions or falsifications for persuasive purposes (Herman and Chomsky 1988, Norris 1992), or of falsifying ideological representations. Many ideologies are evaluations (e.g. *women are less intelligent than men*) for which well-groundedness rather than truth is at issue. Of course, discourse analysis cannot *per se* judge the truth or well-groundedness of a proposition, but then critical discourse analysis is just one method to be used within wider critical projects. Judgements of truth and well-groundedness are not just a prerogative arrogantly claimed by intellectuals, they are a constant and necessary part of social life for everyone, including Foucaultians (Dews

1988). Of course there are structures and mechanisms for privileging the judgements of particular social groups and the particular discourses they deploy, including intellectuals. An important emancipatory political objective is to minimize such effects and maximize the conditions for judgements of truth to be compared and evaluated on their merits. Judgements of truth made by intellectuals, including critical analysts, should be seen (like ideology critique in general – see above) in terms of relationships between intellectuals and social classes and groups. Intellectuals should not feel embarrassed about making judgements of truth; on the contrary, like other social groups, they have a responsibility to bring the particular perspective they can contribute into the public domain in debates over the great social and political issues (Norris 1992). Retreating into a helpless relativism when faced with issues such as war crimes in ex-Yugloslavia, which require judgements of truth and falsity, is in my view serious ethical failure, whatever theoretical voices may be used to rationalize it.

Critical discourse analysts sometimes fail adequately to *historicize* their data, that is, on the one hand to specify the particular historical conditions within which it was generated and what its properties and shape owe to these conditions, and on the other hand, to specify what part it plays in wider historical processes. I think that CDA ought in contemporary circumstances to focus its attention upon discourse within the history of the present – changing discursive practices as part of wider processes of social and cultural change – because constant and often dramatic change affecting many domains of social life is a fundamental characteristic of contemporary social experience, because these changes are often constituted to a significant degree by and through changes in discursive practices, and because no proper understanding of contemporary discursive practices is possible that does not attend to that matrix of change. For instance, one major tendency in current sociocultural change thematized in paper 6 is marketization – the reconstruction on a market basis of domains which were once relatively insulated from markets, economically, in terms of social relations, and in terms of cultural values and identities. I argue that marketization is to a significant degree a discoursal process – it is partly constituted through colonization by the discursive practices of market domains, such as advertising. Similarly, sociologists have talked about a process of 'informalisation' (Featherstone 1991) which can in part be discoursally construed as the colonization of public orders of discourse by the discursive practices of the private sphere – what I have called the 'conversationalization' of public discourse (see Fairclough 1994, and paper 6). CDA has a major opportunity here to establish its credentials as a method to be used alongside others in social research on change (see paper 8).

CONCLUSION

CDA has now passed through the first flush of youth, and is embarked upon the maturation process. It is the moment for some consolidation, for some collective thought to be given to the unity and coherence of CDA, its theoretical bases, its methods of analysis, and to its relationship with adjacent areas of study (including linguistics, sociolinguistics, sociology, and other social sciences). This process is already under way.[3] My hope is that the issues I have raised in this introduction will contribute to that debate.

NOTES

1. The papers have been edited to avoid duplication of material and to ensure cross-references.
2. I use the term critical theory here in a generic sense for any theory concerned with critique of ideology and the effects of domination, and not specifically for the critical theory of the Frankfurt School.
3. The establishment of an international journal which focuses on CDA, *Discourse and Society*, is one indicator. Another is the setting up in the European Union and the European Free Trade Area of an Erasmus programme of academic exchange in CDA, and plans by those involved in that programme for a jointly authored introduction to CDA. The authors are to include Ruth Wodak (Austria), Teun van Dijk (Holland), Paul Thibault (Italy), Gunther Kress, Theo van Leeuwen and myself (UK), and Per Linell (Sweden).

LANGUAGE, IDEOLOGY AND POWER

Introduction

The three papers in this section (written 1983–87 and published 1985–89) were mainly working towards the development of an analytical framework for studying connections between language, power and ideology. I called this framework 'critical discourse analysis' (CDA). This work culminated in the publication of *Language and Power* (Fairclough 1989), where critical discourse analysis is viewed as integrating (a) analysis of text, (b) analysis of processes of text production, consumption and distribution, and (c) sociocultural analysis of the discursive event (be it an interview, a scientific paper, or a conversation) as a whole.

Paper 1, 'Critical and descriptive goals in discourse analysis' distinguishes critical discourse analysis from the dominant noncritical, descriptive trend within discourse analysis which was establishing itself within Linguistics departments at the time. The latter is criticized for its lack of concern with explanation – with how discursive practices are socially shaped, or their social effects. I also criticize the concept of 'background knowledge' as an obfuscation of ideological processes in discourse, the preoccupation with 'goals' as based upon an untenable theory of the subject, and the neglect of relations of power manifested for instance in the elevation of conversation between equals to the status of an idealized archetype for linguistic interaction in general.

The critical alternative claims that naturalized implicit propositions of an ideological character are pervasive in discourse, contributing to the positioning of people as social subjects. These include not only aspects of ideational meaning (e.g. implicit propositions needed to infer coherent links between sentences) but also for instance assumptions about social relations underlying interactional practices (e.g. turn-taking systems, or pragmatic politeness conventions). Such assumptions are quite generally naturalized, and people are generally unaware of them and of how they are subjected by/to them. The emphasis in this paper is upon discourse within the social reproduction of relations of domination. The paper suggests a view of critique as embedded within oppositional practice. Opposition and struggle are built into the view of the 'orders of discourse' of social institutions as 'pluralistic', each involving a configuration of potentially antagonistic 'ideological-discursive formations' (IDFs), which are ordered in dominance. The dominance of one IDF over others within an order of discourse results in the naturalization of its (ideological) meanings and practices. Resistance is most likely to come from subjects whose positioning within *other* institutions and orders of discourse provides them with the resources to resist.

The paper does take a dialectical view of the relationship between structure and action. But the emphasis, under the influence of Althusser and French discourse analysis (Althusser 1971, Pêcheux 1982), is upon the determination of action by structures, social reproduction, and the ideological positioning of subjects. Later papers have increasingly emphasized agency and change, and ideology has in some cases become relatively backgrounded. The concept of IDF did not survive this paper; it gave an overly monolithic view of ideological diversity and struggle – well-defined forces in clear relations of opposition. Another characteristic of this early work is the centrality of social class in its view of power. The later relative retreat from a classical left perspective focusing class, ideology and social reproduction is comprehensible in view of political changes and the shifts in theoretical fashions in the 1980s, but I would now see it as rather too hasty.

I would highlight three themes of the paper as particularly significant for later work. First, the claim that ideologies are primarily located in the 'unsaid' (implicit propositions). I later draw upon French discourse analysis for an intertextual account of presuppositions as the 'already-said' or 'preconstructed' (Fairclough 1989, Pêcheux 1982). The second theme is that norms of interaction involving aspects of the interpersonal meaning and forms (e.g. turn-taking systems) may be ideological, in addition to the more widely discussed case of ideational meanings and forms – the 'content' of texts. The third theme is the theorization of power as in part 'ideological/discoursal', the power to shape orders of discourse, to order discursive practices in dominance. Even casual conversation has its conditions of possibility within relations of ideological/discoursal power.

Paper 2, 'Discourse representation in media discourse' contrasts with the preceding theoretical paper in its focus upon linguistic details of texts. On the basis of an analysis of a set of newspaper articles, it suggests tendencies in the representation of discourse ('reported speech') in the media; that the reported discourse is not generally clearly demarcated from the report itself, and that there is generally a focus upon the ideational meaning (the 'content') of the reported discourse and a neglect of its interpersonal meanings and its context. The paper argues that the fine detail of text is in this regard tuned to the social structures and power relations within which the media operate, and has ideological effects in mystifying relations of domination, and sustaining a view of public language and practice as transparent. The paper is thus an application of the emergent critical discourse analysis framework to a specific case. One of the tendencies in media discourse representation that it identifies is what I discuss in later papers as the 'conversationalization' of public discourse – see especially paper 6 below.

Paper 3 'Language and ideology' suggests that the language–ideology relation should be conceptualized within the framework of research on discoursal and sociocultural change. Following Gramsci (Forgacs 1988), the conception of ideology here focuses upon the effects of ideologies rather than questions of truth, and features of texts are seen as ideological in so far as they affect (sustain, undermine) power relations. Ideology is seen as 'located' in both structures (discourse conventions) and events. On the one hand, the conventions drawn upon in actual discursive events, which are structured together within 'orders of discourse' associated with institutions, are ideologically invested in particular ways. On the other hand, ideologies are generated and transformed in actual discursive events – the example I refer to is of ideological creativity in a Margaret Thatcher radio interview. An order of discourse may incorporate in Gramscian terms an 'ideological complex', a configuration of ideologies, and both the ideological complex and the order of discourse may be reconstructed in the course of discursive events. These possible discursive restructurings arise from contradictions in social practice which generate dilemmas for people, which they try to resolve through mixing available discourse conventions in new ways the mixtures being realized in heterogeneities of form and meaning in texts. Orders of discourse are viewed as domains of hegemony and hegemonic (ideological) struggle, within institutions such as education as well as within the wider social formation. In this process the ideological investments of particular discursive practices may change – for instance, the genre of counselling may operate, now counter-hegemonically within resistance to impersonal institutions, now hegemonically as a personalizing stratagem within such institutions. The paper concludes by identifying a role for ideological analysis and critique of discourse within social struggles.

It will be clear from the General Introduction that I am no longer happy with the view of ideology in this paper. But certain features of the discussion of ideology are worth noting; the idea that discourse may be ideologically creative and productive, the concept of ideological complex, the question of whether discursive practices may be reinvested ideologically, and the broad sweep of features of texts that are seen as potentially ideological.

ONE

Critical and descriptive goals in discourse analysis

ABSTRACT

I view social institutions as containing diverse 'ideological-discursive formations' (IDFs) associated with different groups within the institution. There is usually one IDF which is clearly dominant. Each IDF is a sort of 'speech community' with its own discourse norms but also, embedded within and symbolized by the latter, its own 'ideological norms'. Institutional subjects are constructed, in accordance with the norms of an IDF, in subject positions whose ideological underpinnings they may be unaware of. A characteristic of a dominant IDF is the capacity to 'naturalize' ideologies, i.e. to win acceptance for them as non-ideological 'common sense'.

It is argued that the orderliness of interactions depends in part upon such naturalized ideologies. To 'denaturalize' them is the objective of a discourse analysis which adopts 'critical' goals. I suggest that denaturalization involves showing how social structures determine properties of discourse, and how discourse in turn determines social structures. This requires a 'global' (macro/micro) explanatory framework which contrasts with the non-explanatory or only 'locally' explanatory frameworks of 'descriptive' work in discourse analysis. I include a critique of features of such work which follow from its limited explanatory goals (its concept of 'background knowledge', 'speaker-goal' explanatory models, and its neglect of power), and discuss the social conditions under which critical discourse analysis might be an effective practice of intervention, and a significant element in mother tongue education.

1. INTRODUCTION: ORDERLINESS AND NATURALIZATION

In this section of the paper I shall distinguish in a preliminary way between 'critical' and 'descriptive' goals in discourse analysis. Data extracts are used to show (i) how the orderliness of interactions depends upon taken-for-granted 'background knowledge' (BGK for short), and (ii) how BGK subsumes 'naturalized' ideological representations, i.e. ideological representations which come to be seen as non-ideological 'common sense'. Adopting critical goals means aiming to elucidate such naturalizations, and more generally to make clear social determinations and effects of discourse which are characteristically opaque to participants. These concerns are absent in currently predominant 'descriptive' work on discourse. The critical approach has its theoretical underpinnings in views of the relationship between 'micro' events (including verbal events) and 'macro' structures which see the latter as both the conditions for and the products of the former, and which therefore reject rigid barriers between the study of the 'micro' (of which the study of discourse is a part) and the study of the 'macro'. I shall discuss these theoretical issues at the end of this section of the paper.

When I refer to the 'orderliness' of an interaction, I mean the feeling of participants in it (which may be more or less successfully elicited, or inferred from their interactive behaviour) that things are as they should be, i.e. as one would normally expect them to be. This may be a matter of coherence of an interaction, in the sense that individual speaker turns fit meaningfully together, or a matter of the taking of turns at talking in the expected or appropriate way, or the use of the expected markers of deference or politeness, or of the appropriate lexicon. (I am of course using the terms 'appropriate' and 'expected' here from the perspective of the participant, not analytically.)

Text 1 gives an example of 'orderliness' in the particular sense of coherence within and between turns, and its dependence on naturalized ideologies. It is an extract from an interview between two male police officers (B and C), and a woman (A) who has come to the police station to make a complaint of rape.[1]

Text 1
1. *C*: you do realize that when we have you medically examined ... and
2. *B*: they'll come up with nothing

3. C: the swabs are taken ... it'll show ... if you've had sexual intercourse with three men this afternoon ...

    it'll ⌈ show

4. A: ⌊ it'll show each one

5. C: it'll ⌈ show each one ...

    B: ⌊ hmm

6. A: yeah I ⌈ know

7. C: ⌊ alright ... so ...

8. A: so it would show ⌈ (indist.)

9. C: ⌊ it'll confirm that you've had

       ⌈ sex ... or

    B: ⌊ hm

    C: not with three men alright ... so we can confirm it's happened ... that you've had sex with three men ... if it does confirm it ... then I would go so far as to say ... that you went to that house willingly ... there's no struggle ... you could have run away quite easily ... when you got out of the car ... to go to the house ... you could have got away quite easily ... you're well known ... in Reading ... to the uniformed ... lads for being a nuisance in the streets shouting and bawling ... couple of times you've been arrested ... for under the Mental Health Act ... for shouting and screaming in the street ... haven't you ...

10. A: when I was ill yeah

11. C: yeah ... right ... so ... what's to stop you ... shouting and screaming in the street ... when you think you're going to get raped ... you're not frightened at all ... you walk in there ... quite blase you're not frightened at all ...

12. A: I was frightened

13. C: you weren't ... you're showing no signs of emotion every now and again you have a little tear ...

14. B: (indist.) if you were frightened ... and you came at me I think I would dive ... I wouldn't take you on

     ⌈ you frighten me

15. C: ⌊ (indist.)

16. A: why would I frighten ⌈ you (indist.) only a little (indist.)

                 ⌊ you   you just   it doesn't

17. B: matter ... you're female and you've probably got a hell of a temper ... if you were to ⌈ go

18. A: ⌊ I haven't got a temper

    (indist.) a hell of ⌈ a temper

               ⌊ oh I don't know ...

19. *C*:
20. *B*: I think if things if if things were up against a a wall ... I think you'd fight and fight very hard ...

I imagine that for most readers the most striking instance of ideologically-based coherence in this text is in 17 (*you're female and you've probably got a hell of a temper*), with the implicit proposition 'women tend to have bad tempers' which, with a further implicit proposition ('people in bad tempers are frightening to others') and certain principles of inference, allows 16 and 17 to be heard as a coherent question–answer and complaint–rejection pair. There are other, perhaps rather less obvious instances, including the following (I have taken the example in 17 as 'case' (1)).

(2) It is taken as given (as mutually assumed background knowledge) that fear or its absence, and perhaps affective states in general, can be 'read off' from behavioural 'symptoms' or their absence. The orderliness of *C*'s talk in 9 (from *there's no struggle*) and 11, i.e. its coherence as the drawing of a conclusion (*you're not frightened at all*) from pieces of evidence (*there's no struggle*, *A* could have got away but didn't, *A* has a proven capacity for creating public scenes but did not do so in this case), depends upon this implicit proposition. Similar comments apply to 13.

(3) It is taken as given that persons have, or do not have, capacities for particular types of behaviour irrespective of changes in time, place, or conditions. This is a version of the doctrine of the 'unified and consistent subject' (Coward and Ellis (1977: 7)). Thus, again in 9 and 11, evidence of *A*'s capacity for creating a public scene in the past, and when she was suffering from some form of mental illness, is taken, despite 10, as evidence for her capacity to do so in this instance. As in the case of (2), the coherence of *C*'s line of argument depends upon the taken-as-given proposition.

(4) It is taken as given that if a woman willingly places herself in a situation where sexual intercourse 'might be expected to occur' (whatever that means), that is tantamount to being a willing partner, and rules out rape. *C*'s apparent objective in this extract is to establish that *A* went willingly to the house where the rape is alleged to have occurred. But this extract is coherently connected with the rest of the interview only on the assumption that what is really at issue is *A*'s willingness to have sexual intercourse. To make this connection, we need the above implicit proposition.

The four implicit propositions which I have identified represent BGK of a rather particular sort, which is distinct from, say, the assumed BGK that there is some identifiable door which is closed when some speaker asks some addressee to 'open the door'. I argue below (section 3.1) that the tendency in the literature to conflate all of the 'taken-for-granted' under the rubric of 'knowledge' is an unacceptable reduction. For present purposes, I propose to refer to these four propositions as 'ideological', by which I mean that each is a particular representation of some aspect of the world (natural or social; what is, what can be, what ought to be) which might be (and may be) alternatively represented, and where any given representation can be associated with some particular 'social base' (I am aware that this is a rather crude gloss on a complex and controversial concept. On ideology, see Althusser (1971) and Therborn (1980)).

These propositions differ in terms of the degree to which they are 'naturalized' (Hall (1982: 75)). I shall assume a scale of naturalization, whose 'most naturalized' (theoretical) terminal point would be represented by a proposition which was taken as commonsensically given by all members of some community, and seen as vouched for by some generally accepted rationalization (which referred it, for instance, to 'human nature').

Cases (1) and (4) involve only limited naturalization. The proposition 'women tend to have bad tempers' could, one imagines, be taken as given only within increasingly narrow and embattled social circles – one achievement of the women's movement has been precisely the denaturalization of many formerly highly naturalized sexist ideologies. Case (4) corresponds to traditional judicial views (in English law) of rape as well as having something of a base outside the law, but it is also under pressure from feminists.

The degree of naturalization in cases (2) and (3) is by contrast rather high, and they are correspondingly more difficult to recognize as ideological representations rather than 'just common sense'. Such ideological propositions are both open to lay rationalization in terms of 'what everyone knows' about human behaviour and 'human nature', and traceable in social scientific theories of human behaviour and the human subject.

Texts 2–4 illustrate other ways in which orderliness may depend upon ideological BGK. My aim here is merely to indicate some of the range of phenomena involved, so my comments on these texts will be brief and schematic.

Text 2

1. *T*: Now, let's just have a look at these things here. Can you tell me, first of all, what's this?
2. *P*: Paper.
3. *T*: Piece of paper, yes. And, hands up, what cutter will cut this?
4. *P*: The pair of scissors.
5. *T*: The pair of scissors, yes. Here we are, the pair of scissors. And, as you can see, it's going to cut the paper. Tell me what's this?
6. *P*: Cigarette box.
7. *T*: Yes. What's it made from?

(Sinclair and Coulthard (1975: 96))

The orderliness in this instance is a matter of conformity on the part of both teacher and pupils to a framework of discoursal and pragmatic rights and obligations, involving the taking of turns, the control of topic, rights to question and obligations to answer, rights over metacommunicative acts and so forth (see Sinclair and Coulthard (1975) and Stubbs (1983: 40–46) for a detailed discussion of these properties of classroom discourse). The implicit ideological propositions identified in text 1 appertain to language in its 'ideational' function, whereas the discoursal and pragmatic norms of text 2 appertain to the 'interpersonal' function of language (Halliday (1978; 45–46)). Moreover, while in text 1 ideologies are formulated in (implicit) propositions, in text 2 ideological representations of social relationships are symbolized in norms of interaction. Michael Halliday's claim that the linguistic system functions as a 'metaphor' for social processes as well as an 'expression' of them, which he formulated in the context of a discussion of the symbolization of social relationships in dialectal and registerial variants (Halliday (1978: 3)) also applies here. In these respects, text 3 is similar to text 2:

Text 3

1. *X*: oh hellŏ Mrs Norton
2. *Y*: oh hellŏ Súsan
3. *X*: yès erm wèll I'm afraid I've got ^ afraid I've got a bit of a pròblem
4. *Y*: you mean about tomorrow *night*
5. *X*: yès ^ erm you [knów I
6. *Y*: oh dèar]
7. *X*: *knòw* that that you said
8. *Y*: yéah
9. *X*: er you *wàn*ted me tomorrow night
10. *Y*: uhúh yéah

11. *X*: well I just thought erm (clears throat) I've got something else
     on which I just didn't think about when I arranged it with you
     you know and er
12. *Y*: (sighs) yés
13. *X*: I'm just wondering if I could possibly back dòwn on tomorrow
                                            (Edmondson (1981: 119–120))[2]

Again, this is a matter of orderliness arising from conformity with
interactive norms, though in this case pragmatic norms of politeness
and mitigation: *X* uses a range of politeness markers, including a title
+ surname mode of address (in 1), 'hedges' (e.g. *a bit of a* in 3), and
indirect speech acts (as in 13). These markers are 'appropriate' given
the status asymmetry between *X* and *Y* (*Y* is *X*'s employer, and no
doubt older than *X*), and given the 'face-threatening' act which *X* is
engaged in (Brown and Levinson (1978: 81)).

The interactive norms exemplified in texts 2 and 3 can be seen
in terms of degrees of naturalization like the implicit propositions
of text 1, though in this case it is a matter of the naturalization
of practices which symbolize particular ideological representations
of social relationships, i.e. relationships between teachers and
pupils, and between babysitters and their employers. The more
dominant some particular representation of a social relationship, the
greater the degree of naturalization of its associated practices. I
will use the expression 'ideological practices' to refer to such
practices.

Texts 1–3 are partial exemplifications of the substantial range of
BGK which participants may draw upon in interactions. We can very
roughly differentiate four dimensions of participants' 'knowledge base',
elaborating Winograd (1982: 14) who distinguishes only the first, third
and fourth:

knowledge of language codes,
knowledge of principles and norms of language use,
knowledge of situation, and
knowledge of the world.

I wish to suggest that all four dimensions of the 'knowledge base'
include ideological elements. I will assume without further discussion
that the examples I have given so far illustrate this for all except the
first of these dimensions, 'knowledge of language code'. Text 4 shows
that this dimension is no exception. It is a summary by Benson and
Hughes (1983: 10–11) of one of the case studies of Aaron Cicourel

from his work on the constitution and interpretation of written records which are generated in the juvenile judicial process (Cicourel (1976)).

Text 4
The probation officer was aware of a number of incidents at school in which Robert was considered to be 'incorrigible'. The probation file contained mention of 15 incidents at school prior to his court appearance, ranging from 'smoking' to 'continued defiance'. The probation officer's assessment and recommendation for Robert contained a fairly detailed citation of a number of factors explaining Robert's 'complete lack of responsibility toward society' with the recommendation that he be placed in a school or state hospital. Among the factors mentioned were his mother's 'severe depression', divorced parents, unstable marriage, and his inability to comprehend his environment: the kind of factors, we should note, assembled in conventional sociological reasoning explaining the causes of delinquency.

Cicourel is concerned to show 'how "delinquents get that way" as a process managed and negotiated through the socially organised activities that constitute "dealing with crime"' (Benson and Hughes (1983: 11)). What I want to highlight is the role which the lexicon itself plays in this process. Let us focus on just four items among the many of interest in the text: *incorrigible, defiance, lack of responsibility, deliquency.* These belong to a particular lexicalization of 'youth', or more specifically of young people who do not 'fit' in their families, their schools, or their neighbourhoods. The 'conditions of use' of this lexicon as we may call them, are focused upon by Cicourel – the unwritten and unspoken conventions for the use of a particular word or expression in connection with particular events or behaviours, which are operative and taken for granted in the production and interpretation of written records. But the lexicon itself, as code, is only one among indefinitely many possible lexicalizations; one can easily create an 'anti-language' (Halliday (1978: 164–182)) equivalent of this part of the lexicon – *irrepressible* for *incorrigible, debunking* for *defiance, refusal to be sucked in by society* for *lack of responsibility toward society,* and perhaps *spirit* for *delinquency.* Alternative lexicalizations are generated from divergent ideological positions. And lexicalizations, like the implicit propositions and pragmatic discoursal practices of the earlier texts, may be more or less naturalized: a lexicalization becomes naturalized to the extent that 'its' IDF achieves dominance, and hence the capacity to win acceptance for it as 'the lexicon', the neutral code.

It may be helpful for me to sum up what I have said so far before moving to a first formulation of 'critical' goals in discourse analysis. I am suggesting (a) that ideologies and ideological practices may become dissociated to a greater or lesser extent from the particular social base, and the particular interests, which generated them – that is, they may become to a greater or lesser extent 'naturalized', and hence be seen to be commonsensical and based in the nature of things or people, rather than in the interests of classes or other groupings; (b) that such naturalized ideologies and practices thereby become part of the 'knowledge base' which is activated in interaction, and hence the 'orderliness' of interaction may depend upon them, and (c) that in this way the orderliness of interactions as 'local', 'micro' events comes to be dependent upon a higher 'orderliness', i.e. an achieved consensus in respect of ideological positions and practices.

This brings me to certain theoretical assumptions which underpin the proposed adoption of critical goals in discourse analysis. Firstly, that verbal interaction is a mode of social action, and that like other modes of social action it presupposes a range of what I shall loosely call 'structures' – which are reflected in the 'knowledge base' – including social structures, situational types, language codes, norms of language use. Secondly, and crucially, that these structures are not only presupposed by, and necessary conditions for, action, but are also the *products* of action; or, in a different terminology, actions *reproduce* structures. Giddens (1981) develops this view from a sociological perspective in terms of the notion of 'duality of structure'.

The significance of the second assumption is that 'micro' actions or events, including verbal interaction, can in no sense be regarded as of merely 'local' significance to the situations in which they occur, for any and every action contributes to the reproduction of 'macro' structures. Notice that one dimension of what I am suggesting is that language codes are reproduced in speech, a view which is in accordance with one formulation in Saussure's *Cours*: 'Language and speaking are thus interdependent; the former is both the instrument and the product of the latter' (1966: 19). My concern here, however, is with the reproduction of social structures in discourse, a concern which is evident in Halliday's more recent work:

> By their everyday acts of meaning, people act out the social structure, affirming their own statuses and roles, and establishing and transmitting the shared systems of value and of knowledge. (Halliday (1978: 2))

But if this is the case, then it makes little sense to study verbal interactions *as if* they were unconnected with social structures: 'there can be no theoretical defence for supposing that the personal encounters of day-to-day life can be conceptually separated from the long-term institutional development of society' (Giddens (1981: 173)). Yet that seems to be precisely how verbal interactions have in fact been studied for the most part in the currently predominant 'descriptive' work on discourse. Thus the adoption of critical goals means, first and foremost, investigating verbal interactions with an eye to their determination by, and their effects on, social structures. However, as I have suggested in discussing the texts, neither determinations nor effects are necessarily apparent to participants; opacity is the other side of the coin of naturalization. The goals of critical discourse analysis are also therefore 'denaturalizing'. I shall elaborate on this preliminary formulation in the following sections.

My use of the term 'critical' (and the associated term 'critique') is linked on the one hand to a commitment to a dialectical theory and method 'which grasps things . . . essentially in their interconnection, in their concatenation, their motion, their coming into and passing out of existence' (Engels (1976: 27)), and on the other hand to the view that, in human matters, interconnections and chains of cause-and-effect may be distorted out of vision. Hence 'critique' is essentially making visible the interconnectedness of things; for a review of senses of 'critique', see Connerton (1976: 11–39). In using the term 'critical', I am also signalling a connection (though by no means an identity of views) between my objectives in this paper and the 'critical linguistics' of a group of linguists and sociologists associated with Roger Fowler (Fowler *et al.* (1979), Kress and Hodge (1979)).

2. SOCIAL INSTITUTIONS AND CRITICAL ANALYSIS

The above sketch of what I mean by 'critical goals' in discourse analysis gives rise to many questions. For instance: how can it be that people are standardly unaware of how their ways of speaking are socially determined, and of what social effects they may cumulatively lead to? What conception of the social subject does such a lack of awareness imply? How does the naturalization of ideologies come about? How is it sustained? What determines the degree of naturalization in a particular instance? How may this change?

I cannot claim to provide answers to these questions in this paper. What I suggest, however, is that we can begin to formulate answers to these and other questions, and to develop a theoretical framework which will facilitate researching them, by focusing attention upon the 'social institution' and upon discourses which are clearly associable with particular institutions, rather than on casual conversation, as has been the fashion (see further section 3.3 below). My reasoning is in essence simply that (a) such questions can only be broached within a framework which integrates 'micro' and 'macro' research, and (b) we are most likely to be able to arrive at such an integration if we focus upon the institution as a 'pivot' between the highest level of social structuring, that of the 'social formation',[3] and the most concrete level, that of the particular social event or action. The argument is rather similar to Fishman's case for the 'domain' (Fishman (1972)): the social institution is an intermediate level of social structuring, which faces Janus-like 'upwards' to the social formation, and 'downwards' to social actions.

Social actions tend very much to cluster in terms of institutions; when we witness a social event (e.g. a verbal interaction), we normally have no difficulty identifying it in institutional terms, i.e. as appertaining to the family, the school, the workplace, church, the courts, some department of government, or some other institution. And from a developmental point of view, institutions are no less salient: the socialization of the child (in which process discourse is both medium and target), can be described in terms of the child's progressive exposure to institutions of primary socialization (family, peer group, school, etc.). Given that institutions play such a prominent role, it is not surprising that, despite the concentration on casual conversation in recent discourse analysis referred to above, a significant amount of work is on types of discourse which are institutionally identified, such as classroom discourse (e.g. Sinclair and Coulthard (1975)); courtroom discourse (e.g. Atkinson and Drew (1979), O'Barr (1982)), or psycho-therapeutic discourse (e.g. Labov and Fanshel (1977)). However, most of this work suffers from the inadequacies characteristic of descriptive discourse analysis, which I detail in section 3.

One can envisage the relationship between the three levels of social phenomena I have indicated – the social formation, the social institution, and social action – as one of determination from 'top' to 'bottom': social institutions are determined by the social formation, and social action is determined by social institutions. While I would accept that this direction of determination is the fundamental one, this formulation is inadequate in that it is mechanistic (or undialectical): that is, it does not allow that determination may also be 'upwards'. Let us take education as an example. I would want to argue that features of the school as an institution (e.g. the ways in which schools define relationship between teachers and pupils) are ultimately determined at the level of the social formation (e.g. by such factors as the relationship between the schools and the economic system and between the schools and the state), and that the actions and events that take place in the schools are in turn determined by institutional factors. However, I would also wish to insist that the mode of determination is not mechanical determination, and that changes may occur at the level of concrete action which may reshape the institution itself, and changes may occur in the institution which may contribute to the transformation of the social formation. Thus the process of determination works dialectically.

A social institution is (amongst other things) an apparatus of verbal interaction, or an 'order of discourse'. (I suggest later in this section that this property only *appears* to belong to the institution itself.) In this perspective, we may regard an institution as a sort of 'speech community', with its own particular repertoire of speech events, describable in terms of the sorts of 'components' which ethnograhic work on speaking has differentiated – settings, participants (their identities and relationships), goals, topics, and so forth (Hymes (1972)). Each institution has its own set of speech events, its own differentiated settings and scenes, its cast of participants, and its own norms for their combination – for which members of the cast may participate in which speech events, playing which parts, in which settings, in the pursuit of which topics or goals, for which institutionally recognized purposes. It is, I suggest, necessary to see the institution as simultaneously facilitating and constraining the social action (here, specifically, verbal interaction) of its members: it provides them with a frame for action, without which they could not act, but it thereby constrains them to act within that frame.[4] Moreover, every such institutional frame includes formulations and symbolizations of a particular set of ideological representations: particular ways of talking are based upon particular 'ways of seeing' (see further below in this section).

I shall use the terms 'subject', 'client', and '(member of) public' for the parties to verbal interaction, rather than the more familiar term 'participant'. I use 'subject' for 'members' of an institution – those who have institutional roles and identities acquired in a defined acquisition period and maintained as long-term attributes. The 'client' is an outsider rather than a member, who nevertheless takes part in certain institutional interactions in accordance with norms laid down by the institution, but without a defined acquisition period or long-term maintenance of attributes (though attribute-maintenance is no doubt a matter of degree). Examples would be a patient in a medical examination, or a lay witness in a court hearing. Finally, some institutions have a 'public' to whom messages are addressed, whose members are sometimes assumed to interpret these messages according to norms laid down by the institution, but who do not interact with institutional subjects directly. The primary concept is 'subject': 'client' and 'public' might be defined as special and relatively peripheral types of subject.

The term 'subject' is used in preference to 'participant' (or 'member') because it has the double sense of agent ('the subjects of history') and affected ('the Queen's subjects'); this captures the concept of the subject as qualified to act through being constrained – 'subjected' – to an institutional frame (see above). I shall refer to 'social subjects' as well as 'institutional subjects': the social subject is the whole social person, and social subjects occupy subject positions in a variety of institutions. The choice of terms here is not a trivial matter: I suspect the term 'participant' tends to imply an essential, integral 'individual' who 'participates' in various institutionally defined types of interaction without that individuality being in any way shaped or modified thereby. In preferring 'subject', I am emphasizing that discourse makes people, as well as people make discourse.

We may usefully distinguish various facets of the subject (either 'institutional' or 'social'), and talk of 'economic', 'political', 'ideological' and 'discoursal' subjects. What I have been suggesting above can be summed up by saying that institutions construct their ideological and discoursal subjects; they construct them in the sense that they impose ideological and discoursal constraints upon them as a condition for qualifying them to act as subjects. For instance, to become a teacher, one must master the discursive and ideological norms which the school attaches to that subject position – one must learn to talk like a teacher and 'see things' (i.e. things such as learning and teaching) like a teacher. (Though as I shall show in section 1.4, these are not mechanically deterministic processes.) And, as I have suggested above, these ways of talking and ways of seeing are inseparably intertwined in that the latter constitute a part of the taken-for-granted 'knowledge base' upon which the orderliness of the former depends. This means that in the process of acquiring the ways of talking which are normatively associated with a subject position, one necessarily acquires also its ways of seeing, or ideological norms. And just as one is typically unaware of one's ways of talking unless for some reason they are subjected to conscious scrutiny, so also is one typically unaware of what ways of seeing, what ideological representations, underlie one's talk. This is a crucial assumption which I return to below.

However, social institutions are not as monolithic as the account so far will have suggested: as ideological and discursive orders, they are pluralistic rather than monistic, i.e. they provide alternative sets of discoursal and ideological norms. More accurately, they are pluralistic to an extent which varies in time and place, and from one institution to another in a given social formation, in accordance with factors including the balance of power between social classes at the level of the social formation, and the degree to which institutions in the social formation are integrated or, conversely, autonomous.[5] The significance of the first of these factors, is that pluralism is likely to flourish when non-dominant classes are relatively powerful; the significance of the second is that a relatively autonomous institution may be relatively pluralistic even when non-dominant classes are relatively powerless.

I shall say that, as regards the ideological facet of pluralism, a given institution may house two or more distinguishable 'ideological forma-tions' (Althusser (1971)), i.e. distinct ideological positions which will tend to be associated with different forces within the institution. This diversity of ideological formations is a consequence of, and a condition for, struggles between different forces within the institution: that is, conflict between forces results in ideological barriers between them, and ideological struggle is part of that conflict. These institutional struggles are connected to class struggle, though the relationship is not necessarily a direct or transparent one; and ideological and discoursal control of institutions is itself a stake in the struggle between classes (see below on 'ideological and discoursal power').

I propose to use for talking about institutional pluralism Pêcheux's term 'discursive formation' as well as Althusser's 'ideological formation'. Pêcheux defines a discursive formation as 'that which in a given ideological formation, i.e. from a particular position in a given conjunc-ture determined by the state of the class struggle, determines *"what can and should be said"*' (Pêcheux (1982: 111)). I shall refer to 'ideological-discursive formations' (IDFs for short), in accordance with what I have said above about the inseparability of 'ways of talking' and 'ways of seeing'. In so doing, I shall make the simplifying assumption, which further work may well challenge, that there is a one-to-one relationship between ideological formations and discursive formations.

I have referred above to the social institution itself as a sort of speech community and (to extend the image) ideological community; and I have claimed that institutions construct subjects ideologically and discoursally. Institutions do indeed give the appearance of having these properties – but only in cases where one IDF is unambiguously dominant (see below). I suggest that these properties are properly attributed to the IDF, not the social institution: it is the IDF that positions subjects in relation to its own sets of speech events, participants, settings, topics, goals and, simultaneously, ideological representations.

As I have just indicated, IDFs are ordered in dominance: it is generally possible to identify a 'dominant' IDF and one or more 'dominated' IDFs in a social institution. The struggle between forces within the institution which I have referred to above can be seen as centring upon maintaining a dominant IDF in dominance (from the perspective of those in power) or undermining a dominant IDF in order to replace it. It is when the dominance of an IDF is unchallenged to all intents and purposes (i.e. when whatever challenges there are do not constitute any threat), that the norms of the IDF will become most naturalized, and most opaque (see section 1), and may come to be seen as the norms of the institution itself. The interests of the dominant class at the level of the social formation require the maintenance in dominance in each social institution of an IDF compatible with their continued power. But this is never given – it must be constantly fought for, and is constantly at risk through a shift in relations of power between forces at the level of the social formation and in the institutions. I shall refer to the capacity to maintain an IDF in dominance (or, at the level of the social formation, a network of IDFs) as 'ideological/discoursal power', which exists alongside economic and political power, and can normally be expected to be held in conjunction with them. I shall use 'power' in this sense in contrast with 'status': the latter relates to the relationship between subjects in interactions, and their status is registered in terms of (symmetrical or asymmetrical) interactional rights and obligations, which are manifested in a range of linguistic, pragmatic and discoursal features. The group which has ideological and discoursal power in an institution may or may not be clearly status-marked.

We are now in a position to develop what has been said so far about the naturalization of ideologies, and what I described at the end of section 1 as 'the other side of the coin of naturalization', their opacity to participants in interactions; since the case for a discourse analysis with critical goals (which it is the primary objection of this paper to argue) rests upon the assumption that the naturalization and opacity of ideologies is a significant property of discourse, it is important to be as clear as possible about these effects and their origins.

Naturalization gives to particular ideological representations the status of common sense, and thereby makes them opaque, i.e. no longer visible as ideologies. These effects can be explained given (a) the process of subject-construction referred to above, and (b) the notion of a dominant IDF. I have argued that in the construction of the subject, the acquisition of normative 'ways of talking' associated with a given subject position must simultaneously be the acquisition of the associated 'ways of seeing' (ideological norms); that is, since any set of discursive norms entails a certain knowledge base, and since any knowledge base includes an ideological component, in acquiring the discursive norms one simultaneously acquires the associated ideological norms.

If, moreover, the process of acquisition takes place under conditions of the clear dominance of a given IDF in an institution, such that other IDFs are unlikely to be evident (at least to the outsider or novice), there is no basis internal to the institution for the relativization of the norms of the given IDF. In such cases, these norms will tend to be perceived first as norms of the institution itself, and second as merely skills or techniques which must be mastered in order for the status of competent institutional subjects to be achieved. These are the origins of naturalization and opacity.

If it is also the case (as it typically is) that those who undergo the process of subjection are unaware of the functioning of the institution concerned in the social formation as a whole, then the institution will tend to be seen in isolation and there will be no basis external to the institution, either, for the relativization and rationalization of the norms of the given IDF.

Subjects, then, are typically unaware of the ideological dimensions of the subject positions they occupy. This means of course that they are in no reasonable sense 'committed' to them, and it under-lines the point that ideologies are not to be equated with views or beliefs. It is quite possible for a social subject to occupy institutional subject positions which are ideologically incompatible, or to occupy a subject position incompatible with his or her overt political or social beliefs and affiliations, without being aware of any contradiction.[6]

3. CRITICAL AND DESCRIPTIVE GOALS
I am using the term 'descriptive' primarily to characterize approaches

to discourse analysis whose goals are either non-explanatory, or explanatory within 'local' limits, in contrast to the 'global' explanatory goals of critical discourse analysis outlined above. Where goals are non-explanatory, the objective is to describe without explaining: if for instance a speaker in some interaction uses consistently indirect forms of request, one points this out without looking for causes. Where goals are explanatory but 'local', causes are looked for in the immediate situation (e.g. in the 'goals' of the speaker – see below), but not beyond it; that is, not at the higher levels of the social institution and the social formation, which would figure in critical explanation. Moreover, although 'locally' explanatory descriptive work may seek to identify at least local determinants of features of particular discourses, descriptive work generally has been little concerned with the *effects* of discourse. And it has certainly not concerned itself with effects which go beyond the immediate situation. For critical discourse analysis, on the other hand, the question of how discourse cumulatively contributes to the reproduction of macro structures is at the heart of the explanatory endeavour.

Descriptive work in discourse analysis tends to share other characteristics which can be seen as following from its at best limited explanatory goals. These include a reliance upon the concept of 'background knowledge', adoption of a 'goal-driven' local explanatory model, and neglect of power in discourse and, to an extent, status; all of these are discussed below. I shall refer for convenience to 'a descriptive approach' which has these characteristics in addition to descriptive goals in the above sense, but this is to be understood as a generalized characterization of a tendency within discourse analysis and not as a characterization of the work of any particular discourse analyst. Thus I would regard all of the following as basically descriptive in approach, diverse though they are in other respects: Atkinson and Drew (1979), Brown and Yule (1983), Labov and Fanshel (1977), Sinclair and Coulthard (1975), Stubbs (1983). But this does not mean that I am attributing to each of them all the descriptive (or, indeed, none of the critical) characteristics.

3.1. Background knowledge [7]

My primary contention in this sub-section is that the undifferentiated concept of BGK which has such wide currency in descriptive discourse analysis places discourse analysis in the position of ('uncritically') reproducing certain ideological effects.

The concept of BGK reduces diverse aspects of the 'backgrounded material' which is drawn upon in interaction – beliefs, values, ideologies, as well as knowledge properly so called – to 'knowledge'. 'Knowledge' implies facts to be known, facts coded in propositions which are straightforwardly and transparently related to them. But 'ideology', as I have argued above, involves the representation of 'the world' from the perspective of a particular interest, so that the relationship between proposition and fact is not transparent, but mediated by representational activity. So ideology cannot be reduced to 'knowledge' without distortion.[8]

I suggested in section 2 that where an IDF has undisputed dominance in an institution, its norms tend to be seen as highly naturalized, and as norms of the institution itself. In such instances, a particular ideological representation of some reality may come to appear as merely a transparent reflection of some 'reality' which is given in the same way to all. In this way, ideology creates 'reality' as an effect (see Hall (1982: 75)). The undifferentiated concept of BGK mirrors, complements and reproduces this ideological effect: it treats such 'realities' as objects of knowledge, like any other reality.

It also contributes to the reproduction of another ideological effect, the 'autonomous subject' effect. The autonomous subject effect is a particular manifestation of the general tendency towards opacity which I have taken to be inherent to ideology: ideology produces subjects which appear not to have been 'subjected' or produced, but to be 'free, homogeneous and responsible for (their) actions' (Coward and Ellis (1977: 77)). That is, metaphorically speaking, ideology endeavours to cover its own traces. The autonomous subject effect is at the bottom of theories of the 'individual' of the sort I referred to in section 2.

Seeing all background material as 'knowledge' is tantamount to attributing it to each participating person in each interaction as a set of attributes of that person ('what that person knows'). Interactions can then be seen as the coming-together of so many constituted, autonomous persons, 'of their own free will', whose 'knowledge bases' are mobilized in managing and making sense of discourse. This conception is cognitive and psychological at the expense of being asociological; the sociological is reduced to the cognitive through the 'competence' metaphor, so that social factors do not themselves figure, only the 'social competence' of persons. The 'competent' subject of cognitive conceptions of interaction is the autonomous subject of ideology.

I am not of course suggesting that descriptive discourse analysts are consciously conspiring to give social scientific credence to ideological effects. The point is rather that unless the analyst differentiates ideology from knowledge, i.e. unless s/he is aware of the ideological dimensions of discourse, the chances are that s/he will be unconsciously implicated in the reproduction of ideologies, much as the lay subject is. To put the point more positively and more contentiously, the concept of ideology is essential for a scientific understanding of discourse, as opposed to a mode of understanding which emulates that of the partially unsighted discourse subject. But the concept of ideology is incompatible with the limited explanatory goals of the descriptive approach, for it necessarily requires reference outside the immediate situation to the social institution and the social formation in that ideologies are by definition representations generated by social forces at these levels.

3.2. Goals[9]

'Goal-driven' explanatory models of interaction tend, I suggest, to exaggerate the extent to which actions are under the conscious control of subjects. In referring to goal-driven models, I mainly have in mind 'speaker goal' models which set out to explain the strategies adopted by speakers, and the particular linguistic, pragmatic and discoursal choices made, in terms of speakers' goals (e.g. Leech (1983: 35–44), Winograd (1982: 13–20)). But I shall also comment on what one might call an 'activity-goal' model, which claims that features of the 'activity type' are explicable by reference to its 'goal', i.e. 'the function or functions that members of the society see the activity as having' (Levinson 1979: 369)). I include activity-goals because Levinson also suggests that there might be a connection between them and speaker-goals: in essence, the former determine the latter. Atkinson and Drew (1979) attribute analogous explanatory value to activity-goals.

My objection to the 'activity-goal' model is that it regards properties of a particular type of interaction as determined by the *perceived* social functions of that type of interaction (its 'goal'), thus representing the relationship between discourse and its determinants as transparent to those taking part. The properties which Levinson sees as so determined broadly correspond to what I have called 'ideological practices' (see section 1), i.e. discoursal practices which vary between IDFs, and which are explicable immediately in terms of the ideological facets of IDFs and indirectly in terms of the social determinants of these ideologies. An example of ideological practices is the unequal distribution of discoursal and pragmatic rights and obligations in classroom discourse, illustrated in text 2. A distinction needs to be made between the ideologies which underlie such practices, and *rationalizations* of such practices which institutional subjects may generate; rationalizations may radically distort the ideological bases of such practices. Yet the activity type model portrays such rationalizations – the function(s) which these practices are *seen* (Levinson's term) as having – as *determinants* of these practices.

The objection to 'speaker-goal' models is similar: they imply that what speakers do in interaction is under their conscious control, and are at odds with the claim that naturalization and opacity of determinants and effects are basic features of discourse. I have no doubt that this will be a contentious view of speaker-goal models; it will be objected that I am using 'goal' in its ordinary language sense of 'conscious objectives' ('goal 1') rather than in the technical sense ('goal 2') of 'a state which regulates the behaviour of an individual' (Leech (1983: 40)), which misrepresents speaker-goal models. However, I would argue that such an objection underestimates the power of a metaphor: goal 2 includes goal 1; there is no obvious reason why one should accept this conflation of conscious goals and unconscious 'goals'; but given this conflation, it is inevitable that the sense of goal 1 will predominate, and hence that interactions will be essentially seen as the pursuit of conscious goals. Such a view is in harmony with the local explanatory goals of the descriptive approach, for it seems to offer an explanation without needing to refer to institutions or the social formation.

3.3. Power and status

Either the descriptive approach offers pseudo-explanations of norms of interaction such as that of the activity-goal model, or it regards norms of interaction as requiring descriptions but not explanation. I shall be suggesting here that in either case, given that the capacity to maintain an IDF in dominance is the most salient effect of power in discourse, the absence of a serious concern with explaining norms results in a neglect of power; that, furthermore, there has been such an emphasis on cooperative conversation between equals that even matters of status have been relatively neglected (see section 2 for 'power' and 'status').

The descriptive approach has virtually elevated cooperative conversation between equals into an archetype of verbal interaction in general.

As a result, even where attention has been given to 'unequal encounters' (the term is used in the Lancaster work referred to in note 1 for interactions with status asymmetries), the asymmetrical distribution of discoursal and pragmatic rights and obligations according to status (see below) has not been the focal concern. The archetype has developed under influences which prominently include two which I shall comment upon: the 'Cooperative Principle' of Grice (1975), and ethnomethodological work on turn-taking.

I think it is clear that Grice primarily had in mind, when formulating the 'Cooperative Principle' and the maxims in the 1975 paper, interaction between persons capable of contributing (more or less) equally; this is the implication of his focus on 'the *exchange* of information' (my emphasis, see below). But for persons to be able to contribute equally, they must have equal status. Having equal status will presumably mean having equal discoursal and pragmatic rights and obligations – for instance, the same turn-taking rights and the same obligations to avoid silences and interruptions, the same rights to utter 'obligating' illocutionary acts (such as requests and questions), and the same obligations to respond to them. I take it that having equal status also means having equal control over the determination of the concepts presupposed by Grice's maxims: over what for interactional purposes counts as 'truth', 'relevance', adequate information, etc. (see Pratt (1981: 13)).

Of course, there do occur interactions which at least approximate to these conditions, but they are by no means typical of interactions in general. Grice himself pointed out that the maxims were stated as if the purpose which 'talk is adapted to serve and primarily employed to serve' were 'a maximally effective exchange of information', and noted that 'the scheme needs to be generalized to allow for such general purposes as influencing or directing the actions of others' (1975: 47). This proviso seems to have been often overlooked.

The impact of ethnomethodological work on turn-taking on the archetype must surely involve an influential paper by Sacks, Schegloff and Jefferson (1978), which proposes a simple but powerful set of rules to account for properties of conversational turn-taking, where 'conversation' is again very much cooperative interaction between equals. These rules tend to be taken as generally relevant for turn-taking, even though they are explicitly formulated for conversation. The paper itself argues that the 'exchange system' for conversation which it characterizes 'should be considered the basic form of speech-exchange system, with other systems ... representing a variety of transformations on conversation's turn-taking system' (Sacks *et al.* (1978: 47)). Levinson has suggested an analogous primacy for Grice's maxims, which we might view as 'specifications of some basic *unmarked* communicative context, deviations from which however common are seen as special or *marked*' (1979: 376). Any such assignment of primacy or 'unmarked' status to conversation strengthens the archetype I have referred to.

The neglect of 'unequal encounters' and questions of status which has resulted from the appeal of the archetype is not unconnected with the neglect of power I referred to above. For if one focuses upon 'unequal encounters', or the comparison of 'equal' and 'unequal' interactions, the variability and relativity of norms of interaction is likely to be highlighted, giving rise to questions about their origins and rationales which may in turn lead to questions about ideological and discursive power; whereas if one concentrates heavily upon data where the distribution of rights and obligations is more or less symmetrical, there seems to be nothing to explain. Though from a critical perspective, of course, there is: the possibility of, and constraints upon, cooperative conversation between equals, which are themselves effects of power.

Such conversation does not occur freely irrespective of institution, subjects, settings, and so forth. A reasonable hypothesis perhaps is that the most favourable conditions for its occurrence would be in an institution whose dominant IDF represented (certain) subjects as diversely contributing to a cooperative venture of equals; and that those with power would be most likely to endeavour to maintain such an IDF in dominance where the conditions existed for them (or required of them) to maintain their power through actively involving the 'powerless' in the organization and control of the institution. In contemporary Britain, academic communities approximate rather closely to these conditions.

From the critical perspective, a statement of the conditions under which interactions of a particular type may occur is a necessary element of an account of such interactions, and I have suggested that such a statement cannot be made without reference to the distribution and exercise of power in the institution and, ultimately, in the social formation. Given the limited explanatory goals of the descriptive approach, however, the concept of power lies outside its scope.

3.4. Conclusion: research objectives

I have suggested that from the at best 'locally' explanatory goals of the descriptive approach there follow certain other characteristics – its conception of BGK and its 'complicity' in certain ideological effects, its interest in goal-driven models and its image of subjects in conscious control of interactions, the absence of serious explanatory work on norms and the neglect of power and status.

I referred in section 3.1 to the 'cognitive' conception of interaction which is implicit in the concept of BGK. Interest in cognitive theories of language and discourse is on the increase, at least in part because of their 'computer-friendliness'; Winograd (1982) presents a 'computational paradigm' as a new synthesis of the work of linguists, psychologists, students of artificial intelligence and others, around a computer-friendly cognitive theory of language. Winograd's proposals have much in common with what I have called the 'descriptive approach', including a speaker-goal model, and local goals. I suspect that the current computational explosion might make this an increasingly attractive direction for discourse analysis, which will no doubt produce significant advances in certain directions, much as tranformational-generative grammar did, and at much the same cost in terms of the desocialization of language and discourse.

Any such development must however come to terms with what I would see as a major problem for non-critical discourse analysis, that of what I shall call the *rationality* of its research programme. I take a 'rational' research programme to be one which makes possible a systematic development in knowledge and understanding of the relevant domain, in this case discourse. Given the in principle infinite amount of possible data, a principled basis for sampling is necessary for such a programme. No such principled basis is possible so long as discourse analysts treat their samples as *objets trouvés* (Haberland and Mey (1977: 8)), i.e. so long as bits of discourse are analysed with little or no attention to their places in their institutional matrices.

A principled basis for sampling requires minimally (a) a sociological account of the institution under study, its relationship to other institutions in the social formation, and relationship between forces within it; (b) an account of the 'order of discourse' of the institution, of its IDFs and the dominance relationships among them, with links between (a) and (b); (c) an ethnographic account of each IDF. Given this information, one could identify for collection and analysis interactions which are representative of the range of IDFs and speech events, interactional 'cruxes' which are particularly significant in terms of tensions between IDFs or between subjects, and so forth. In this way a systematic understanding of the functioning of discourse in institutions and institutional change could become a feasible target.

The same is true for 'comparative' research on discourse across institutions. The descriptive approach to such research may show interesting similarities or differences in discourse structure and organization, as does work in the Birmingham discourse analysis model (Sinclair and Coulthard (1975: 115–18), Coulthard and Montgomery (1981)). But such comparison requires a principled basis for selecting cases, given which it can contribute to the investigation of substantive social issues such as: the degree to which social institutions are integrated or autonomous in a given social formation, and centralizing or decentralizing tendencies; or the positions of social institutions on a hierarchy of relative importance to the function of the social formation, and how this relates to influences from one institution to another on various levels, including the ideological and discoursal. The work of Foucault (1979) is a suggestive starting point for such research.

4. CONCLUDING REMARKS: RESISTANCE

The following piece of data is, like text 1, an extract from a police interview, though in this case the interviewee is a youth suspected of involvement in an incident during which a bus window was broken. *A* is the youth, *B* is the police interviewer, and the conventions are the same as for text 1.

Text 5

```
 1. B:   so why did ⎡ you get the other fellows to come up with
 2. A:              ⎣ some went up first
 3. B:   you as well
 4. A:   I'm not getting on a bus with a bus load of coons me sitting
         there jack the lad d'you know what I mean ...
 5. B:   why's ⎡ that
 6. A:         ⎣ get laid into what do you mean why's that ...
 7. B:   well they weren't attacking any other white people on the
         bus were they
 8. A:   no ... that's coz there was no other skinhead on the bus that's
         why ... if there was a skinhead on the bus that was it they
         would lay into him
 9. B:   so there's a feud is there
10. A:   yeah ...
11. B:   between skinheads and blacks
12. A:   yeah ...
```

13. *B:* so when you went on the upstairs on the bus because let's face it if there was none of them downstairs was there
14. *A:* no
15. *B:* so why did you go upstairs
16. *A:* like I say there was no room downstairs anyway I don't sit on the bottom of the bus that's where all the grannies sit ... I can't sit down there[10]

In contrast to the orderliness of the texts discussed in section 1.1 of this paper, text 5 manifests a certain 'disorderliness', in the sense that the interviewee is in a number of respects not constraining his contributions to the interaction in accordance with institutional norms for the subject position he is in. This is a case where we have a 'client' rather than an institutional subject; as I indicated earlier, clients can normally be expected to comply with institutional norms. The client here is non-compliant in the following ways:

(a) *A* interrupts *B* (2,5)
(b) *A* challenges *B's* questions rather than answering them (3,5)
(c) *A* questions *B* (5)
(d) *A* questions *B's* sincerity. In 9 and 11, *A* signals prosodically as well as non-vocally that *B* is already in possession of information he purports to be asking for (and therefore not to have).
(e) *A* maintains a different 'orientation' (Sinclair and Coulthard (1975: 130–32)) from *B's*. This is marked by his use of the lexis of his peer group rather than that of police interviews (*coon, jack the lad, grannies*).

One might add that there are indications that *A* gets *B* to adapt to his orientation, whereas one would expect the reverse, i.e. one would expect the client to adapt to the orientation of the subject (and of the institution). For instance, in 6 *B* anaphorically refers to (*a bus load of*) *coons*, rather than using a different lexicalization as one might expect him to if he were 'asserting' his orientation (and as he does in 10, with *blacks*).

Text 5 will no doubt correct any impression that may have been given in this paper that norms are necessarily faithfully mirrored in practices (see note 4). One factor determining how likely it is that a client will comply with the norms which an institution attaches to a subject position, is the particular configuration of processes of subjection in other institutions which have contributed to the social formation of that client. In this instance one might wish to look into the subject positions associated with the client's peer-group, i.e. the relevant 'youth culture'. One dimension of institutional subject construction which I have not referred to in the paper so far is that the institution also constructs the subject's stance towards 'outsiders', including subjects in other institutions. In this case, it could be that the client is constructed into an oppositional stance towards the police and perhaps other public authorities.

The critique of institutional discourse, as part of the critique of social institutions and the social formation, does not take place in glorious academic isolation from the practices of institutional subjects, clients and publics. On the contrary, it is continuous with such practices, and it is only in so far as such practices include significant elements of resistance to dominant IDFs, be it through clients rejecting subject positions as in text 5, or, analogously, readers rejecting the 'preferred reader' positions which writers 'write into' their texts; or through challenges to the dominance of an IDF from other IDFs, that the critique of institutional discourse can develop into a 'material force' with the capacity to contribute to the transformation of institutions and social formations.

Given the existence of such conditions across social institutions, which may occur in a period when the struggle between social forces at the level of the social formation is sharp, it may be possible to introduce forms of critical discourse analysis in the schools, as part of the development of 'language awareness', in the teaching of the mother tongue. The desirability in principle of such a development follows from what I have claimed above: if speakers are standardly operating in discourse under unknown determinants and with unknown effects, it is a proper objective for schools to increase discoursal consciousness. However, I have stressed the conditions for such a development, because it would be naïve to think that its desirability in principle would be sufficient for it to be achieved. On the contrary, it is likely to be fiercely resisted.

NOTES

1. The transcription conventions are: turns are numbered, excluding 'back channels'; beginnings of overlaps are marked with square brackets; pauses are marked with dots for a 'short' pause and a dash for a 'long' pause; material in round brackets was indistinct. For texts 2 and 3 I retain the conventions used in their sources, which are indicated. Text 1 was part of

the data used in a presentation to the Language Study Group of the British Sociological Association (Lancaster Conference, June 1982) by myself and colleagues Christopher Candlin, Michael Makosch, Susan Spencer, Jennifer Thomas. It is taken from the television series *Police* as is text 5.

2. Italicized syllables carry primary stress; intonation is selectively marked; utterance segments which overlap are enclosed within one pair of square brackets; short pauses are marked '^'.

3. I use the term 'social formation' to designate a particular society at a particular time and stage of development (e.g. Britain in 1984). The term 'society' is used too loosely and variously to serve the purpose.

4. The relationship between norms and action is not as simple as this suggests. Sometimes, which norms are the appropriate ones is itself a matter for negotiation; then there may be alternative sets of norms available (see below); and, as I show in section 4, norms may be rejected.

5. I have in mind throughout class societies, and more specifically capitalist social formations such as the one I am most familiar with: that of modern Britain.

6. Nor are ideologies to be equated with 'propaganda' or 'bias'; the latter are associated with particular communicative intentions (such as 'persuading'), the former are not.

7. The concept of BGK has a wide currency across a number of disciplines. The following, for instance, are representative of pragmatics, discourse analysis and sociology: Levinson (1983), Brown and Yule (1983), Giddens (1976).

8. I assume for present purposes that 'knowledge' and 'ideology' are clearly separable, which presupposes a much more categorical distinction between science and ideology than may be sustainable.

9. I use the term 'goal' here with respect to parties in discourse, whereas my use of the term earlier has been with respect to analytical goals. I don't believe there should be any confusion.

10. This text and some of my comments on it derive from a part of the presentation referred to in note 1 which was jointly produced by Michael Makosch, Susan Spencer and myself. I am grateful to all the colleagues referred to in note 1 for providing the stimuli which led to the writing of this paper. I am grateful to my wife Vonny for showing me how to be more coherent; remaining incoherence is my own responsibility.

TWO

Discourse representation in media discourse

The purpose of this paper is to identify tendencies in the representation of spoken and written discourse in newspapers, and to suggest how these tendencies accord with ideologies which are implicit in practices of news production. I use 'discourse representation' rather than the more familiar 'speech reporting' because (a) writing, as well as speech, may be represented, and (b) rather than a transparent 'report' of what was said or written, there is always a decision to interpret and represent it in one way rather than another. I have drawn upon accounts of discourse representation in Leech and Short (1981), McHale (1978), Quirk et al. (1972), but I am particularly indebted to Volosinov (1973). I shall refer to articles which appeared in five British national newspapers on Friday 24 May 1985, all of which are about a report of the House of Commons Home Affairs Committee on hard drug abuse which will be referred to below as 'the Report' (HMSO 1985). Three of the articles are reproduced, in the Appendix.[1] I have selected articles which are about a publicly available written report in order to be in a position – which readers of newspapers usually are not – to compare their representation of discourse with an 'original'. This paper is intended as a contribution to 'critical linguistics' (Fowler et al. 1979, Fairclough 1985, 1989), in that it sets out to explain specific linguistic properties of a particular type of discourse in terms of ideologies and relations of power.

1. TENDENCIES IN DISCOURSE REPRESENTATION

In this section I shall focus upon discourse representation in the five newspaper articles referred to above, using a framework based upon Volosinov's account. Let me briefly identify three salient aspects of this account, using a distinction between 'primary discourse' (the representing or reporting discourse) and 'secondary discourse' (the discourse represented or reported). First, he suggests a typology of discourse representation built around 'the dynamic interrelationship' of primary discourse and secondary discourse: in one major 'style' of representation, primary and secondary discourse are clearly differentiated, in the other they are merged. Secondly, overlapping this distinction is another between types of representation which represent, in Hallidayan terms, only the 'ideational' meaning (or 'message') of secondary discourse, and types which also represent 'interpersonal' ('stylistic', 'expressive') meanings (Halliday (1978): 112–13). Thirdly, Volosinov notes that the way in which secondary discourse is interpreted may be controlled by the way it is contextualized in primary discourse.

My framework draws upon these aspects of Volosinov's account. It incorporates five parameters in terms of which texts or types of discourse can be compared with respect to discourse representation: *mode, boundary maintenance, stylisticity, situationality*, and *setting*. I shall discuss these in turn with reference to the five articles.

Mode

I distinguish here Direct Discourse (DD) and Indirect Discourse (ID) in the same terms as Quirk *et al.* (1972): DD is 'converted' into ID by (a) subordination of the secondary discourse, in the form of a *that*-clause, to the 'reporting clause'; (b) shift from 1 and 2 person pronouns to 3 person pronouns; (c) shift of deictics (e.g. *here* becomes *there*); (d) 'back-shift' of tense. For instance, *Mrs Thatcher warned Cabinet colleagues: 'I will not stand for any backsliding'* is DD, whereas *Mrs Thatcher warned Cabinet colleagues that she would not stand for any backsliding* is ID. One also needs a category for cases of 'slipping' between modes, such as *Mrs Thatcher warned Cabinet colleagues that she would 'not stand for any backsliding'*. Slipping is always into DD in the five articles, and I treat it as a sub-type of DD, coded as 'DD(S)'. A further mode, coded as UNSIG(nalled), is necessary for cases where what is clearly secondary discourse appears in primary discourse without being explicitly marked as represented discourse – *Mrs Thatcher will not stand for any backsliding* as a newspaper headline, for instance. UNSIG includes what Quirk *et al.* (1972) and other standard accounts call Free Indirect Discourse (FID), which is illustrated below. The most significant contrast as far as this article is concerned is between DD and DD(S) where there is explicit demarcation between the 'voice' of the reporter or the newspaper and the 'voice' of the person whose discourse is being

Table 1: Mode of representation

DD	DD(S)	ID	UNSIG		
5	2	15	6	G(28)	
4	0	9	12	M(25)	
4	4	9	5	MS(22)	
6	2	4	4	S(16)	
15	8	12	13	T(48)	
34	16	49	40	139	TOTALS

represented, and ID and UNSIG where these 'voices' are not clearly demarcated.

Table 1 shows the incidence of modes of discourse representation in the five articles. The figures on the right in brackets give total instances of discourse presentation for each newspaper – *The Guardian* (G), *The Mirror* (M), *The Morning Star* (MS), *The Sun* (S), and *The Daily Telegraph* (T). There is a grand total of 139 instances. This includes each example of slipping being coded twice, for the mode it begins in, and for the mode – always DD(S) – it 'slips' into.

DD (if one includes DD(S)) is used overall as frequently as ID, though there are contrasts in their relative frequency between different newspapers. DD appears to be used where (a) the secondary discourse is important, dramatic, pithy, witty, etc., (b) the secondary discourse emanates from an authoritative source, (c) the representer wishes to associate with, or distance from, the secondary discourse – a common motivation for slipping, (d) the report has ample space assigned to it.

In contrast with Leech and Short (1981), I found it impossible to give a precise semantic value to ID. Leech and Short suggest that the use of ID involves a commitment to give the full ideational meaning of the secondary discourse. DD carries a commitment to give also the exact form of the words used. They distinguish both from 'narrative report of speech act' (NRSA), which reports that speech acts have taken place without giving their full ideational meaning (e.g. *she refused the offer*).

I found ID to be inherently ambivalent as to what it represents. It may in some cases represent the full ideational meaning as Leech and Short suggest, but it may also represent less than that. For instance, the italicized instance of ID in the following paraphrases two sentences in the Report:

The committee also attacks the softer attitude towards marijuana, and says *it must be bracketed with the campaign against heroin and cocaine*. (G)

ID may also accurately represent the actual words used, or alternatively a transformation of those words into the 'voice' (in the sense of the style distinctive for, say, a newspaper or some sections of it) of the primary discourse – see 'Boundary maintenance' below for examples. In general, where ID occurs there is ambivalence as to voice.

This ambivalence is part of a wider tendency for primary and secondary discourse not to be clearly differentiated. This accounts for the frequency of UNSIG, where secondary discourse appears without being explicitly marked as such and seems to be primary discourse. The second sentence of the following is an example:

Britain must take immediate draconian measures against hard drugs or be overwhelmed within five years by addiction on the scale which is sweeping America, according to a committee of MPs.
The group has just returned from observing the drugs scene in the United States, where it is estimated that 12 million Americans are regular users of the 'devastating' drug cocaine. (T)

Of course, one only knows that this is UNSIG by checking it against the Report. Under normal reading conditions that possibility would of course not exist, and such instances are likely to be taken simply as primary discourse.

5 of the 40 instances of UNSIG are examples of FID – which in the Quirk *et al.* (1972) account is ID without a 'reporting clause'. For example, the second sentence of:

Stripping of these assets would allow the battle against drugs to be partly self-financing. This had proved so successful in the United States that the assets and money seized had been used to build prisons and buy high-speed launches and aircraft to fight the drug traffickers. (T)

My reason for not treating FID as a separate mode is illustrated in the first sentence of this example: in a number of cases, we have a modal verb (here *would*) which could be taken either as a 'back-shifted' form of a modal in secondary discourse marking FID (here *would* back-shifted from *will* with the meaning of 'prediction'), or as a modal belonging to primary discourse (*would* with a hypothetical meaning).

Boundary maintenance

I referred above to an ambivalence of 'voice' characteristic of ID. 'Boundary maintenance' measures the extent to which the voices of primary and secondary discourse are kept apart or, on the contrary, merged. Merging can occur in either direction. Suppose for instance that the Labour leader Neil Kinnock says 'Margaret Thatcher must resign', and this is represented in two different headlines as *Maggie must get out, says Kinnock* and *Margaret Thatcher must resign.* The former is typical of the case where the secondary discourse is being translated into the voice of the primary discourse, through vocabulary and other changes. I shall call this 'incorporation'. In the latter, the secondary discourse 'takes over' the primary, in the sense that the voice (manifested in vocabulary and other linguistic features) of the secondary discourse directly affects the primary discourse. Notice the mode is UNSIG. I shall call this 'dissemination'.

Boundary maintenance is generally low in the five articles, which means that incorporation and dissemination frequently occur. If we restrict attention to the Report itself, excluding press conferences which were reported in the articles, there is a total of 81 instances of discourse representation, and 58 of these (71%) involve incorporation. The most common form of incorporation is change in the interpersonal or stylistic meanings of secondary discourse. Compare for instance this extract from the Report with its representation in *The Sun*:

> The Government should consider the use of the Royal Navy and the Royal Air Force for radar, airborne or ship surveillance duties. We recommend . . . that there should be intensified law enforcement against drug traffickers by H.M. Customs, the police, the security services and possibly the armed forces. (Report)

> *Call Up Forces in Drug Battle!*
> The armed forces should be called up to fight off a massive invasion by drug pushers, MPs demanded yesterday. (S)

S uses vocabulary items wholly absent from the Report (*call up, battle, fight off, massive, invasion, pushers,* and *forces* without modification). It uses a (dramatic) imperative, in the headline. But S also changes the ideational meaning of the Report – it represents a cautious recommendation that armed forces might be involved as a demand for them to be involved.

The ambivalence of ID referred to earlier is partly a matter of incorporation. ID may represent the actual words used, or it may incorporate the secondary discourse into the primary discourse. These are illustrated respectively by MS, which here reproduces the Report apart from omitting *big* from *big drug dealers*, and S, which substitutes (along with other changes) *pedlars* for *traffickers* and *the country's way of life* for *our national well-being*:

> The MPs say that the ruthlessness of the drug dealers must be met by equally ruthless penalties once they are caught, tried and convicted. (MS)

> Cocaine pedlars are the greatest threat ever faced by Britain in peace time, and could destroy the country's way of life, they said. (S)

The following illustrates dissemination:

> Premier Margaret Thatcher pledged tough new laws against the drug barons yesterday after hearing a shock report.
> The evil traffickers are the most serious peace-time threat to Britain, warned a top team of MPs.
> And unless the Government launches all-out war on them cities could be racked with terror, despair and squalor by 1990. (M)

There is a close link between dissemination and UNSIG. UNSIG is the main mode for dissemination, and all instances of UNSIG involve dissemination. The third sentence is a case. But dissemination may occur with other modes. For example, the second sentence above does have a reporting clause and is ID. But there are various features of its organization which lead one to attribute the voice of the secondary discourse at least partially to the primary discourse: the reporting clause occurs finally, so that the status of what preceeds it as secondary discourse is backgrounded; tense is not back-shifted in the represented clause, so that modally its 'source of authority' appears to be the representer, in the primary discourse; the definite subject noun phrase (*the evil traffickers*) 'rememberships' *the drug barons* from the preceding paragraph, and again the authority source for this (and the evaluation it includes) appears to be the representer.

Although incorporation and dissemination appear on the face of it to be opposite tendencies, there are instances of represented discourse which simultaneously involve both – the second and third sentences of the last example, for instance. Sentence 2 represents the following sentence from the Report:

> We see this (i.e. Britain and Europe inheriting the American drug problem) as the most serious peacetime threat to our well-being.

Although M sticks close to most of the wording, it introduces *traffickers* (which does occur elsewhere in the Report) and *evil* (which does not). Incorporation-plus-dissemination actually occurs in 28 of the 81 instances of represented discourse referring to the Report itself, and is particularly common in S and M. I suggest a reason for its frequency below.

Stylisticity and situationality

These two parameters are closely connected, so I take them together. Stylisticity measures the extent to which the non-ideational, interpersonal meanings of secondary discourse are represented, and situationality the degree to which the context of situation of secondary discourse is represented. Stylisticity is very low – there are just five cases in total where interpersonal aspects of meaning are represented. Representations of context of situation are about four times as common. But even where stylisticity and situationality do occur, they occur overwhelmingly as devices for 'setting' the interpretation of secondary discourse – and for that reason I illustrate them below. There is no evidence that the interpersonal meanings and situational contexts of secondary discourse are regarded as parts of what an adequate representation should include.

Setting

Setting is concerned with the extent to which and ways in which reader/listener interpretation of secondary discourse is controlled by placing it in a particular textual context (or 'cotext'). The incidence of setting was high, occurring in 37 per cent of instances. Here is an example of DD which uses a range of setting devices:

> In one of the hardest-hitting Commons reports for years, the committee – chaired by Tory lawyer MP Sir Edward Gardner – warned gravely: 'Western society is faced . . .'. (S)

One device used here is predisposing interpretation by representing the illocutionary force of the secondary discourse (*warned*). This example also illustrates the contribution of stylisticity to setting, with the style adjunct *gravely* underscoring the weightiness of Gardner's words. What is most striking, though, is the contribution to establishing weightiness of the representation of the context of situation – the extensive membershipping of Gardner as Tory, lawyer, MP, and knight, and the contextualization of Gardner's words within the Report.

These devices cumulatively but implicitly ascribe massive legitimacy to the secondary discourse. A further setting device not illustrated by this example is 'formulation' (Heritage and Watson 1979), usually a summarizing gist of the secondary discourse before it occurs in a fuller representation. This is a function of headlines, and formulations in headlines are often repeated in the initial sentence of a news article. An example is the opening of the S article cited earlier, where both the headline and the initial sentence formulate the third and fourth sentences.

2. EXPLAINING THE TENDENCIES

Let me summarize the main tendencies in the representation of discourse in the five articles: (a) a high incidence of ambivalence between primary and secondary discourse, involving both ID and UNSIG; (b) low boundary maintenance and correspondingly high incorporation and dissemination, and incorporation-plus-dissemination; (c) low stylisticity and situationality; (d) a high degree of setting. It would be rash to draw general conclusions from five articles, but it is my impression that these tendencies have wider validity for media discourse.

They can I think be reduced to two main tendencies. Both (a) and (b) are indicative of a low level of demarcation between primary and secondary discourse. And there is a close connection between incorporation within (b) and setting in (d): in both, primary discourse is shaping secondary discourse, either in terms of its form (incorporation) or in terms of its reception (settings). This gives one main tendency corresponding to (a), (b) and (d), and another corresponding to (c):

Tendency 1: low demarcation between primary and secondary discourse

Tendency 2: focus upon representation of the ideational meaning of the words used

Tendency 1

Hall *et al.* (1978: 61) have referred to a trend in media towards 'the translation of official viewpoints into a public idiom' which not only 'makes the former more "available" to the uninitiated', but also 'invests them with popular force and resonance, naturalizing them within the horizon of understandings of the various publics'. I think that we can best understand tendency 1 as a part of this trend.

If they are effectively to bring about this 'translation', what we might collectively refer to as 'newsgivers' (the perceived source of news, be it a newsreader or a journalist) need to be in a particular rapport with audiences. Newsgivers have come to adopt the position of *mediators*, figures who cultivate 'characteristics which are taken to be typical of the "target" audience' and a relationship of solidarity with it, and can mediate newsworthy events to the audience in the latter's 'common sense' terms (Hartley 1982: 87). This shift in the role of newsgiver reflects economic pressures to make news a more 'saleable commodity' in order to win bigger audiences, and more advertising revenue in some cases. It is easy to see how incorporation fits into this picture: the process of 'translation' is from the 'voice' of the secondary discourse to the 'voice' of the primary discourse, where the latter is presented as the voice of mediator and audience. But what about the other elements of tendency 1?

Goffman (1981: 144) has suggested that what we normally think of as simply the role of 'speaker' or 'writer' in fact conflates three roles: *animator* – the person who is actually making the sounds, or the marks on paper; *author* – the one who put the words together; and *principal*, the one whose position is represented by the words. Newsgivers are at least animators. Sometimes they are also authors; but sometimes they act as if they were authors, or indeed principals, when they are not. We can relate this latter tendency to the mediator role: if one is a mediator, one cannot come across as a mere animator or mouthpiece, there is pressure to put one's own position on the line. The mediator can affect a degree of commitment by simulating authorship, which is often innocent enough. But the status of principal is more complicated. The mediator cannot be seen as speaking or writing simply on her or his own behalf, and yet needs to appear committed. One 'solution' is for the mediator to purport to speak on behalf of the audience, with the audience/mediator as principals. Since actual principals will often be other than the mediator or audience – others in media organizations, or 'sources' in public life – a degree of mystification of principalship is common. This is where two other elements of tendency 1 come in: ambivalence of mode and dissemination, where authorship or principalship which originate in secondary discourse appear to attach to primary discourse.

There is an added twist when we consider which sectors of the society actually come to have their positions represented in the news media. Access to the media is most open to socially dominant sectors, both as 'reliable sources' and as 'accessed voices' appearing in represented discourse and interviews (Hartley 1982: 111). According to Halloran *et al.*, for example, 'preferred sources are ... identifiable individuals with known views and, ideally, well-known public figures who occupy some "official" or semi-official position' (1970: 137). As a consequence, the set of potential principals for the utterances of the news media is very much a socially contracted set. In so far as principalship is mystified, the news media can be regarded as covertly transmitting the voices of social power-holders. And the final element of tendency 1, *setting*, gives the possibility of control of the reception of pieces of represented discourse through the adjustment of their primary discourse context.

It is not necessary to see these transformations of secondary discourse as always or generally conscious distortion or manipulation; they can perhaps rather be regarded as built into common-sense professional practices. But whatever the motivations of media personnel, the social function of the media in effecting such transformations as a part of the trend identified by Hall *et al.* is to legitimize and reproduce existing asymmetrical power relationships by putting across the voices of the powerful as if they were the voices of 'common sense'. Although the chain is a complex one, it is thus possible to trace links between structural properties of the system of social relationships, and the favouring of particular forms of discourse representation.

The case of incorporation-plus-dissemination, which I commented upon in the last section as an apparent paradox and yet very common in the sample, now appears to be archetypical for tendency 1: secondary discourse is both translated into the familiar voice of primary discourse, and portrayed as if it originated in primary discourse.

The 'mediator' role for newsgivers is better developed in some media outlets than others, and one would expect tendency 1 to be most in evidence in these outlets. The five articles I have referred to offer some modest evidence of this. Within the press, it is the 'popular' newspapers such as S and M which have most developed the mediator role, and the S and M articles are clearly ahead of the others in respect of one element of tendency 1, boundary maintenance. This is most evident in the case of incorporation-plus-dissemination, which occurs in 6 out of the 8 representations of the Report in S, 9 out of 16 in M, 9 out of 25 in T, 2 out of 13 in MS, and 2 out of 19 in G.

Tendency 2

It may be that ours is a highly ideational culture, that 'another's speech is received as one whole block of social behaviour, as the speaker's indivisible, conceptual position – in which case only the "what" of speech is taken in and the "how" is left outside reception' (Volosinov 1973: 119). But there are certainly gradations in this respect: oral narrative, for instance, would appear to be significantly more oriented towards representing non-ideational, interpersonal aspects of meaning than media discourse. Also, the fact that the articles I have referred to are representing a written document may lead to a greater orientation to ideational meaning, though there seems to be no more of an orientation to interpersonal meaning and situational context in those parts of the articles which represent the press conference rather than the Report.

News tends to be seen as very much a conceptual and ideational business, a matter of statements, claims, beliefs, positions – rather than feelings, circumstances, qualities of social and interpersonal relationships, and so forth. Correspondingly the focus is upon *what* is said by the mainly public figures and organizations whose discourse is reported – to the extent that there is rarely any concession to the commonplace in social studies of language that what is said, the ideational meaning, may depend upon how it is said and under what social circumstances. The assumption is that the words themselves are ideationally transparent. We can regard this as an ideological representation of language which underlies tendency 2, and which seems to be characteristic of what is generally regarded as within the 'public' domain as opposed to the 'private' domain. There is also a system of values here: the 'public' has greater prestige than the 'private', and implicitly those aspects of discourse which merit public representation – the ideational aspects – are ascribed greater import than those which are of merely private significance.

Another related explanation for tendency 2 is the myth that the media are a 'mirror' to reality. To sustain this myth, one needs another: that reality is transparent and can be 'read' without mediation or interpretation. It is just plausible (though mistaken) to maintain that the ideational meaning of secondary discourses is transparently 'there' in the words used, but it would be quite impossible to sustain the same claim about interpersonal meanings, which so obviously depend upon discourse situation and wider social context, and which so obviously need to be interpreted and represented. These myths are the by-product of the tendency for dominant ideological representations of reality to be naturalized as the only possible ways of seeing reality, which is consequently construed as transparent.

3. CONCLUSION

I have suggested in this paper that the representation of discourse in news media can be seen as an ideological process of considerable social importance, and that the finer detail of discourse representation, which on the face of it is merely a matter of technical properties of the grammar and semantics of texts, may be tuned to social determinants and social effects. It is I believe important both for linguists to be sensitive to how discourse is shaped by and helps to shape social structures and relations, and for sociologists to be sensitive to how social structures and relations are instantiated in the fine detail of daily social practices, including discourse.

NOTE

1. I am grateful to *The Guardian*, *The Daily Mirror* and *The Sun* for permission to reproduce the articles included in the appendix.

APPENDIX

Three of the articles referred to are reproduced on pages 67–9. In the case of the S article, I have numbered (1–14) those sentences which contain discourse representation, and shown my analysis for them in Table 2 on the next page.

Table 2: Analysis of discourse representation in S

Instance	Mode	B/Maintenance	Setting
1	DD	INC/DISS	IF
2	UNSIG	INC/DISS	—
3	ID	INC/DISS	F, IF
4	ID	INC/DISS	—
5	UNSIG	INC/DISS	IF
6	UNSIG	INC/DISS	—
7	UNSIG	DISS	SIT
8	DD	INC	SIT, IF, STYLE
9	DD	/	—
10	DD	/	—
11	DD(S)	/	SIT
12	DD	/	F
13	UNSIG	/DISS	—
14	DD(S)	/	SIT

Table notes

1. DD(S) codes slipping from ID into DD.

2. INC/DISS codes incorporation-plus-dissemination. The slash (/) in 9–14 relates to incorporation, and means 'not applicable' – these instances report the press conference rather than the Report.

3. Types of setting are distinguished as follows: IF = representation of illocutionary force, F = formulation, SIT = representation of aspects of context of situation, STYLE = representation of interpersonal meaning.

1 Britain faces a war to stop pedlars, warn MPs

CALL UP FORCES
2 # IN DRUG BATTLE!

By DAVID KEMP

3 THE armed forces should be called up to fight off a massive invasion by drug pushers, MPs demanded yesterday.

4 Cocaine pedlars are the greatest threat ever faced by Britain in peacetime — and could destroy the country's way of life, they said.

5 The MPs want Ministers to consider ordering the Navy and the RAF to track suspected drug-running ships approaching our coasts.

6 On shore there should be intensified law enforcement by Customs, police and security services.

Profits

7 The all-party Home Affairs Committee visited America and were deeply shocked by what they saw.

8 In one of the hardest-hitting Commons reports for years, the committee—chaired by Tory lawyer MP Sir Edward Gardner — warned gravely:

❝ Western society is faced by a warlike threat from the hard-drugs industry.

The traffickers amass princely incomes from the exploitation of human weakness, boredom and misery.

They must be made to lose everything — their homes, their money and all they possess which can be attributed to their profits from selling drugs. ❞

9 Sir Edward said yesterday: "We believe that trafficking in drugs is tantamount to murder and punishment ought to reflect this."

The Government is expected to bring in clampdown laws in the autumn.

Photo of Miss Fookes

Miss Fookes ... "There was evil in the air" **10**

Horror watch on addicts

11 ● THE investigators' "horrifying" trip to America was described by Tory MP Miss Janet Fookes last night. She **12** said: "You felt there was evil in the air."

13 ● In New York's East Side they saw drug dealers in the boarded-up buildings push drugs through make-shift hatchways to addicts in the streets.

14 ● Committee chairman Sir Edward Gardner said his escort moved him away because "a man watching us from ninth storey of the building was preparing to drop a lump of concrete on us."

The Sun

MPs urge harsher heroin penalties

By David Hencke, Social Services Correspondent

Tough legal action to counter what MPs describe as the biggest threat to the stability of peace time Britain — the burgeoning heroin and cocaine trade — was demanded yesterday by the all-party Commons home affairs committee.

Its report calls for harsher penalties for drug traffickers than currently given to IRA terrorists, murderers and child molesters.

The Prime Minister, Mrs Thatcher said yesterday in the Commons that the Home Secretary, Mr Leon Brittan, was working on precise proposals for legislation "to seize and confiscate the proceeds of drug traffickers."

The home affairs committee wants to bring in the Navy and the RAF to survey and possibly intercept ships suspected of bringing in heroin or cocaine.

The report says that life sentences — equivalent to the penalty for premeditated murder — should be meted out for all people convicted of drug-trafficking, including foreigners who would stand trial in Britain rather than being deported. Sir Edward Gardner, the chairman, wanted the death penalty restored.

The seizure and forfeiture of all assets acquired by a drug trafficker his wife and children if they can be connected to money obtained through heroin is also recommended. This process would be helped by revising the burden of proof from the police to the defendant in civil proceedings, so that even a person acquitted of drug trafficking would still have to provide the police with evidence of how they purchased their houses, boats, cars, aircraft, jewellery and clothing to prevent their being seized.

The home affairs committee also calls for a change in international banking laws to allow the police to obtain information to stop the "laundering" of money obtained by crime from being transferred elsewhere. This would allow banking assets to be seized even if they went abroad.

On a more mundane level the MPs also called for police attaches with diplomatic status to be attached to the Washington Embassy and to the Consulate in Atlanta, plus more cash to persuade Third World countries to eradicate drug crops.

The committee also attacks the softer attitude towards marijuana, and says it must be bracketed with the campaign against heroin and cocaine. One committee member, Mr Robin Corbett, Labour MP for Birmingham Erdington, said that those who had argued for the legalisation of marijuana had been proved wrong because people did progress from one drug to another. "The equivalent is switching from shandy to whisky," he said.

Sir Edward Gardner, said the MPs had been heavily influenced and shaken by their visit to the United States. Their report found that an estimated 12 million Americans regularly use cocaine, with the wealthy and successful middle classes spending up to $3,000 each a week to satisfy their craving.

"We fear that unless immediate and effective action is taken Britain and Europe stand to inherit the American drug problem in less than five years. We see this as the most serious peacetime threat to our national well-being," the report says "Western society is faced by a warlike threat from the hard drugs industry."

It adds: "All those whom we consulted in the US made no attempt to conceal their anxieties about the future of drug abuse. Given that the richest nation on earth has now mobilised its resources to the maximum possible extent against the drug traffickers, we found it frightening to be told that they aimed to do no more than 'hold the line,' and never claimed to be able to intercept more than 10 per cent of the drugs sent to the US Borders."

Sir Edward and Miss Janet Fookes, a Conservative member of the committee, placed great store on the seizing of assets to provide funds for governments to build up their policing of the drug trade.

Miss Fookes said she hoped that seizures would make policing "self-funding," while Sir Edward said that in the United States the confiscated assets had been used to build prisons and buy high speed launches and aircraft.

The Guardian

Shock report warns of worst peacetime threat

PREMIER Margaret Thatcher pledged tough new laws against drug barons yesterday after hearing a shock report.

The evil traffickers are the most serious peace-time threat to Britain, warned a top team of MPs.

And unless the Government launches all-out war on them cities could be racked with terror, despair and squalor by 1990.

The MPs probed the drug crisis in the US.

And chairman Sir Edward Gardner, QC, said: "Without swift action what is happening in New York, Atlanta and Miami will undoubtedly happen in London, Manchester and Liverpool."

To combat the threat the Commons Home Affairs Committee want to:

MOBILIZE the Army, Navy and RAF to intercept drug supplies.

SEIZE assets from people suspected for drug trafficking–even if they have not been convicted.

STRIP the secrecy from banks which allow traffickers to hide their huge profits.

SENTENCE the drug barons to life.

THE MPs were horrified by what they saw on their 10-day investigation in America.

Committee member Robin Corbett said: "We have seen the future and it is frightening."

The committee said America's most devastating drug is cocaine with 12 million people regularly using it and 50,000 new addicts a day.

They spend up to £2,500 each a week to satisfy their craving.

Up to 60 per cent of all crime

WAR ON DRUG PUSHERS

BY JOHN DESBOROUGH

against property is to finance drug-taking.

The MPs fear that when the American market becomes saturated the flood of hard drugs will cross the Atlantic.

US officials warned the MPs that Britain would inherit exactly the same problems within five years unless action is taken now.

The stability of society is threatened by the drug barons who use their huge profits to corrupt.

The MPs said they, their wives and children should be stripped of money, homes, cars and any other assets – even if they are acquitted by a criminal court.

The burden of proof should be on defendants to show their assets came from honest money – a complete reversal of the present system.

The MPs also called for the appointment of police attaches in Washington and Atlanta –

nerve centre of the US's battle to stem imports through Florida and the Caribbean.

Sir Edward said he wanted to see major traffickers hanged – but conceded it was politically impossible.

But the MPs said penalties must be so ruthless that no major dealer would risk taking on the United Kingdom.

Mrs Thatcher said in the Commons new laws would be introduced next session.

They would make it possible to seize the assets of traffickers.

Britain had a 30 per cent rise in drug trafficking last year.

Scotland Yard's head of CID, Assistant Commissioner John Dellow, warned he had too few officers to stem the flood of heroin and cocaine.

"It was a bad year. Some very, very evil men are making a massive amount of money," he said.

Daily Mirror

THREE

Language and ideology

1. INTRODUCTION

This paper explores the theoretical question of what sort of relationships there are between language and ideology, and the methodological question of how such relationships are shown in analysis (which together I refer to as 'language/ideology'). It is an attempt to build from the achievements and limitations of explorations of these questions within Marxism, especially Althusser's contribution to the theory of ideology and its development by Pêcheux into a theory of discourse and a method for discourse analysis (see Althusser 1971; Larrain 1979; Haroche, Henry, Pêcheux 1971; Pêcheux 1975 (1982)). I have found the self-criticism of Pêcheux and his associates in their most recent work a valuable resource for going beyond structuralist accounts of language/ideology (Conein *et al.* 1981; Maldidier 1984; Pêcheux 1988).

I discuss the merits of 'locating' ideology in language structures or language events and conclude it is present in both. I outline a conception of discourse and discourse analysis which is compatible with this conclusion, and suggest that a more diverse range of linguistic features and levels may be ideologically invested than is usually assumed, including aspects of linguistic form and style as well as 'content'. I then argue that language/ideology issues ought to figure in the wider framework of theories and analyses of power, for which the Gramscian concept of hegemony is fruitful. This implies a focus in studies of language/ideology upon change in discoursal practice and structures, seen as a dimension of change in the balance of social forces. I conclude with a discussion of the limits of ideology and the possibilities for combating ideological discourse.

2. LOCATION OF IDEOLOGY

I want to argue that ideology invests language in various ways at various levels, and that we don't have to choose between different possible 'locations' of ideology, all of which seem partly justified and none of which seems entirely satisfactory. The key issue is whether ideology is a property of structures or a property of events, and the answer is 'both'. And the key problem is to find a satisfactory account of the dialectic of structures and events.

A number of accounts place ideology in some form of system of potential underlying language practice – be it a 'code', 'structure', 'system' or 'formation' (e.g. a set of expressions in specified semantic relations). These structures are defined for various varieties of a language, not for a language *per se*. The 'structure' option, as I shall call it, has the virtue of showing events, actual discoursal practice, to be constrained by social conventions, norms, histories. It has the disadvantage of tending to defocus the event on the assumption that events are mere instantiations of structures, whereas the relationship of events to structures would appear to be less neat and less compliant. This privileges the perspective of reproduction rather than that of transformation, and the ideological conventionality and repetitiveness of events. Pêcheux is a case in point, though he represents an advance on Althusser in opening up the possibility of resistance through 'counteridentification' and 'disidentification'. It also tends to postulate entities (codes, formations, etc.) which appear to be more clearly bounded than real entities are, thus privileging the synchronic moment of fixity over historical processes of fixation and dissolution.

An alternative location for ideology would be the discursive event itself. This has the virtue of representing ideology as a process which goes on in events, and it permits transformation and fluidity to be highlighted. But it can lead to an illusory view of discourse as free processes of formation unless there is a simultaneous emphasis on structures. There is a textual variant of this location: ideologies reside in texts. While it is true that the forms and content of texts do bear the imprint of ideological processes and structures, it is not possible to 'read off' ideologies from texts. This is because meanings are produced through interpretations of texts and texts are open to diverse interpretations, and because ideological processes appertain to discourses as whole social events – they are processes between people – not to the texts which are produced, distributed and interpreted as moments of such events. Claims to discover ideological processes solely through text analysis run into the problem now familiar in media sociology that text 'consumers' (readers, viewers) appear sometimes to be quite immune to the effects of such ideologies (Morley 1983).

Both the structure and discourse options (as well as the text option) have the limitation of being localized and particular. Ideologies cut across the boundaries of situation types and institutions, and we need to be able to discuss how they transcend particular codes or types of discourse (a simple example would be metaphors of the nation as a family), how ideology relates to the structuring and restructuring of relations between such entities. The concept of 'interdiscourse' is helpful here, so too is Foucault's concept of 'order of discourse' (Foucault 1971) which I shall use. Once again, the structural focus on orders of discourse needs a complementary focus on events, where these restructurings concretely take place.

An issue is what sort of entities are involved in the (re)structuring of orders of discourse. Without attempting a detailed account of the structuring of orders of discourse, I would like to suggest the entities which make them up are (a) more or less clearly defined, (b) variable in scale, and (c) in various relationships to each other, including the relationships of complementarity, inclusion, and contradiction. I re-marked above that structures are sometimes conceived of as more clearly bounded than they are; some entities seem to be sharply differentiated, others fuzzy. The entities which are articulated and rearticulated in discourse are not all fully-fledged codes or registers; they may be smaller scale entities such as turn-taking systems, lexicons which incorporate particular classifications, generic scripts for narratives (for instance), sets of politeness conventions, and so forth. Finally, orders of discourse should I suggest be seen as heterogeneous in the sense that they articulate both compatible and complementary entities and contradictory entities – such as contrasting lexicalizations, or turn-taking systems. These suggested properties of orders of discourse accord with thinking in 'second-generation' French discourse analysts. They also, as I shall show, harmonize with the concept of hegemony.

Ideology is located, then, both in structures which constitute the outcome of past events and the conditions for current events, and in events themselves as they reproduce and transform their conditioning structures. In the following two sections I shall present a way of conceptualizing (use of) language and a matrix for conceptualizing ideology in its relation to economic and political relations which harmonize with this position.

3. DISCOURSE AND TEXT

The Saussurean conception of language use or parole sees it in individualistic and asocial terms. In using the term 'discourse' I am claiming language use to be imbricated in social relations and processes which systematically determine variations in its properties, including the linguistic forms which appear in texts. One aspect of this imbrication in the social which is inherent to the notion of discourse is that language is a material form of ideology, and language is invested by ideology.

Also inherent to discourse is the dialectical relation of structure/ event discussed above: discourse is shaped by structures, but also contributes to shaping and reshaping them, to reproducing and transforming them. These structures are most immediately of a discoursal/ ideological nature – orders of discourse, codes and their elements such as vocabularies or turn-taking conventions – but they also include in a mediated form political and economic structures, relationships in the market, gender relations, relations within the state and within the institutions of civil society such as education.

The relationship of discourse to such extra-discoursal structures and relations is not just representational but constitutive: ideology has material effects, discourse contributes to the creation and constant recreation of the relations, subjects (as recognized in the Althusserian concept of interpellation) and objects which populate the social world. The parent–child relationships of the family, the determination of what positions of 'mother', 'father' and 'child' are socially available as well as the subjection of real individuals to these positions, the nature of the family, or of the home, are all shaped in the ideological processes of discourse. This could easily lead to the idealist inversion referred to earlier whereby the realities of the social world are seen as emanating from ideas. However, there are two provisos which together block this. First, people are always confronted with the family as a real institution (in a limited number of variants) with concrete practices: existing family structures are also partly constituted in ideology and discourse, but reified into institutions and practices. Second, the constitutive work of discourse necessarily takes place within the constraints of the complex of economic, political and discoursal/ideological structures referred to above – and I shall argue later in relation to particular hegemonic projects and struggle. The result is that the ideological and discoursal shaping of the real is always caught up in the networks of the real.

I see discourse as a complex of three elements: social practice, discoursal practice (text production, distribution and consumption), and text, and the analysis of a specific discourse calls for analysis in each of these three dimensions and their interrelations. The hypothesis is that significant connections exist between features of texts, ways in which texts are put together and interpreted, and the nature of the social practice (see paper 5 for details of this framework).

Ideology enters this picture first in the ideological investment of elements which are drawn upon in producing or interpreting a text, and the ways they are articulated together in orders of discourse: and second in the ways in which these elements are articulated together and orders of discourse rearticulated in discoursal events (detailed below). In the former connection, it should be noted that the richness of the ideological elements which go into producing and interpreting a text may be sparsely represented in the text. An example might be the way in which scare quotes are used to signal a point of confrontation between ideologies (and discourses) which are not further represented in the text – around the word 'personal' in the expression 'the "personal" problems of young people' in a left-wing newspaper (for which many 'personal' problems will be social).

A further substantive question about ideology is what features or levels of language and discourse may be ideologically invested. A common claim is that it is 'meanings' (sometimes specified as 'content' as opposed to 'form') that are ideological (e.g., Thompson (1984)), and this often means just or mainly lexical meanings. Lexical meanings are of course important, but so too are presuppositions, implicatures, metaphors, and coherence, all aspects of meaning. For instance, coherent interpretations of texts are arrived at by interpreters on the basis of cues in the text, and resources (including internalized ideological and discoursal structures) which they bring to text interpretation. Coherence is a key factor in the ideological constitution and reconstitution of subjects in discourse: a text 'postulates' a subject 'capable' of auto-matically linking together its potentially highly diverse and not explic-itly linked elements to make sense of it. In postulating such a subject, a text contributes to constituting such a subject.

The 'form'–'content' opposition is itself misleading, however. If content is to enter the realm of practice, it must do so in formal clothing, in texts or other material forms, though it is possible to study forms as if they were unrelated to content, as linguists sometimes do. In fact, formal features of texts at various levels may be ideologically invested. For example, the representation of slumps and unemployment as akin to natural disasters may involve a preference for intransitive and attributive rather than transitive sentence structures ('the currency has lost its value', 'millions are out of work', as opposed to 'investors are buying gold', 'firms have sacked millions' – see Fowler *et al.* (1979)). At a different level, crime stories in newspapers are written according to relatively predictable scripts which embody ideological representations of crime (Jordanidou (1990)). Again, the turn-taking system in a classroom or politeness conventions operating between a manager and a secretary imply particular ideologial representations of teacher–pupil and manager–secretary relations. Nevertheless, it may be useful to think of ideologies in terms of content-like entities which are manifested in various formal features, and perhaps frame, schema, script and related concepts are of value in this respect (Schank and Abelson (1977)).

Even aspects of the 'style' of a text may be ideologically significant. When for instance public bodies such as government ministries produce public information on their schemes and activities, they select a style of writing (or indeed televising) partly on the basis of the image they thereby construct for themselves. This can be regarded as a special sort of ideological process of subject constitution. A topical case in point is the Department of Trade and Industry's publicity for its 'enterprise' initiatives. The Department seems to be trying to create for itself the image of the entrepreneur of 'enterprise culture', in its efforts to persuade others to adopt the same image and identity. It does this in part stylistically. Its publicity for instance is full of categorical, authoritative and unmitigated statements about business practice aimed at businessmen (e.g. 'It's no good expecting to make the right decisions for your business if you don't start with decent information') which have I think more to do with establishing a categorical and authoritative and decisive image than with giving 'information' (or rather opinions) which addressees must already have.

4. HEGEMONY

The concept of hegemony originates in Lenin but is the centrepiece in an elaborated form of Gramsci's analysis of Western capitalism and revolutionary strategy in Western Europe. I shall make use of it both because it harmonizes with the dialectical conception of structure/ event advocated above, and because it provides a framework for theorizing and analysing ideology/discourse which avoids both economism and idealism. Hegemony cuts across and integrates economy, politics and ideology, yet ascribes an authentic place to each of them within an overall focus upon politics and power, and upon the dialectical relations between classes and class fragments.

Hegemony is leadership as well as domination across the economic, political, cultural and ideological domains of a society. Hegemony is the power over society as a whole of one of the fundamental economically defined classes in alliance (as a bloc) with other social forces, but it is never achieved more than partially and temporarily, as an 'unstable equilibrium'. Hegemony is about constructing alliances, and integrating rather than simply dominating subordinate classes, through concessions or through ideological means, to win their consent. Hegemony is a focus of constant struggle around points of greatest instability between classes and blocs, to construct or sustain or fracture alliances and relations of domination/subordination, which takes economic, political and ideological forms. Hegemonic struggle takes place on a broad front which includes the institutions of civil society (education, trade unions, family), with possible unevenness between different levels and domains.

Ideology is understood within this framework in terms which bear the seeds of all Althusser's advances (Buci-Glucksmann (1980): 66), in, for instance, its focusing of the implicit and unconscious materialization of ideologies in practices (which contain them as implicit theoretical 'premisses'), ideology being 'a conception of the world that is implicitly manifest in art, in law, in economic activity and in the manifestations of individual and collective life' (Gramsci 1971: 328). While the interpellation of subjects is an Althusserian elaboration, there is in Gramsci a conception of subjects as structured by diverse ideologies implicit in their practice which gives them a 'strangely composite' character (1971: 324), and a view of 'common sense' as both a depositary of the diverse effects of past ideological struggles, and a constant target for restructuring, in ongoing struggles. In common sense, ideologies become naturalized, or automatized. For Gramsci, ideology is tied to action, and ideologies are judged in terms of their social effects rather than their truth values. Moreover, Gramsci conceived of 'the field of ideologies in terms of conflicting, overlapping, or intersecting currents or formations' (Hall 1988: 55–6), which highlights the question of how the elements of what he calls 'an ideological complex' (Gramsci 1971: 195) come to be structured and restructured, articulated and rearticulated, in processes of ideological struggle. This is a perspective developed by Laclau and Mouffe (1985), though in terms which reject basic Gramscian positions such as the rootedness of hegemony in class (see also Laclau (1979)).

The ideological dimensions of hegemonic struggle can be conceptualized and analysed in terms of the view of discourse I have introduced above. An order of discourse constitutes the discoursal/ideological facet of a contradictory and unstable equilibrium (hegemony); notice that the view outlined above of an order of discourse as complex, heterogeneous and contradictory harmonizes with the concept of ideological complex. And discoursal practice is a facet of struggle which contributes in varying degrees to the reproduction or transformation of the existing order of discourse, and through that of existing social and power relations. Let us take the political discourse of Thatcherism as an example. Thatcherite discourse can be interpreted as a rearticulation of the existing order of political discourse which has brought traditional conservative, neo-liberal and populist discourse elements into a new mix that has also constituted an unprecedented discourse of political power for a woman leader. This discoursal rearticulation materializes an ideological project for the constitution of a new political base, new political subjects, and a new agenda, itself a facet of the political project of restructuring the hegemony of the bloc centred upon the bourgeoisie in new economic and political conditions. Thatcherite discourse has been described along these lines by Hall (1988), and Fairclough (1989) shows how such an analysis can be carried out in terms of the conception of discourse introduced above, in a way which accounts for (as Hall does not) the specific features of the language of Thatcher's political texts. I should add that the rearticulated order of discourse is a contradictory one: authoritarian elements coexist with democratic and egalitarian ones (textually, for instance, inclusive *we* coexists with indefinite *you*), patriarchal elements with feminist elements, but always with the latter member of each pair being contained and constrained by the former. The rearticulation of orders of discourse, however, is achieved not only in productive discoursal practice, but also in interpretation: because of the heterogeneous elements which go into their production, texts are open to many ambivalences which are reduced if not eliminated by particular interpretative practices which draw upon particular configurations of discoursal elements as parts of their interpretative procedures.

However, most discourse does not bear upon hegemonic struggle in such a direct way as Thatcherite discourse. In most discourse, the protagonists (as it were) are not classes or political forces linked in such relatively direct ways to classes or blocs, but for instance teachers and pupils, counsellors and clients, police and public, women and men. Hegemony is a process at the societal level, whereas most discourse has a more local character, being located in or on the edges of particular institutions – the family, schools, neighbourhoods, work-places, courts of law, etc. We have to honour the specificity of such institutional domains. However, hegemony still provides both a model and a matrix. It provides a model: in, let us say, education, the dominant groups also appear to exercise power through constituting alliances, integrating rather than merely dominating subordinate groups, winning their consent, achieving a precarious equilibrium which may be undermined by other groups, and doing so in part through discourse and ideology, through the constitution of and struggle around local orders of discourse, no less heterogeneous and contradictory than their societal counterpart. It provides a matrix: the achievement of hegemony at a societal level requires a degree of integration of local and semi-autonomous institutions and power relations, so that the latter are partially shaped by hegemonic relations. This directs attention to links across institutions, and links and movement between institutional orders of discourse. What is necessary but difficult to accomplish is giving proper weight to integration without thereby playing down the relative autonomy and integrity of non-class struggles: between the sexes, ethnic groups, and the various categories of institutional agent.

From the perspective of hegemony, it is processes which are in focus: local processes of constituting and reconstituting social relations through discourse, global processes of integration and disintegration transcending particular institutions and local orders of discourse. Dis-coursal change, and its relationship to ideological change and to social struggle and change in a broader sense, is where the emphasis must be placed, and where the language/ideology problem should be con-fronted. And in accordance with the dialectical view of structure/event above, a study of discoursal change needs a double focus on the discoursal event and on the societal and institutional orders of discourse.

By change in discoursal events I mean innovation or creativity which in some way goes against conventions and expectations. Change involves forms of transgression, crossing boundaries, such as putting together existing codes or elements in new combinations, or drawing upon orders of discourse or their elements in situations which conven-tionally preclude them in a way which gives a sense of a struggle between different ways of signifying a particular domain of experience. Change leaves traces in texts in the form of the co-occurrence of contradictory or inconsistent elements – mixtures of formal and informal styles, technical and non-technical vocabularies, markers of authority and familiarity, more typically written and more typically spoken syntactic forms, and so forth. The immediate origins and motivations of change lie in contradictions which may problematize conventions in a variety of ways. For example, contradictions which occur in the positioning of subjects, such as those involving gender-relations, where gender-linked discoursal and other practices have been problematized and changed under the impact of contradictions between traditional gendered subject positions which many of us were socialized into, and new gender relations. People are faced with what Billig et al. (1988) call 'ideological dilemmas', which they attempt to resolve or contain through discoursal forms of struggle. On a rather different plane, Thatcher's political discourse can be seen to arise out of the problematisation of traditional rightwing discoursal practices in circumstances where contradictions become apparent between the social relations, subject positions and political practices they are based in and a changing world. Such subjective apprehensions of problems in concrete situations have their social conditions in stuctural contradictions at the institutional and societal levels, upon which discoursal events have cumulative effects. In terms of the framework for discourse analysis introduced in the previous section, social conditions and effects are analysed in the dimension of social practice, 'ideological dilemmas' and attempts to resolve them in the dimension of discourse practice, and textual traces in the dimension of text.

In respect of structural change, changes which appear to move across boundaries between institutional orders of discourse are of particular interest in their possible links to wider hegemonic projects. Let me refer to two changes of this sort. One is an apparent democratization of discourse which involves the reduction of overt markers of power asymmetry between people of unequal institutional power – teachers and pupils, academics and students, employers/managers and workers, parents and children, doctors and patients. This tendency is manifested in a great many different institutional domains. Although there are variations between them, it appears to be generally interpretable not as the elimination of power asymmetry but its transformation into covert forms. For example, teachers may exercise control in discourse with pupils less through direct orders and overt constraints on their rights to speak than through indirect requests and suggestions and the way they react and respond (facially and physically as well as verbally) to pupils' contributions. Such discourse can be seen in terms of contradictory mixtures of discourses of equality and power. The second example is what I have called 'synthetic personalisation' (Fairclough (1989)). This is the simulation of private, face-to-face, person-to-person discourse in public mass-audience discourse – print, radio, television. Both examples are I think interpretable in hegemonic terms, though to do so properly would require more space than I have here. Discoursal democratization is of course linked to political democratization, and to the broad shift from coercion to consent, incorporation and pluralism in the exercise of power. Synthetic personalization is I think a facet of a concomitant process of the breaking down of divisions between public and private, political society and civil society, as the state and its mechanisms (especially ideological) of generating consent expand into private domains. Although both cases can perhaps be seen in pessimistic terms as illusions of democracy, informality and so forth being projected for ulterior motives, the fact that orders of discourse do incorporate these elements if only in ways limited and constrained by others renders them open, if we adopt a hegemonic model, to discoursal struggle directed at promoting these elements, as it were. In this sense democratization and personalization as strategies are high risk.

Are discoursal changes of this order necessarily ideologically invested, and what are their implications for the language/ideology problem? It is quite conceivable that changes in discoursal practices and restructuring of orders of discourse could come about for purely rational reasons. For example, it could well be that doctors are more likely to arrive at sound medical judgements if they talk with their patients conversationally on a roughly (at least apparently) equal footing than if they merely subject them to batteries of preconstructed verbal and physical examinations. But the rational motivations for such a change are virtually bound to attract an ideological overlay by the fact that the change takes places within existing power relations inside and outside medicine. Let me spell this out: in so far as changes in practices and restructurings can be said to embody representations, propositions or assumptions which affect (sustain, undermine) relations of power, they can be said to be ideological. This is broadly similar to Thompson's view of ideology as meaning in the service of relations of domination (though I would add resistance to domination), or Frow's view of ideology as a 'political functionalization of speech' (Thompson (1984): 4, Frow (1985): 204). For discourse, being ideological does not therefore preclude being other things as well.

This does not mean however that the specific ideological import of a particular element is fixed. Consider for example the apparently nondirective, nonjudgemental, empathizing way of talking to people one-to-one about themselves and their problems which we call 'counselling'. Counselling has its origins in therapy, but it now circulates as a technique across many institutional domains. It is highly ambivalent ideologically. Most counsellors see themselves as giving space to people as individuals in a world which increasingly treats them as ciphers, which makes counselling look like a counter-hegemonic practice. However, counselling is now used in preference to practices of an overtly disciplinary nature in various institutions, which makes it look like a hegemonic technique for subtly drawing aspects of people's private lives into the domain of power. Hegemonic struggle of an ideological order is partly through counselling and partly over counselling.

The picture of language/ideology which emerges from this discussion is moving towards Frow's view of ideology as 'a state of discourse . . . in relation to the class struggle' (1985: 204). That is, rather than attributing specific and fixed ideological 'contents' to elements, ideology is seen more dynamically as the shifting relationship of discoursal practices to hegemonic (and more local-institutional) struggle. Clearly some elements are more ideologically fixed than others – think for instance of vocabularies it would be difficult not to regard as sexist or racist. The point is however that many discoursal elements at least which may manifest a degree of ideological fixity may nevertheless be turned around. Foucault makes the same point in referring to the 'tactical polyvalence of discourses':

> Discourses are tactical elements or blocks operating in the field of force relations; there can exist different and even contradictory discourses within the same strategy; they can, on the contrary, circulate without changing their form from one strategy to another, opposing strategy. (Foucault 1981: 101)

This suggests a homology between discoursal 'strategies' and hegemonic political strategies for constructing alliances and incorporating subordinate groups, which underscores the value of the hegemony concept for exploring discoursal change and language/ideology. It also suggests that perhaps the relationship between discourse and hegemony is a matter of the latter limiting the potential of the former: there is no specifically discoursal reason why there should not be an unlimited articulation and rearticulation of elements. It is hegemony – history – that curtails this discoursal potential and constrains which articulations actually come about, their durability, and so forth. I should add that the view I have set out of changes in the structure of orders of discourse as facets of an evolving hegemonic struggle will hopefully evoke Foucault's explorations of discourse and the technologies of power (Foucault 1972, Dreyfus and Rabinow 1982).

5. LIMITS OF IDEOLOGY

I have suggested that discoursal practices are ideologically invested in so far as they contribute to sustaining or undermining power relations. Relations of power may in principle be affected by discoursal practices in any type of discourse, even in scientific and theoretical discourse. This precludes a categorical opposition between ideology on the one hand and science or theory on the other which some writers on language/ideology have suggested (Pêcheux 1982, Zima 1981). This does not however imply that all discourse is irredeemably ideological. Ideologies arise in class societies characterized by relations of domination, and in so far as human beings are capable of transcending such societies they are capable of transcending ideology. I do not therefore accept the view of 'ideology in general' as a form of social cement which is inseparable from society itself.

On a less Utopian level, it is also quite possible to combat ideology now. The fact that all types of discourse are open in principle and no doubt to some extent in fact in our society to ideological investment does not mean that all types of discourse are ideologically invested to the same degree. It should not be too difficult to show that advertising is in broad terms more heavily invested than the physical sciences, though the thrust of Foucault's work (even if he resists the concept of ideology) is to show that the social sciences have a heavy ideological investment. There are structural determinants of degrees of ideological investment, but that does not mean that ideology cannot be effectively combated in any circumstances. Ideology works, as Althusser reminds us, by disguising its ideological nature. It becomes naturalized, automatized – 'common sense' in Gramsci's terms. Subjects are ideologically positioned as independent of ideological determination. Yet subjects are also contradictorily positioned, and when contradictory positions overlap they provide a basis for awareness and reflexivity, just as they lead to problematization and change. A critically orientated discourse analysis can systematize awareness and critique of ideology (which does not of course mean it is itself automatically immune from it).

From awareness and critique arise possibilities of empowerment and change (Fairclough (1989), chapter 9). Since all such movements take place within the matrix of hegemonic struggle, however, they are liable not only to be resisted but also to be incorporated. A critical discourse analysis must aim for constant vigilance about who is using its results for what, and about whether its critique of certain practices is not helping to naturalize other equally but differently ideological practices.

ACKNOWLEDGEMENTS

I am grateful to Raman Selden for comments on a draft of this paper.

DISCOURSE AND SOCIOCULTURAL CHANGE

Introduction

The papers in this section, which were written between 1989 and 1992, are all centred in one way or another upon the theme of change; changing discursive practices as an important part of wider processes of social and cultural change.

'Discourse, change and hegemony' links the 'macro' domain of state, government and policy with the 'micro' domain of discursive practice, by way of the concept of 'technologization of discourse'. The technologization of discourse is a specifically contemporary form of top-down intervention to change discursive practices and restructure hegemonies within orders of discourse (in places of work, for instance), as one element within wider struggles to reconstruct hegemonies in institutional practices and culture. It is a technology of government in a Foucaultian sense, and linked to what Gramsci calls the 'ethical state' – the state as involved in engineering its subjects to fit in with the demands of the economy (Forgacs 1988). It involves redesign of discursive practices on the basis of research into their institutional effectivity, and retraining of personnel. I discuss the emergence of various aspects of discourse technologization; expert discourse technologists, a shift in the policing of discursive practices associated with technologization of discourse, the role within it of context-free 'skills', and strategically motivated simulation of conversation.

The paper sketches out a version of the 'three-dimensional' CDA framework which I have used extensively elsewhere – CDA looks to establish connections between properties of texts, features of discourse practice (text production, consumption and distribution), and wider sociocultural practice. An extract from a medical interview is analysed in these terms, and I argue that the link between sociocultural practice and the other two dimensions involves the integration of 'macro' and 'micro' analysis of discursive events, where the former includes analysis of discourse technologization processes. On the one hand, no instance of discursive practice can be interpreted without reference to its context; in this example, for instance, one cannot determine whether the 'conversationalization' of medical discourse is democratizing or manipulative without reference to the 'macro' context and to discourse technologization processes. But on the other hand, 'macro' phenomena such as technologization of discourse cannot be properly analysed without the evidence of their actual effects on practice, which comes from analysis of discursive events. I demonstrate this with an extract from a university prospectus, which illustrates the dilemmas that people are placed in by discourse technologization, and strategies for resolving them through accommodation, compromise or resistance.

'What might we mean by "enterprise discourse"?' began life as a paper within a series of interdisciplinary seminars organized by the Centre for the Study of Cultural Values at Lancaster University on the theme of 'enterprise culture', and is published in a book of that title which brings together a number of those papers (Keat and Abercrombie 1990). It is an analysis of 'enterprise discourse' in the political speeches of a minister in Margaret Thatcher's government, and in a brochure produced by his ministry, the Department of Trade and Industry. The paper highlights the potentially diffuse nature of changes in discursive practices which constitute changes in culture; a change which appears explicitly in the political speeches as shifting relations between word meanings (of the word *enterprise*) and vocabularies, manifests itself implicitly in the brochure in a clash between different and contradictory subject positions. I suggest that different meanings of a word may be hierarchically ordered in salience, and that sociocultural change may be discoursally realized through a restructuring of such hierarchical rela-tions (as in the case of *enterprise*), by means of a manipulation of context and cotext. I suggest that 'enterprise discourse' be conceptual-ized not in terms of a unitary variety or 'code' (or even a 'discourse' in that sense), but as a field open to strategically motivated transforma-tions, and I show how this analysis fits into the sort of framework developed in the previous paper, with its emphasis on orders of discourse and discoursal change as a mode of hegemonic struggle.

'Critical discourse analysis and the marketization of public discourse', published in 1993, is a recent formulation of the theory and method of CDA, here seen as one of the array of analytical resources available for researching contemporary society and culture in transition. The paper opens with a sketch of a social theory of discourse and a framework for its critical analysis, which is centred around a combination of a Gramscian theory of power as hegemony and a Bakhtinian theory of intertextuality: the creative potentialities implicit in the latter are limited by the state of hegemonic relations and hegemonic struggle. I suggest that the place and role of discourse in society and culture is a historical variable, and discuss the role of discourse within modern and especially contemporary ('late modern' according to Giddens (1991)) society. Specifically, I consider the role of discourse in a range of major contemporary cultural changes which have been thematized in recent sociological analysis: shifts towards 'post-traditional' forms of social life, more reflexive forms of social life, and a 'promotional culture'. The bulk of the paper is taken up with an analysis of discourse samples which illustrate the marketization of higher education in contemporary Britain, as an instance of contemporaneity in discursive practices tied in with these three cultural tendencies. My examples are (extracts from) advertisements for academic posts, materials for a conference, a curriculum vitae, and undergraduate prospectuses. The focus is upon shifts in the identities of groups within higher education, especially academics, and upon authority relations between groups, for example, between institutional managements and academic staff or students. The paper concludes with a discussion of CDA as a resource for people who are trying to cope with the alienating and disabling effects of changes imposed upon them.

The next paper, 'Ideology and identity change in political television' is an application of the framework of the last paper to analysis of media discourse – specifically, one section of a late-night political discussion and analysis programme which was broadcast during the 1992 General Election in Britain. The paper argues that the discourse practice of the programme effects a restructuring between the orders of discourse of politics, private life (the 'lifeworld'), and entertainment, through a mixing of some of their constituent genres and discourses. One notable presence is the emergent television genre of 'chat', which is an institutionalized simulation of ordinary conversation as a form of entertainment and humour. I suggest that humour is a design feature of the mixed genre of the programme; participants are shown to be orientating to a groundrule that requires any serious political talk to be lightened with humour. This complex discourse practice is seen as part of an unstable and shifting social practice, the scenario Habermas refers to as a 'structural transformation of the public sphere' of politics (Habermas (1989)), in which the domain of politics is being restructured through a redrawing of its boundaries with leisure and the media and with the lifeworld. The complex discourse practice is realized in heterogeneities of meaning and form in the text. I focus in particular on the effect upon the textual construction of identities, for the presenter of the programme and the politicians he is interviewing, suggesting that the restructuring of boundaries between forms of life and orders of discourse is condensed into their complex personalities. The complexity of the discourse practice gives rise to a high level of ambivalence, in that the mixture of genres entails uncertainty over which interpretative principles apply. The complex format also appears to place heavy demands upon participants and cause difficulties for them which are manifest in disfluencies and in failures to observe the groundrule identified above, which are treated as sanctionable behaviour by other participants. The paper concludes with a discussion of the ideological effects of these changes in political discourse.

FOUR

Discourse, change and hegemony

ABSTRACT

In this paper I use the term 'technologization of discourse' to identify a distinctively contemporary mode of language policy and planning, the application specifically to discourse of the sort of 'technologies' which Foucault (1979) identified as constitutive of power in modern society. Technologization of discourse involves the combination of (i) research into the discursive practices of social institutions and organizations, (ii) redesign of those practices in accordance with particular strategies and objectives, usually those of managers or bureaucrats, and (iii) training of institutional personnel in these redesigned practices. It is being used in a widening range of types of institution, notably within the service industries and the professions, and in increasingly systematic ways.

I regard technologization of discourse as an important resource in attempts by dominant social forces to direct and control the course of the major social and cultural changes which are affecting contemporary societies. This argument is developed below within the framework of a Gramscian theory of power in modern capitalist societies as 'hegemony', together with an assumption that hegemony and hegemonic struggle are constituted to a significant degree in the discursive practices of institutions and organizations. Discourse conventions may embody naturalized ideologies which make them a most effective mechanism for sustaining hegemonies. Moreover, control over the discursive practices of institutions is one dimension of cultural hegemony. Technologization of discourse is part of a struggle on the part of dominant social forces to modify existing institutional discursive practices, as one dimension of the engineering of social and cultural change and the restructuring of hegemonies, on the basis of strategic calculations of the wider hegemonic and ideological effects of discursive practices. However, hegemonic projects are contested in discursive and other modes of practice, and technologization of discourse is no exception. I argue that this mode of language policy and planning needs to be investigated not only at more 'macro' levels of policy formation and implementation, but also through a critical method of discourse analysis which can show how technologization of discourse is received and appropriated by those who are subjected to it, through various forms of accommodation and resistance which produce hybrid combinations of existing and imposed discursive practices.

The paper is structured as follows. The first section is theoretical. It gives a necessarily skeletal account of social class, political power and the state in modern society in terms of Gramsci's concept of hegemony, and a view of how discourse and discursive change, and specifically the technologization of discourse, fit into such a framework. The second section is methodological. It sketches out, with examples, a multidimensional 'critical' approach to discourse analysis, based upon the theoretical positions adopted in the first section, which is I suggest a suitable approach for use in research on social and cultural change and its discursive aspects. The third and final section focuses upon the policy and planning dimension of the paper and the concept of technologization of discourse, locating it within the theoretical and methodological frameworks set out in the first two sections.

DISCOURSE AND HEGEMONY

In the sphere of language as in other spheres, the nature of policy formation and implementation varies according to the political and organizational structures within which it takes place. For example, simple models of policies radiating outwards and downwards from central government do not match the complexities of modern states in developed capitalist societies such as Britain or the USA. In the case of technologization of discourse, there are clear tendencies at national and even transnational levels which can be linked to state and dominant class (including capitalist multinational) interests without too much difficulty; yet it is not possible to trace them to one or even several particular moments of locations of central policy formation. Rather, the policies and planning which underlie processes of discourse technologization have been determined at different levels and different times, in many different institutions and organizations, within the private domain as well as within the public domain. Of course, these instances are linked together in various ways (e.g., through a common relationship to the social scientific expertise which discourse technologization depends upon), but the decision-making and implementational processes are autonomous.

We need therefore a theory of power, class and state in modern capitalist societies which can account for the relationship of such developments as technologization of discourse to class and state interests, without reducing complex relationships between organizations, institutions and levels to a 'conveyor belt' view of state power. Such a theory is available in Gramsci's studies of the structures of power in Western capitalist societies after the First World War, and the sort of revolutionary strategies they implied. (See Gramsci 1971, Forgacs 1988, Buci-Glucksmann 1980. Quotations from Gramsci are taken from Forgacs 1988.) For Gramsci, the political power of the dominant class in such societies is based upon a combination of 'domination' – state power in the narrow sense, control over the forces of repression and the capacity to use coercion against other social groups – and 'intellectual and moral leadership' or 'hegemony' (Forgacs (1988): 249). (On hegemony, see paper 4, pp. 103ff.) Correspondingly, the state is a combination of 'political society' (the public domain, the domain of state power in the narrow sense) and 'civil society' (the private domain, the domain of hegemony) – or as Gramsci graphically puts it, 'hegemony protected by the armour of coercion' (Forgacs (1988): 235). It is the hegemonic control of the dominant class over the institutions of civil society (education, work, family, leisure etc.) within the 'outer defences' of the repressive state apparatus that makes revolutionary transformation of modern capitalist societies so difficult, and imposes upon the revolutionary party the long-term ideological and hegemonic struggles of a 'war of position', rather than direct confrontation with the state in a 'war of manoeuvre'.

Gramsci links hegemony to the functioning of the state as an 'ethical state'; 'every state is ethical in as much as one of its most important functions is to raise the great mass of the population to a particular cultural and moral level, a level (or type) which corresponds to the needs of the productive forces of development, and hence to the interests of the ruling classes' (Forgacs (1988): 234). And, referring to Fordism and Taylorism in the USA, Gramsci discusses 'the need to elaborate a new type of man suited to the new type of work'. One aspect of hegemony is thus cultural and ethical engineering, the reshaping of subjectivities or 'selves' (Keat and Abercrombie 1990), and technologization of discourse is one aspect of this process as I shall argue in more detail later. However, it is necessary first to provide an account of how discourse fits into Gramsci's theoretical framework. (See also the account of the interaction of hegemony and discourse provided in Laclau and Mouffe 1985 and Hall 1988, working with a somewhat different concept of discourse. A fuller account is given in Fairclough (1992a).)

There is a dual relationship of discourse to hegemony. On the one hand, hegemonic practice and hegemonic struggle to a substantial extent take the form of discursive practice, in spoken and written interaction. Indeed, my use of the term 'discourse' rather than (say) 'use of language' implies the imbrication of speaking and writing in the exercise, reproduction and negotiation of power relations, and in ideological processes and ideological struggle. The concept of hegemony implies the development in various domains of civil society (e.g., work, education, leisure activities) of practices which naturalize particular relations and ideologies, practices which are largely discursive. A particular set of discourse conventions (e.g., for conducting medical consultations, or media interviews, or for writing crime reports in newspapers) implicitly embodies certain ideologies – particular knowledge and beliefs, particular 'positions' for the types of social subject that participate in that practice (e.g., doctors, patients, interviewees, newspaper readers), and particular relationships between categories of participants (e.g., between doctors and patients). In so far as conventions become naturalized and commonsensical, so too do these ideological presuppositions. Naturalized discourse conventions are a most effective mechanism for sustaining and reproducing cultural and ideological dimensions of hegemony. Correspondingly, a significant target of hegemonic struggle is the denaturalization of existing conventions and replacement of them with others.

An example I develop in the next section is doctor–patient consultations. In contemporary British society (for example), there is a dominant traditional mode of conducting consultations, and emergent alternative modes. In the dominant mode, doctors ask questions according to preset agendas, patients are limited to answering questions, and trying to squeeze anything which does not fit into the doctors' agendas into elaborations of their answers. The tone is impersonal and often brusque, the patient being treated as a bundle of symptoms rather than a person. (See Mishler (1984) and Fairclough (1992a) chapter 5, for a more detailed account.) This traditional mode of consultation corresponds to conventional hegemonic relations within medicine, and it is based upon and reproduces ideological assumptions about the nature of medicine, the social identities of doctors and patients, and the nature of the doctor–patient relationship, which partly constitute those hegemonic relations. Conversely, alternative modes of consultation which have more conversational properties, often drawing upon counselling as a model, are emerging as a part of struggles to challenge and restructure existing hegemonic relations. In my view, any analysis of hegemony and hegemonic struggle within an institution such as medicine must include analysis of discursive practices and of relationships (of dominance, or of opposition and confrontation) between diverse discursive practices.

The second aspect of the dual relationship of discourse to hegemony is that discourse is itself a sphere of cultural hegemony, and the hegemony of a class or group over the whole society or over particular sections of it (or indeed, these days, hegemony on a transnational scale) is in part a matter of its capacity to shape discursive practices and orders of discourse (see paper 4). The importance of cultural hegemony in the sphere of discourse follows from the ideological potency of discursive practices and conventions referred to in the last paragraph. Hegemony in this sphere also includes, as Gramsci himself pointed out (Forgacs 1988: 357ff), the relationships set up between different language varieties (different languages, different dialects), and the emergence of a dominant standard variety. The hegemony of a class or group over an order of discourse is constituted by a more or less unstable equilibrium between its constitutive discursive practices, which may become unbalanced and open to being restructured in the course of hegemonic struggle. For example, in traditional forms of medical practice, doctors did act as counsellors ('lay priests') to their patients as well as body-menders, but the two sets of (discursive) practices tended to be kept distinct; in the struggle of alternative forms of medical practice against traditional forms, this boundary within the order of discourse tends to be weakened, so that the discursive practices of counselling and medicine in the narrow sense merge to produce a new discursive practice. See the next section for an illustration. I should add that hegemonic struggle includes struggle on the part of dominant forces to preserve or restructure and renew their hegemony in the sphere of discourse, as well as struggle on the part of dominated groups.

The two aspects of the relationship of discourse to hegemony distinguished above are of course closely connected, in that it is in concrete discursive practice that hegemonic structurings of orders of discourse are produced, reproduced, challenged and transformed. Any instance of discursive practice can thus be interpreted in terms of its relationship to existing orders of discourse and discursive practices (is it broadly normative, reproducing them, or creative, contributing to their transformation?), as well as its relationship to existing social structures, ideologies and power relations (e.g., in the case of consultations between male doctors and women patients, do they reproduce or challenge dominant gender relations and ideologies?).

In the paragraphs above I have already introduced a historical and dynamic dimension into the relationship between discourse and hegemony through references to hegemonic struggle: hegemonic struggle takes place to a significant extent in discourse, where the 'stakes' include the structuring of orders of discourse as well as other dimensions of hegemonies. This has important theoretical and methodological implications for the study of social and cultural change: accounts of social change need to give more serious attention to discourse than they have done in the past, and to the question of how discursive change relates to (instantiates, constitutes or reflects) social and cultural change; and discourse analysis needs to be used alongside other types of analysis (e.g., sociological, ethnographic) in research on change. The general point is that the investigation of change requires a combination of 'micro' forms of analysis (discourse analysis is one) and more 'macro' forms of analysis (see Fairclough (1992a)). These conclusions have considerable current relevance, because of the radical changes which are affecting contemporary societies, and more especially because discourse is coming to be an increasingly salient and defining element in certain areas of social life such as many types of work (notably in the service industries), so that social and cultural changes *are* largely changes in discursive practices (see further below). This is the context in which technologization of discourse is becoming increasingly prominent as a conscious and strategic intervention to reshape discursive practices on the basis of calculations of their wider hegemonic and ideological effects.

A CRITICAL APPROACH TO DISCOURSE ANALYSIS

My purpose in this section is to give a brief description, with illustrative examples, of an approach to discourse analysis which is based upon the theoretical positions above (see Fairclough (1989), Fairclough (1992a)). It is an approach which is, I believe, suitable for use in the sort of research into social and cultural change I referred to above. What in particular makes it suitable for such work is that it foregrounds links between social practice and language, and the systematic investigation of connections between the nature of social processes and properties of language texts. (I use 'text' for the language 'product' of discursive processes, whether it be written or spoken language; a spoken 'text' can of course be turned into a written text by being transcribed.) It also facilitates the integration of 'micro' analysis (of discourse) and 'macro' analysis (including analysis of language policy and planning). It is moreover a 'critical' approach to discourse analysis in the sense that it sets out to make visible through analysis, and to criticize, connections between properties of texts and social processes and relations (ideologies, power relations) which are generally not obvious to people who produce and interpret those texts, and whose effectiveness depends upon this opacity.

The approach I have adopted is based upon a three-dimensional conception of discourse, and correspondingly a three-dimensional method of discourse analysis. Discourse, and any specific instance of discursive practice, is seen as simultaneously (i) a language text, spoken or written, (ii) discourse practice (text production and text interpretation), (iii) sociocultural practice. Furthermore, a piece of discourse is embedded within sociocultural practice at a number of levels; in the immediate situation, in the wider institution or organization, and at a societal level; for example, one can read an interaction between marital partners in terms of their particular relationship, relationships between partners within the family as an institution, or gender relationships in the larger society. The method of discourse analysis includes linguistic *description* of the language text, *interpretation* of the relationship between the (productive and interpretative) discursive processes and the text, and *explanation* of the relationship between the discursive processes and the social processes. A special feature of the approach is that the link between sociocultural practice and text is mediated by discourse practice; how a text is produced or interpreted, in the sense of what discursive practices and conventions are drawn from what order(s) of discourse and how they are articulated together, depends upon the nature of the sociocultural practice which the discourse is a part of (including the relationship to existing hegemonies); the nature of the discourse practice of text production shapes the text, and leaves 'traces' in surface features of the text; and the nature of the discourse practice of text interpretation determines how the surface features of a text will be interpreted. On page 98 there is a diagrammatic representation of this approach.

I want to illustrate the approach by applying it to an example which exemplifies:

1. Texts with heterogeneous and contradictory features;
2. A complex relationship between discourse practice (text production)

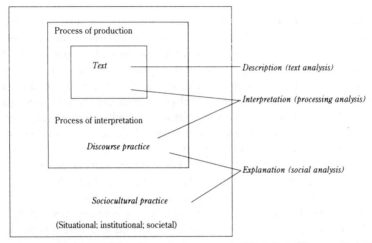

Process of production

Text ———————————— Description (text analysis)

——— Interpretation (processing analysis)

Process of interpretation

Discourse practice

Explanation (social analysis)

Sociocultural practice

(Situational; institutional; societal)

Dimensions of discourse   *Dimensions of discourse analysis*

and discourse conventions; one could show a similarly complex relationship between text interpretation and conventions, but I shall not do so here;

3. A relationship between such heterogeneous textual features and such complexity of discourse processes, and processes of sociocultural change.

The example is an extract from a consultation between a doctor (a 'general practitioner' in the British medical system) and his female patient (a dot indicates a short pause, a dash a longer pause, and overlaps are shown with square brackets).

1. *Patient*: but she really has been very unfair to me . got ⌈no
   Doctor: ⌊hm
   Patient: respect for me at ⌈all and I think . that's one of the
   Doctor: ⌊hm
5. *Patient*: reasons why I drank s⌈o much you ⌈know ⌈—
   Doctor: ⌊hm   ⌊hm   ⌊hm
   Patient: a⌈nd em
   Doctor: ⌊hm   are you you back are you back on it have you
              started drinking ⌈again
10. *Patient*:   ⌊no
   Doctor: oh you haven't (unclea⌈r)
   Patient: ⌊no . but em one thing that
              the lady on the Tuesday said to me was that . if my
              mother did turn me out of the ⌈house which she
15. *Doctor*:   ⌊yes

Patient: thinks she may do ⌈ . coz . she doesn't like the way
Doctor: ⌊ hm
Patient: I've been she has turned me ⌈ out be ⌈ fore . and em .
Doctor: ⌊ hm ⌊ hm
20. Patient: she said that . I could she thought that it might be
possible to me for me to go to a council ⌈ flat
Doctor: ⌊ right
yes ⌈ yeah
Patient: ⌊ but she said it's a very em she wasn't
25. ⌈ pushing it because . my mother's got to sign a
Doctor: ⌊ hm
Patient: whole ⌈ lot of ⌈ things and e: . she said it's difficult
Doctor: ⌊ hm ⌊ hm
Patient: ⌈ and em . there's no rush over it . I I don't know
30. Doctor: ⌊ hm
Patient: whether . I mean one thing they say in AA is that
you shouldn't change anything ⌈ . for a year
Doctor: ⌊ hm
Doctor: hm   yes I think I think that's wise . I think that's
35. wise (5 second pause) well look I'd like to keep you
know seeing you keep . you know hearing how things
are going from time to time if that's possible

The *text* is characterized by a configuration of heterogeneous and contradictory properties. I want to illustrate that in terms of a contrast between the *fact* of certain occurrences and their *manner* of occurrence. On the one hand, the fact of the occurrence of the doctor's question about whether the patient (an alcoholic) has started drinking again (*are you back are you back on it have you started drinking again*) in lines 8–9, which breaks topic and which is repeated as a check (*oh you haven't (indistinct)*) in line 11; and the fact of the occurrence of the doctor's assessment of the advice the patient has received (*I think that's wise. I think that's wise*) in line 34; and of the doctor's directive to the patient to see him again in lines 35–37 – *well look I'd like to keep you know seeing you keep . you know hearing how things are going from time to time if that's possible*. On the other hand, the manner of these contributions from the doctor: the doctor's question in lines 8–9 both in its working (the vague initial formulation – *are you back are you back on it* – and the reformulation – *have you started drinking again*), and in a strikingly quiet and fast delivery (which I have not tried to represent) which give this presumably vital medical question the appearance of an aside; and the assessment in line 34, which includes an explicit subjective modality marker (*I think*) which modulates its authoritativeness; and the directive (lines 35–37), which is extremely tentative, hedged (*you know* etc.) and indirect.

In terms of *discourse practice*, it appears to me that the doctor is creatively articulating two different discourse conventions, that associated with traditional medical consultations, and that associated with counselling. Of course this is not just this doctor's personal achievement; this is a common and widespread articulation. On the one hand, the doctor as in traditional consultations pursues an agenda which controls and determines the structure of the interaction, and this is manifest in the fact of occurrence of the doctor's question, assessment and directive. On the other hand, the doctor like the counsellor in a counselling session appears to cede much of the control and leadership of the interaction to the patient. The typical apparent non-directiveness of counselling is manifest in the manner of occurrence of the question, assessment and directive. The contradictory demands of medical practice and counselling are tenuously reconciled through the choice of forms of realization for these speech acts. A more overtly counselling feature is the degree of empathy shown by the doctor, in the textual form of his substantial backchannelling activity (*hm, right, yes,* and so on).

The nature of the discourse production process can itself be referred to the wider sociocultural practice within which it occurs. For instance, at the institutional level, the doctor belongs to a minority oppositional group within official medicine which is open to the practices of alternative medicine and counselling. Institutional members with a knowledge of relations and struggles within medicine may well interpret the doctor's articulation of diverse conventions in this instance as anti-authoritarian – against the authority of the doctor over the patient, and the authority of the medical establishment over the profession; breaking down the professional elitism of doctors by giving the patient greater control in the consultation, and sanctioning the introduction via counselling of more informal and conversational discursive practices which patients are familiar with and at the same time treating the patient as a person, an individual.

However, this particular mix of medical discourse and counselling discourse is one institutionally local instance of a global feature of the contemporary societal order of discourse; the colonization of institutions in the public domain by types of discourse which emanate from the private domain. This tendency could be called the 'conversationalization' of institutional discourse. Conversationalization entails greater informality, and interactions which have a person-to-person quality in contrast with the interaction between roles or statuses which characterizes more traditional institutional discourse. It also entails more democratic interaction, with a greater sharing of control and a reduction of the asymmetries which mark, say, conventional doctor–patient interaction. Conversationalization can I think be seen as a discursive part of social and cultural changes associated at some levels at least with increased openness and democracy, in relations between professionals and clients for instance, and greater individualism.

However, while these developments cannot be simply equated with a spread of consumerism, they have come to be tied in with – one might say appropriated by – consumerism to some extent. Correspondingly, commercial organizations, including increasingly organizations like the professions, social services and even the arts which are being drawn into commercial and consumerist modes of operation, are under pressure to transform their organizational practices and 'cultures' in this direction, undertaking in many cases systematic strategies of training and other forms of intervention to achieve these ends. Technologization of discourse is a part of this process, and in many cases a central objective of technologization of discourse is the achievement of a shift towards more conversationalized discursive practices as a part of these broader organizational and cultural changes. Thus conversationalized discursive practices are open to contradictory investments, being linked either to democratization or to new strategies of control, and being therefore themselves a focus of hegemonic struggle.

Returning to the example, I would suggest that it is difficult to interpret the mixing of medical discourse and counselling discourse, in the sense of arriving at a conclusion about the social value and import that it has, without placing it in the context of longer-term transformations affecting orders of discourse, tendencies of the sort referred to in the previous paragraph, and the current state of hegemonies and hegemonic struggles (including deployment of technologization of discourse) in the discursive sphere within the institution concerned. In this case, I suspect there is at least an ambivalence about the mixing of discursive practices; it may instantiate a democratic and anti-authoritarian stance on the part of the doctor, but it may also constitute the imposition upon the patient of a new mode of control more in accordance with contemporary cultural emphases.

This discussion points to the necessary interdependence of 'micro' analyses of specific discourse samples and more 'macro' analysis of longer term tendencies affecting orders of discourse, the construction and restructuring of hegemonies in the sphere of discursive practices, and language policy and planning. These 'macro' dimensions constitute part of the context of any discursive event, and are necessary for its interpretation. Conversely, as I shall argue in the next section, no account of discourse technologization (or other 'macro' developments) can forgo an investigation of how planning initiatives are received and responded to (adopted, paid lip service to, accommodated, opposed), which can come only from analyses of specific discourse samples. 'Micro' and 'macro' analyses of discourse and discursive change are mutually dependent.

TECHNOLOGIZATION OF DISCOURSE[1]

Technologization of discourse is a process of intervention in the sphere of discourse practices with the objective of constructing a new hegemony in the order of discourse of the institution or organization concerned, as part of a more general struggle to impose restructured hegemonies in institutional practices and culture. In terms of the analytical method introduced in the last section, it involves an attempt to shape a new synthesis between discourse practice, sociocultural practice and texts. This is done through a process of redesigning existing discursive practices and training institutional personnel in the redesigned practices, on the basis of research into the existing discursive practices of the institution and their effectivity (be it in terms of the efficiency of organizational operations, the effectiveness of interaction with clients or 'publics', or the successful projection of 'image').

My use of the term 'technology' derives ultimately from Foucault's analyses of the alliance between social sciences and structures of power which constitutes modern 'bio-power', which has 'brought life and its mechanisms into the realm of explicit calculations and made knowledge/power an agent of transformation of human life' (Foucault 1981). Technologies of discourse are more specifically a variety of what Rose and Miller call 'technologies of government': 'the strategies, techniques and procedures by means of which different forces seek to render programmes operable, the networks and relays that connect the aspirations of authorities with the activities of individuals and groups' (Rose and Miller 1989). Referring to liberalism as a mode of government, these authors see the 'deployment' of 'political rationalities and the programmes of government' as 'action at a distance', involving the 'enrolment' of those they seek to govern through 'networks of power' incorporating diverse agents and 'the complex assemblage of diverse forces – laws, buildings, professions, routines, norms'. Discourse is, I would suggest, one such 'force' which becomes operative within specific 'assemblages' with other forces.

Technologization of discourse has, I think been accelerating and taking on firmer contours in the past decade or so, but its lineage is longer. For example, 'social skills training' (Argyle 1978) is a well-established application of social psychological research, and technology of government, which has a partially discursive nature. Large units of practice such as interview are assumed to be composed of sequences of smaller units which are produced through the automatic application of skills which are selected on the basis of their contribution to the achievement of goals. It is assumed that these skills can be isolated and described, and that inadequacies in social (including discursive) practice can be overcome by training people to draw upon these skills. Social skills training has been widely implemented for training mental patients, social workers, health workers, counsellors, managers, salespeople and public officials. One example given by Argyle is training in the 'personnel interview' (used for instance for disciplinary interviews in workplaces), which (and this quotation points to the design element) 'can make it a pleasanter and more effective occasion' (Argyle 1978).

I shall use the following list of five characteristics of technologization of discourse as a framework for elaborating the definition given above.

1. The emergence of expert 'discourse technologists'.
2. A shift in the 'policing' of discourse practices.
3. Design and projection of context-free discourse techniques.
4. Strategically motivated simulation in discourse.
5. Pressure towards standardization of discourse practices.

There have long been specialists in persuasive and manipulative discourse, but what we might call contempory 'technologists of dis-course' have certain distinguishing features. One is their relationship to knowledge. They are social scientists, or other sorts of expert or consultant with privileged access to scientific information, and their interventions into discursive practice therefore carry the aura of 'truth'. Another is their relationship to institutions. They are likely to hold accredited roles associated with accredited practices and routines in institutions, either as direct employees or as expert consultants brought in from outside for particular projects. For example, 'staff development' and 'staff appraisal' are two recent additions to the institutional practices of British universities. Both the training of staff and the training of appraisers are partly training in a variety of discourse practices – lecturing, organizing seminars, interviewing, designing publicity materials, writing research proposals. And both directly employed staff and outside management consultants are being drawn into specialized institutional roles and practices, partly as discourse technologists. These relationships of discourse technologists to knowledge and to institutions distinguish contemporary forms of discourse technologization from earlier forms of intervention in institutional discourse practices.

Discourse practices are, I think, normally 'policed' – subjected to checks, corrections and sanctions – though there is a great deal of variation in how overtly or how rigorously. One effect of technologization of discourse is, I suggest, to shift the policing of discourse practices from a local institutional level to a transinstitutional level, and from categories of agent within particular institutions (be it education, law, medicine) to discourse technologists as outsiders. In addition to a shift in the location of policing agents, there is a shift in the basis of their legitimacy. It has traditionally been on the basis of their power and prestige within the profession or institution that certain categories of agent claimed the right to police its practices; now it is increasingly on the grounds of science, knowledge and truth. The discourse technologist as expert as well as outsider.

Discourse technologists design and redesign what I shall call 'discursive techniques', such as interviewing, lecturing or counselling, to maximize their effectiveness and change them affectively – recall the objective of making a disciplinary interview 'a pleasanter and more effective occasion'. Argyle recommends that an interview should end with a review of what has been agreed and 'on as friendly a note as possible', suggestions about design which involve the design of particular utterances (to be 'friendly') as well as the overall organization of the interview. I suspect that the tendency is for techniques to be increasingly designed and projected as 'context-free', as useable in any relevant context. This tendency is evident in training, where there is a focus upon the transferability of skills – 'teaching for transfer' is a prominent theme in recent vocational education for example. Moreover, the projection of such context-free techniques into a variety of institutional contexts contributes to a widespread effect of 'colonization' of local institutional orders of discourse by a few culturally-salient discourse types – advertising and managerial and marketing discourse, counselling, and of course interviewing (Fairclough 1989a).

The redesign of discourse techniques involves extensive *simulation*, by which I mean the conscious and systematic grafting onto a discourse technique of discourse practices originating elsewhere, on the basis of a strategic calculation of their effectivity. I have in mind particularly simulation of meanings and forms which appertain to the discursive constitution of social relationships and social identities – which have 'interpersonal' functions in systemicist terminology (Halliday 1978). The recommendation that an interview end on a friendly note is an invitation to the interviewer to simulate the meanings and forms (those of language but also other semiotic modalities) of 'friendliness', meanings and forms which imply and implicitly claim social relations and identities associated more with domains of private life than with institutional events like interviews. Opening frontiers between the private and the institutional; institutional appropriation of the resources of conversation; conversationalization and apparent democratization of institutional discourse (already referred to above) – these are pervasive features of the technologization of discourse.

The final characteristic of discourse technologization in my list is that it constitutes a powerful impetus towards standardization and normalization of discourse practices, across as well as within institutions and different types of work. The importance of expert outsiders as discourse technologists, the shifting of the policing of discourse to a transcendent position 'above' particular institutions, and the trend towards context-free discourse techniques – all of these are centralizing and standardizing pressures upon discourse practice; pressures which meet with resistance, however, as I shall suggest below.

The contemporary prominence of technologization of discourse reflects the increasing relative importance of discursive practices in certain areas of social life, especially various types of work. It is well known that there has been an increase in service industry at the expense of manufacturing industry, and the 'skills' necessary for jobs in service industries are to a substantial extent 'communication skills'. The quality of the 'product' in service industries often depends largely upon discursive practices and capacities of workers. Even within manufacturing industry, discursive practices are becoming more important, as new technologies bring about a shift from repetitive and solitary work on a production line to more variable work in teams. In a context of rapid change in the nature of work, the engineering of change in discursive practices assumes some importance.

The engineering of change in discursive practices is part of a process of cultural engineering and restructuring cultural hegemony – as

Gramsci put it, 'elaborating a new type of man suitable to the new type of work' (Forgacs (1988: 234). For example, the simulation of conversational discourse in institutional settings – the 'conversationaliza-tion' of institutional discourse – has implications for the social identities of, and social relationships between, those who operate in them. A professional such as a doctor or lawyer cannot shift to a conversational mode of interaction with patients or clients without taking on in some degree a new social identity, and projecting a new social identity for the patient or client. These new identities draw upon models in the 'lifeworld', the private sphere. The same is true where interaction between managers and workers, and more generally those at different points on hierarchical scales, becomes more conversational. However, the engineering of social identity may have unforeseen pathological consequences; the widespread simulation of conversation and its cultural values may lead to a crisis of sincerity and a crisis of credibility and a general cynicism, where people come to be unsure about what is genuine and what is synthetic.

People in their actual discoursal practice may react in various ways to pressures for change emanating from the technologization of dis-course; they may comply, they may tactically appear to comply, they may refuse to be budged, or they may arrive at all sorts of accommoda-tions and compromises between existing practices and new techniques. The latter is perhaps the most common and certainly the most interesting case. Study of such accommodations in the discursive practice of workplaces, for example, strikes me as a likely source of insight into the actual impact of technologies of government on practice, and into ongoing processes of change in social relations and social identities.

I want to suggest that the production of discourse under such conditions of change places producers in 'dilemmas' (Billig *et al.* (1988)) which are an effect of trying simultaneously to operate in accordance with divergent constructions of social relationships and social identities, and that these dilemmas lead to accommoda-tions and compromises which are manifested in the ambivalence and heterogeneity of spoken or written texts (see also paper 4).

Let me relate these suggestions to a specific example, an extract from a British university prospectus (see overleaf), using the approach to discourse analysis presented in the last section. The recent evolution of university prospectuses reflects clearly pressures on universities to operate under market conditions, and to 'sell' their courses, using discursive techniques from advertising. Some of the changes that have occurred are immediately evident in the physical appearance of prospectuses; the typical course entry has shifted in ten years from a couple of pages of quite dense writing to a mixture of written text, colour photographs, and sophisticated graphics. But prospectuses also show how academics have responded to the dilemmas that these pressures have placed them in by accommodation and compromise. These dilemmas centre upon the contradiction between a traditional professional- (or producer-) orientated relationship between university and applicant, where the university is the 'authoritor' admitting or rejecting applicants according to its criteria for entry; and a 'consumer-orientated' relationship being forced upon universities by the economic position they have been placed in, where the applicant is the authoritor choosing (as consumers do) among the range of goods on offer. On the former model, a prospectus would focally give information about courses and conditions of entry, on the latter model it would 'sell' courses. In fact, contemporary prospectuses attempt a balancing act between these two discursive practices, and in terms of professional identities, they show academics trying to reconcile being academics and being salespeople.

This dilemma shows up in the heterogeneity of the text, and in particular in how its heterogeneity in terms of semiotic modalities and genres (written text and photograph on the left, list of courses and graphic display on the right) relates to its heterogeneity in terms of meanings, or more precisely speech functions (the main ones are informing, regulating and persuading). Let me begin with regulating. It strikes me as significant that everything to do with requirements imposed by the university upon the applicant − entry requirements, course requirements − is located in the synoptic right-hand section of the entry. This allows requirements to be separated from any source or authoritor, so that the problematic meaning (problematic, that is, in the consumer-orientated model) of the university imposing requirements upon applicants does not have to be overtly expressed. This occlusion is evident in the wording of the graphic display: *you will need* rather than for instance *we require* shifts the onus onto the student, and the agentless passives (*will be accepted, candidates who are offered places will be invited*). In the written text, regulating is avoided, and aspects of the degree scheme which might normally be seen as requirements are semanticized in other terms. For example, in paragraph 3 taking courses in several disciplines comes across as an assurance (*students will gain valuable experience*) rather than a requirement; similarly in paragraph

AMERICAN STUDIES

Enquiries to: Director of Admissions
Teaching staff: members of appropriate departments

Photograph of American scene

Lancaster students have always shown lively interest in American subjects, whether in the English, History, Politics or other departments. Now it is possible to take a specialised degree in American Studies. This degree combines different disciplinary approaches to the study of the United States and offers options covering American history, literature, and politics from the earliest colonial settlements to the present day.

In addition, American Studies majors will spend their second year at an American university, such as the University of Massachusetts at Amherst or another selected American university. Lancaster's close American connections make it possible to integrate the year abroad into the degree, so that, unusually in British universities, the American Studies degree can be completed in *three* years. Special counselling will ensure close integration between the year abroad and the two years at Lancaster.

Degree studies at Lancaster call on specialists in a number of departments,

and, as with most Lancaster degrees, students will gain valuable experience in more than one discipline. But a substantial degree of flexibility is maintained, and it is possible for students to concentrate substantially on either history or literature or politics if they so choose.

The first year is largely devoted to providing a disciplinary grounding, and students pursue the normal first year courses in the History, English and Politics departments, taking American options where they exist. Thereafter the course of study is almost exclusively devoted to American topics, and may include the writing of a dissertation of an American theme.

American Studies graduates pursue careers normally associated with a humanities or social science education: education, business, journalism, publishing, librarianship, and social service, with the wider opportunities which may come from students' transatlantic experience and perspective.

Two pages from the Lancaster University 1990 Undergraduate Prospectus

4, taking the three specified courses in the first year comes across as a description (*students pursue . . .*) rather than a requirement.

Let me turn from regulating to the other two speech functions, informing and persuading. The most fully persuasive modality is the photograph, which positions the applicant in some unspecified but most attractive 'American' scene, co-constructing the potential student, the programme and the university within a mythical 'America'. The sentences of the written text on the other hand are in many cases ambivalent between informing and persuading – persuasion is certainly a significant speech function, but in a mainly covert form which anticipates substantial inferential work on the part of the reader (as of course does the photograph). The opening paragraph for instance appears on the face of it to consist of three bits of information (with

B A Hons **American Studies** *Q400*

First Year

History (American options)
English
Politics

Second Year

Four or five courses in American subjects taken at a United States university, including at least one interdisciplinary course.

Third Year

Four or five courses, normally from:

History:
The History of the United States of America
Religion in America from Jamestown to
   Appomatox, 1607–1865
From Puritan to Yankee: New England,
   1630–1730

The Great Alliance: Britain, Russia and the
   United States, 1941–1945
Cold war America: The United States from
   Truman to Kennedy

English:
American Literature, 1620–1865
American Literature, 1865–1940
American Literature, 1940–1980

Politics:
The Politics of Race
United States Government: The Politics of the
   Presidency
The American Policy Process
United States Foreign Policy since 1945

Assessment: see under appropriate subjects.

YOU WILL NEED

Courses	A-level	O-level/GCSE
Amer-St	**BBC/BCC** **normally incl.** **English**	**A pass in a** **foreign** **language**

or other qualifications (IB, EB, Scottish Highers) at a comparable standard.
AS-levels: will be accepted.
Interview policy: special cases only.
Open days: candidates who are offered a place will be invited.

lively as a transparently persuasive lexicalization) – about the tradition of American Studies at the university, the introduction of a specialized degree, and content of the degree. The first two sentences are in an overtly temporal relationship marked by the contrast between present perfective and simple present verb forms, and the temporal conjunct *now*. A little inferential work on the part of the reader can construct these markers and bits of information into a persuasive narrative according to which the degree is the culmination of a cross-disciplinary tradition. Similarly in other paragraphs, persuasion is mainly covert. The academic's dilemma appears to be resolved through a compromise; the written text is designed to persuade while appearing to be merely informative.

There are many variants of such accommodations and compromises between 'telling' and 'selling', reflecting the dilemmas of professionals in various domains faced with commodification and marketization and pressure to use associated discourse techniques. In paper 2, I analysed the effect of contradictory producer- and consumer-orientations and authoritor–authoritee relations on the modality of a brochure about a bank's financial services. One might also see the text analysed in the last section in similar dilemmatic terms: in terms of the compromises effected by a medical practitioner in attempting to adopt a patient-orientated counselling or therapeutic style of medical interview while maintaining control over medically important aspects of the interview. Similarly, Candlin and Lucas (1986) have shown how a family-planning counsellor tries to reconcile contradictory pressures to control clients' behaviour and yet as counsellors to refrain from any form of direction, through the indirect linguistic realization of speech acts. In all such cases, people are using discourse as one medium in which they can attempt to negotiate their identities and their relationships with others in problematical circumstances of change.

There is however a significant gap between such practices of accommodation and compromise, and the impetus within technologization of discourse towards more standardized and context-free discourse practice; technologies of government generate strategies of resistance. What appear in a social psychological perspective as attempts to resolve dilemmas, appear in the perspective of a politics of discourse as discursive facets of processes of hegemonic struggle in which the structuring of orders of discourse and of relationships between orders of discourse is at stake. The outcomes are restructured orders of discourse, innovative mixing of genres, and the emergence of new genres and sub-genres. One should also not exclude the possible appropriation of discourse technologization by dominated social forces.

Let me note finally that important changes are taking place in language education and training in Britain (and I imagine elsewhere), for example, in the new national curriculum for schools and in the 'communication' elements of prevocational education programmes which seem to be closely linked to technologization of discourse. There is a new emphasis on oracy and spoken language education, on face-to-face interaction and interaction in small groups, sometimes explicitly justified in terms of changing communicative requirements in work. And there is an extension to language of competence-based models of education which see knowledge operationally in terms of what people can do, and see education as training in skills. These new priorities and approaches contrast with more traditional emphases on written Standard English. Their emergence can, I think, be interpreted as the spread of a technologizing orientation to discourse into the general educational system, most obviously into vocationally orientated programmes, but also to a degree into the general school curriculum. The competence- and skill-based approach harmonizes with technologization of discourse in a number of ways: it focuses upon training in context-free techniques (skills), it is a pressure for standardization of practices, it fits with autonomous notions of the self, each individual being construed as housing a configuration of skills which can be worked upon and improved.

CONCLUSION

I have identifed technologization of discourse as an emergent domain of language policy and planning, and have tried to locate it within a view of social and cultural change which highlights the role of discourse, insisting at the same time that discursive aspects of change, including policy and planning dimensions, should be investigated with methods which integrate 'micro' and 'macro' modes of analysis.

NOTE

1. This section of the paper is a modified version of part of 'Technologization of discourse', which will appear in Costas-Coulthard, C. R. and Coulthard, M. (eds) *Critical Discourse Analysis*, Routledge.

FIVE

What might we mean by 'enterprise discourse'?

This paper will refer to political speeches given between 1985 and 1988 by Lord Young of Graffham, until recently Secretary of State for Trade and Industry, and to a publicity brochure produced by his department.[1] My primary objective will be to argue that notions like 'enterprise discourse' ought not to be understood too rigidly, and that enterprise discourse itself is a rather diffuse set of tendencies affecting the 'order of discourse' (Fairclough 1989) of contemporary British society (i.e. the structured whole of its discoursal practices) as part of wider tendencies of cultural change, rather than a well-defined code or 'formation' (in the sense of Pêcheux (1982)).

The chapter is in four parts. The first will concentrate upon the word enterprise itself in Young's speeches. What emerges is an unstable picture of various senses being structured and restructured in relation to each other according to shifting strategies – a field of potential meaning, and sets of transformations upon that field according to wider political strategies – rather than *a* meaning. In the second part, an analogous picture emerges when I extend the field from the various senses of 'enterprise' to relationships between vocabularies – the vocabularies of enterprise, skills and consumption. The third part of the chapter shifts the focus from changes over time in Young's speeches to changes in social space as enterprise discourse moves across discoursal domains. I will discuss a Department of Trade and Industry publicity brochure, and suggest that features of enterprise discourse that are manifest in the vocabulary of the Young speeches are manifest at a quite different level here, mainly in the subject positions, which are implicitly established for producer and audience in the brochure. This leads me to the conclusion that enterprise discourse is best conceived of as a rather diffuse set of changes affecting various aspects of the societal order of discourse in various ways. The final part of the chapter places this conclusion in a wider theoretical framework for exploring discoursal change in its relation to social and cultural change.

MEANINGS OF 'ENTERPRISE'

The word enterprise occurs in Young's speeches almost exclusively as a non-count noun (enterprise as a count noun has singular and plural forms and takes indefinite articles – an enterprise, enterprises). According to the *OED*, enterprise as a non-count noun can have three senses:

1. 'Engagement in bold, arduous or momentous undertakings' (*OED* gives as examples 'times of national enterprise' and 'men fond of intellectual enterprise').
2. 'Disposition or readiness to engage in undertakings of difficulty, risk or danger; daring spirit' (e.g. 'enterprise supplies the want of discipline', 'his lack of enterprise').
3. (In collocation with 'private' or 'free') 'private business', as a collective noun.

I shall refer to these for short as the 'activity', 'quality' (in the sense of personal quality) and 'business' senses. All these senses are manifest in the Young speeches, but they also show a contrast in the case of the quality sense (and marginally for the activity sense) between qualities specifically related to business activity (e.g. the ability to spot and exploit a market opportunity) and more general personal qualities (e.g. willingness to accept responsibility for oneself). I shall refer to these senses collectively as the 'meaning potential' of enterprise.

A noteworthy feature of the speeches is that 'enterprise' in its business sense is generally but not always used without the modifiers 'private' or 'free'. This increases what one might call the 'ambivalence potential' of 'enterprise': in principle, any occurrence of the word is open to being interpreted in any of the three senses or any combination of them. (I use 'ambivalence' where a word may be taken to have a combination of two or more senses, in contrast with 'ambiguity' where a word may be taken to have one sense *or* another (or more than one other).) However, while most occurrences of 'enterprise' are indeed semantically ambivalent and involve some combination of the three senses, this potential ambivalence is reduced by the context, including the more-or-less immediate verbal context in which the word occurs. Verbal context has two sorts of effect. First, it may eliminate one or more of the senses. Second, it may give relative salience to one of the senses without eliminating the others. Examples will be given later in the chapter.

The ambivalence potential of 'enterprise' and the possibilities for manipulating it by varying the verbal context constitute a resource that is open to strategic exploitation, and is indeed strategically exploited in the Young speeches. Different speeches highlight different senses, not by promoting one sense to the exclusion of the others, but by establishing particular configurations of meanings, particular hierarchical salience relationships among the senses of 'enterprise', which can be seen to be suited to wider strategic objectives of the speeches. It should be noted that I am not suggesting a self-conscious awareness of the senses of 'enterprise' and of processes of manipulating its meaning potential. Calculation at such a level of detail is perhaps implausible, and it is more likely that calculation at a more general level about how to achieve specific communicative objectives with respect to particular audiences leads to unselfconscious adaptations of meaning resources to these higher purposes. However, the basic strategic exploitation of the ambivalence of the word enterprise in the speeches is a not insignificant element in achieving these higher purposes – notably in contributing to the revaluation of a somewhat discredited private business sector by associating private enterprise with culturally valued qualities of 'enterprisingness'.

The analysis of enterprise I am suggesting in the speeches has implications for conceptions of meaning both in dictionaries and in specific texts: that the 'dictionary meaning' of a word as a relatively stable entity may be better conceived of as a particular hierarchical configuration of senses rather than a set of complementary senses; that context may not 'disambiguate' words in specific texts in the sense of eliminating all but one of their senses, but may, rather, impose hierarchical salience relations between senses; and that in these textual processes the relatively stable equilibria of dictionary meanings may be open to contestation, destructuring and restructuring. (Such conceptions of meaning are implicit in Williams (1976); see also Hodge (1984.)

The strategic exploitation of the meaning potential of 'enterprise' that I have referred to is evident in Young's speeches both in the explicit definitions that are given for 'enterprise' (which are quite numerous), and in the ways in which the word is used. Let me briefly comment on definitions before looking in more detail at uses. Almost all of Young's definitions of 'enterprise' give it the quality sense. What differentiates them is the contrast I mentioned earlier between qualities that are specific to business activity and more general personal qualities.

In fact there is a scale here rather than a simple opposition, illustrated in examples 1–4 in the following list, which move from the business end of the scale to the general qualities end.

1. By enterprise I mean the ability of an individual to create goods and services that other people will willingly consume. Enterprise meets people's needs and that is the source of jobs. (CPS)
2. Enterprise encompasses flexibility, innovation, risk-taking and hard work – the qualities so essential to the future of our economy and our nation. (FR)
3. ... early in life we all have an abundance of enterprise, initiative, the ability to spot an opportunity and take rapid advantage of it. So when we are young we are all entrepreneurs. (PEJ)
4. Enterprise ... means an acceptance of personal responsibility and a confidence and desire to take action to improve your own circumstances. (BL)

There are short-term strategies at work that involve 'enterprise' being variously defined according to the varying communicative objectives, situations and audiences of the speeches – thus definition 2 occurs in a speech whose focus is tackling unemployment, whereas definition 4, just two months later, occurs in a speech whose focus is inner-city policy and 'enterprise in the community'. There also appears to be a progressive though uneven shift from the earlier to the more recent speeches towards the general personal quality sense.

When we turn to the actual use of the word 'enterprise', strategies become more complex because, as I have already said, what is going on is the establishment of hierarchical configurations of senses rather than just the highlighting of particular elements of the meaning potential. The first speech I shall refer to, entitled 'Enterprise and employment' (EE), was delivered in March 1985 to the Bow Group. Here (apart from the title and the one instance of the expression 'enterprise culture') is the first occurrence of 'enterprise'.

5. Jobs come when enterprise has the freedom and vigour to meet the demands of the market, to produce the goods and services that people want.

The verbal context unambivalently gives the business sense – only persons or collectives like private business take predicates like 'have (the) freedom (to)'. Note that this is an instance of 'enterprise' in the business sense without the usual modifiers.

In every instance except example 5, the verbal context gives salience to one sense without excluding the others. The following is an example:

6. The task of government (is) to produce a climate in which prosperity is created by enterprise.

Example 6 occurs immediately following a paragraph referring to private business in which example 5 occurs, which gives the business sense salience without excluding the other senses: one could replace 'enterprise' by any of the expressions – private enterprise, enterprising activity, enterprising individuals – without making the sentence semantically incongruous in its verbal context.

In other cases, salience relations are established through the conjunction of 'enterprise' with other expressions (my italics):

7. Attitudes which regard *business, enterprise and the job of wealth creation* as a positive benefit to society.
8. Competition provides the spur to greater efficiency. Incentives provide the spur for *individual initiative and enterprise*.

The conjunction of 'enterprise' with expressions from the business domain in example 7 highlights again the business sense, while the conjunction of enterprise with an expression that signifies a personal quality (individual initiative) in example 8 highlights the quality sense, though the preceding verbal context places it at the 'business qualities' end of the scale. Notice that example 8 is syntactically ambiguous: the word individual can be taken as modifying both nouns, or just the word initiative.

The expression 'enterprise culture', which occurs in this speech and throughout the speeches, and is widely used as a label for core components of government policy and strategy, is itself highly ambivalent, not only because 'enterprise' is ambivalent between the three senses, but also because the relationship between the two elements of such nominal compounds is itself open to multiple interpretations.

The second speech I shall discuss is the Gresham lecture (FR), which was delivered just a few months later in July 1985. Here again, most instances of the use of the word 'enterprise' are semantically ambivalent, though there is one where the verbal context requires the activity sense, but in a narrowly business activity variant:

9. Their (the Quakers') enterprise may be explained by legal restrictions on other activities.

The focus of this speech as the title suggests is 'entrepreneurs', glossed as 'those who give us leadership in business and industry', and the qualities of entrepreneurs are highlighted – 'innovator', 'promoter', 'risk taker', 'desire to create', 'willingness to take responsibility'.

The way in which the senses of enterprise are 'hierarchized' in the speech reflect this wider strategic focus, and we find the quality sense being more salient than in the first speech. This relative salience is in fact syntactically marked in two cases, through the conjunction of the word enterprise with expressions that isolate the quality sense (my italics):

10. ... the whole thrust of changes in the structure of our economy ... have been fundamentally harmful to *enterprise –and the enterprising instincts of individuals.*
11. And partly because conscious decisions have been taken to encourage *enterprise* and to encourage *enterprising individuals.*

Notice that the participial adjective 'enterprising', like the noun 'entrepreneur' is associated with the quality sense. Although the quality sense is relatively salient in this speech, it is again the business qualities end of the scale that is most prominent, so that in this speech as in the previous one the structuring of senses of 'enterprise' is business-dominated. At the same time, however, a more general quality sense is implicit in 'enterprising instincts' in example 10 (as well as 'the urge for enterprise'), which prefigure a notion made more explicit in later speeches of enterprise as an inborn human attribute that social circumstances may stifle.

The third and final speech I shall refer to was delivered in November 1987 to the British Institute of Management (BIM). What is striking here in contrast with the previous two speeches is the number of instances where the verbal context reduces ambivalence potential and imposes one of the senses – the quality sense (my italics):

12. The Technical and Vocational Education Initiative, the National Council for Vocational Qualification and Open College strengthened those links and raised the *skills and enterprise of individuals.*
13. Last April I asked chief executives to pledge their companies to recognize the *professionalism and enterprise of their managers* as a key to business success.
14. I hope the same will happen in management education and development so that we can fully use the *talents and enterprise of people.*

The quality sense is imposed in each case by twin properties of verbal context: (a) enterprise is co-ordinated with another noun that signifies personal qualities; (b) enterprise (and the noun it is conjoined with) is modified by prepositional phrases that attribute enterprise – as a quality of course – to (categories of) persons. Furthermore, although the speech is concerned with management education and so very firmly with business, the qualities being referred to are more towards the general personal end of the scale than in the two previous speeches – witness the conjunction of 'enterprise' with the general quality term 'talents' in example 14. This shift in the salience of senses accords with the longer-term strategy I referred to earlier (the third speech came more than 2 years after the second), and with more immediate strategic considerations: the speech refers to the Handy Report on management development, which emphasized the importance of a broad set of qualities acquired in a good general education for managers of the future. However, this is only a relative shift in salience. A significant proportion of instances of the use of the word 'enterprise' remain ambivalent between the three senses, and in some cases the verbal context (in example 15 the conjunction of 'enterprise' with 'wealth creation') still highlights the business sense (my italics):

15.   The whole climate for *wealth creation and enterprise* has changed.

The effect is to contain the shift towards the quality sense and the general personal quality end of the scale within a relatively stable strategic conjunction that gives salience to the business sense and the business end of the quality scale.

The trajectory of 'enterprise' in Young's speeches can be summed up as a process of semantic engineering (Leech 1974: 53–62), whose basic move is the activation of the range of senses associated with 'enterprise' within political discourse and, via the formal device of using 'enterprise', in its business sense, without the usual modifiers ('private', 'free'), the creation of the ambivalence potential I have referred to. A particular meaning potential has been ideologically and politically invested (Frow 1985; paper 4 in this volume) and worked for reasons of political strategy. The result is not something static – we cannot capture it by offering a description of 'the meaning of enterprise in the discourse of enterprise'. It is, rather, a field (a meaning potential and ambivalence potential), and sets of transformations within that field associable with longer- and shorter-term strategies.

CONFIGURATIONS OF VOCABULARIES

The metaphor of a field and sets of transformations within it is also an appropriate conceptual framework for thinking about relationships between the word 'enterprise' and other vocabularies in Young's speeches. 'Enterprise' varies from speech to speech not only in how its senses are hierarchically organized, but also in what wider configurations it enters into, and in what position. One formal way into these patterns of variation is to examine the sorts of expression 'enterprise' is syntactically conjoined with. Here is a sample that is fairly representative of the speeches as a whole: enterprise and employment, initiative and enterprise, enterprise and individual responsibility, self-reliance and enterprise, skills and enterprise, professionalism and enterprise, talents and enterprise.

As the discussion has already shown, what 'enterprise' is conjoined with is a part of its verbal context that can highlight one or other of its senses. But there is more to it than that. Just as establishing particular salience hierarchies among the senses of a word can serve strategic purposes, so, too, can establishing wider configurations – between, say, the vocabularies (what some would call the 'discourses') of enterprise and skill on the one hand, or between the vocabularies of enterprise and individual responsibility on the other. The former combines the vocabularies (and narratives) of 'enterprise' with those of a particular vocationally orientated conceptualization and wording (and ideology) of education and training and of their relationship to work and other dimensions of social life. The latter combines the vocabulary and narratives of 'enterprise' with those of a particular personal morality. These represent contrasting (though potentially complementary) directions of potential alliance for those whose aim is to build an enterprise culture that are matters for important longer-term strategic decisions as well as shorter-term strategic exploitation. They are aspects of the 'intertextuality' of enterprise discourse, the nature of the links between its texts and other categories of text (Kristeva 1980).

The following extract, which is an abbreviated version of a longer passage from Young's NEDC 25th Anniversary Speech (PEJ), gives an extended illustration of strategic configurations of this sort. The italics are mine, and I have numbered the paragraphs for ease of reference.

1. In the schools we have the Technical and Vocational Education Initiative. The main aim of this programme and the big changes in examinations and the curriculum we have introduced, is to *sustain and develop enterprise.* That

is the way to encourage and enable young people to use *their growing skills and knowledge* to solve real problems in today's world.
2. For school leavers there is YTS . . . At heart, the Youth Training Scheme too is about *enterprise*: about *encouraging and helping young people to make and take opportunities, to take responsibility and to welcome change*. A broad foundation of *skills* for the modern world so that our young school leavers can be masters of change and not its victims.
3. Then standards. By 1991 there will be in place the new National Vocational Qualification with at least 5 levels. Those qualifications will be based on *competence what people can do and can show they can do, not academic knowledge alone.*
4. From this September, the Open College will come into every home through the medium of television and radio. The College . . . is unashamedly nailing its colours to the mast of *enterprise, employment, training, skills and competence.*
5. Our system will build on the twin foundations of *competence and enterprise.* There is no room in a modern world for the old divide between 'education' and 'training'. Nor is there any room for the outmoded and outdated distinction between 'academic' and 'vocational'. We are about *competence, the ability to perform and the capacity to be in charge of your own destiny.*
6. And our system must be built on *individual choice and enterprise*, on commitment and enthusiasm, not coercion.
7. To that end, in our system, *the customer, you as employer or individual must be the driving force.*

Examples 1 and 2 show a configuration of vocabularies of enterprise and skill – notice that the relatively greater salience of the former in the configuration is implicit in its appearance before the latter in each paragraph. Example 2 shows, however, that what is going on is not just the placing of two autonomous vocabularies in relation to each other, but some merging: 'enterprise' is glossed in a way that is familiar from Young's definitions of it (to make and take opportunities, to take responsibility and to welcome change) – but these quality senses of enterprise are then referred to as skills. Example 3 sets up a contrast between 'competence' – part of the vocabulary of skills – and 'academic knowledge' and the conjunction of 'enterprise' with 'competence' as well as 'skill' in 4 underscores the implicit opposition between 'enterprise' and 'academic knowledge'. Example 5 is the key paragraph for the configuration of vocabularies of enterprise and skill. Its first sentence explicitly foregrounds the pairing of 'enterprise' and 'competence', and its last sentence effects a further merger between the vocabularies: this time, 'competence' is glossed with a conjunction of an expression that belongs to the vocabulary of skill (ability to perform) and another that belongs to the vocabulary of enterprise (the capacity to be in charge of your own destiny). Examples 6 and 7 add a new vocabulary to the configuration – that of consumption – with its myths and narratives ('the customer is king', and so forth). This is formally marked in the conjunction: individual choice and enterprise. The total configuration that results is the linguistic facet of a major strategic conjunction in government policies: between a promotion of 'enterprise' in the workplace and beyond, consumerism and a vocationally geared education system.

The vocabulary of consumption shows up in a more explicit and self-conscious form in a speech given to the Birmingham Chamber of Commerce in February 1988 (BCC), shortly after the launch by the Department of Trade and Industry of an 'enterprise strategy', which gives private enterprise a major role in creating the 'enterprise culture'. The following is an abbreviated version of a passage from the speech:

> My recent White Paper – 'DTI – The Department for Enterprise' – shows how we are changing our policies and our organisation to work with business; to accept that we too have customers; that you are our customers; and that, in the end, customers are king.
> First, we are expanding our network of contacts with business at a local level.
> In other words we are getting closer to our market, to our customers. We are promoting and marketing DTI's services to you actively. Our use of TV adverts signals a major change in the relationship between business and DTI.
> If we are running schemes FOR business and encouraging activities BY business we have to make sure that what we have to sell TO business is clearly marketed, easy to understand and easy to use. If government is to provide services to business then they must be customer led.

The DTI is cast in the role of marketer and advertiser of the services it has to 'sell' to business, which is cast in the role of customer. I shall shortly discuss how this metadiscoursal representation of DTI practice compares with its actual promotional practice.

TRANSFORMATIONS OF ENTERPRISE DISCOURSE

I have illustrated both for the senses of 'enterprise' and for relations between vocabularies, a conception of 'enterprise discourse' as a field containing a certain potential, and sets of strategically motivated transformations within that field. So far I have stayed with Young's speeches, but it is now time to point out that the transformations that characterize enterprise discourse are not only transformations in time within a particular discoursal domain, but also transformations 'in space' across discoursal domains. Enterprise discourse may originate and evolve initially in political speeches, but it is transported from the domain of political discourse into many others: the media and the various discourses of its various sectors; the educational domains – schools, further education, higher education; training of management and other personnel in industry and the health service; and so forth.

Given this complex distribution, enterprise discourse might be expected to show up in divergent ways and forms in different domains. Part of what is involved here is the question of how it combines with discourses already in place in these various domains – does it replace them, or come to constitute with them complex new forms of merged discourse? There is also the question of resistance: how, if at all, is enterprise discourse opposed in the various domains among which it is distributed, and what are the outcomes of struggle between opposing discourses? This may be, for example, a matter of struggle over the meaning of 'enterprising' by perhaps applying it to activities distant from business, or of drawing upon an alternative vocabulary (e.g. focusing upon cultivating creativity rather than enterprise in education), or constituting alternative subject positions in discourse.

There are, furthermore, variations in what one might call the level of explicitness of enterprise discourse. In Young's speeches, as I have pointed out, the word enterprise is frequently given explicit definition. This is the most explicit level, the metadiscoursal level where aspects of enterprise discourse are overt discourse topics. At a second level, the discoursal level, enterprise discourse is still overtly present in describable features of texts – this is the case with the use of 'enterprise' in the Young speeches. At a third level, what we might call the subdiscoursal level, enterprise discourse is an implicit interpretative resource that one needs to draw upon to arrive at coherent interpretations of the text. I shall exemplify the subdiscoursal level shortly.

I shall illustrate just a small part of this complex set of issues in one piece of Department of Trade and Industry publicity produced in 1988: a 32-page brochure about the 'enterprise initiative', a new label for the services offered by the DTI to business.[2] The enterprise initiative is part of the 'enterprise strategy' launched at the beginning of 1988, which the extracts from BCC in the previous section relate to. I want to focus upon how elements of enterprise discourse function at a subdiscoursal level in the constitution within this text of subject positions for the DTI itself and for the business people the brochure is addressing. All texts express the social identities of their producers and address the assumed social identities of their addressees and audiences. But mass-readership public texts, especially where there are clear instrumental goals as in the case of advertising, actively construct imaginary identities for their producers and audiences, and create subject positions for the latter, which they may or may not compliantly occupy.

The bulk of the brochure is constructed as a series of double-page spreads each detailing one of the 'initiatives' (counselling, marketing, etc.) which cumulatively make up the enterprise initiative. The 'design initiative' is reproduced in Example 1, overleaf.

It is typical in having a heading, an 'orientation' section (printed in bold) that sums up the initiative, then the bulk of the text divided into short headed sections, and a small cartoon and a large photograph (not reproduced in Example 1).

I shall focus upon the orientation sections. Here are four of these, taken from the marketing, design, quality and business-planning initiative texts. I have numbered them for ease of reference.

1. The essence of good marketing is to provide your customers with what they want. Not to spend time and money trying to persuade them to take what you've got. So, whether you're selling at home or abroad, it's important to understand both the market and your competitors.
2. Look behind any successful business and you'll find good design. While knowing your market can help find the product or service your customers want, only good design can translate it into something they will want to buy.
3. It doesn't matter how much time and effort you put into marketing, design and production. If the product or service doesn't live up to your customers' expectations, you're wasting your time.
4. Long-term planning is not a luxury confined to the larger companies. It is essential for any business which is to survive and compete in today's market place.

These orientations have consistent features that cue, so to speak, implicit subject positions for the DTI and the businessperson, and an implicit relationship between them. They consist largely of categorical, bald assertions about matters of business practice that the business people addressed would be assumed to have special knowledge of. The assertions are categorical and bald in the sense that they are not

the
Design
initiative

Look behind any successful business and you'll find good design. While knowing your market can help you find the product or service your customers want, only good design can translate it into something they will want to buy.

Design helps you meet your customers' needs for performance and reliability and meets your needs on ease of manufacture and cost.

Good design helps to position your product and your firm in the market. It doesn't matter if you're manufacturing luxury goods or serving the mass market. The story is the same.

Even if your design is up to scratch now, it will have to evolve to meet changing demands and new opportunities.

If you're not presenting the right image, you're not fulfilling your potential.

How can the Design Initiative help?

The Design Initiative, managed for DTI by the Design Council, offers expert advice on design from product concept to corporate image. Amongst other things they can help you with:-

- product innovation and feasibility studies
- design for efficient production
- mechanical and electrical engineering design
- materials selection and use
- industrial design and styling
- ergonomic and product safety considerations
- packaging and point of sale material
- corporate identity

Who pays what?

DTI will pay half of the cost of between 5 and 15 man-days of consultancy. In Assisted Areas and Urban Programme Areas DTI will pay two thirds (see map on page 32). You pay the rest.

The next step

If you would like to find out more about the Design Initiative contact your nearest Regional Office, Scottish Office or Welsh Office from the list on page 30.

EXAMPLE 1 The design initiative

modulated by markers of tentativeness, indirectness, modality, hedging and so forth (Brown and Levinson 1978). They imply an expert–client relationship between the DTI and the businessperson.

But that is not the end of the story. Even given an expert–client relationship, the expert has various options open to him or her in terms of the forms in which advice and information are given. The forms opted for here appear to be rather face-threatening. Notice for instance the negatives in 1 and 4 in the list, which imply propositions that are likely to hold for many readers (some businesses spend time and money trying to persuade customers to take what they've got; some smaller companies think long-term planning is a luxury). Similarly, many readers will meet the conditions to be wasting their time in the terms of 3. Moreover, a number of propositions in these orientations are likely to be anything but news to most business readers – the first sentence of the first orientation in the list, for example, is surely a crashing truism for business – yet potential readers are given no credit (by adding the word 'obviously' for instance) for what they already know.

One might therefore expect many business readers to find these orientations irritating and insulting, and it would be interesting to do some research on readings to see if this is so. However, I suspect this would not be a general reaction. The categorical and uncompromising style of the orientations may, I think, carry implicit meanings about social identity additional to the expert–client meanings. It is perhaps an attempt at translating values of the enterprise culture that appear at the discoursal level in association with quality senses of the word enterprise in the Young speeches, into a style of writing (and by implication a style of speech – one finds something similar in the DTI's television advertising), which establishes a social identity for an 'enterprising person'. The particular enterprising qualities for which this style is a sort of metaphor are those of self-reliance – as Young says in the Birmingham Chamber of Commerce speech (BCC), the emphasis in the enterprise initiative is upon 'self-help'. A self-reliant person is a person who does not need to be pampered, can face up to things, can be told things straight. The orientations have, I suspect, a double function in these terms: they give the DTI an 'enterprising' identity, and at the same time offer to business people a model for what is becoming a culturally valued identity. If this is so, irritation on the part of business readers may well be overridden.

What about the relationship between DTI practice in this brochure and the new role announced for the DTI by Young in BCC – that of a promoter selling its services to its business customers? There are parts of the brochure that set up subject positions and social identities akin to those of commodity advertising, casting readers in the role of consumers and the DTI in that of advertiser. This involves a reversal of the authority relations of the expert–client relation: in the latter, it is the DTI as expert that is in the authoritor position, whereas in the former it is the businessperson as consumer who is the authoritor and there are correspondingly manifest efforts to persuade him or her. Here is an example from the part of the brochure that deals with the 'consultancy initiatives':

> Over the past few years, we've helped hundreds of small businesses to enlist the help of specialist consultants. We're convinced that it's the most cost effective way for a firm to help itself. So convinced, in fact, that we're planning to support around a thousand consultancies each and every month.
> The (Enterprise) Counsellor will keep an eye out for the untapped resources, inefficient work systems and unrealized potential. You will get impartial (and, of course, confidential) advice based on the Counsellor's considerable experience. Only then will he or she recommend how the Consultancy Initiatives can best help you.

In the first paragraph we find a selling stratagem widely used by advertisers: we believe in x, and our belief is backed up by the resources we have put into x, showing that you, too, can feel secure in believing in x. Even the syntactic pattern – 'We're convinced/confident/etc. that x', 'So convinced, etc. that we are going to/have y (ed), – is an advertising formula, and the use of 'we' to portray a business hierarchy or bureaucracy as a warm community is an advertising device. In the second paragraph, 'keep an eye out' portrays the Counsellor as trustworthy friend; 'of course' both credits the addressees with relevant knowledge (compare the orientations), and claims a rapport between the DTI and addressees; the modification of 'experience' with 'considerable' can be there only to boost addressees' confidence; and the topicalization of 'then' with 'only' in the last sentence implies meticulous care on the Counsellor's part.

What appears in Young's speeches as a strategic configuration of vocabularies, then, appears in the DTI brochure as a strategic configuration of pairings of subject positions for the DTI and the businessperson addressee: expert/client, and advertiser/consumer. There is also another pairing that is more traditional in publicity about government services, which we might refer to as provider/recipient. This pairing is evident, for instance, where the regulations governing availability of services are being set out. Also from the 'consultancy initiatives' text:

> *Who qualifies?*
> If you're an independent firm or group with a payroll of fewer than 500, the Enterprise Initiative offers financial support for between 5 and 15 mandays specialist consultancy in a number of key management functions.

In respect of subject positions, then, the brochure is an amalgam of both traditional and novel practices.

As this example has, I hope, begun to indicate, as one shifts the domain of reference from particular well-defined bodies of texts such as the Young speeches through relatively if loosely homogeneous entities like 'political discourse', to the complex and heterogeneous set of relations between types of discourse in what we might call the 'order of discourse', the discoursal ramifications of enterprise culture become increasingly diffuse. One can, at least in part, associate the notion of enterprise discourse with fairly circumscribed if shifting vocabularies, for instance, in the Young speeches. While one does find a transposition of such vocabularies across the order of discourse, however, the shifting across levels of explicitness I have tried to indicate here suggests a shaping of the order of discourse by enterprise culture that is much less easy to pinpoint. Detailed research into specific discoursal effects in a range of domains is clearly indicated as a concrete means of exploring the progressive political and ideological investment of an order of discourse in the course of social and cultural change.

CONCLUSION

Let me conclude this paper by trying to place the view of enterprise discourse that I have been moving towards in a wider theoretical framework. I have been suggesting that enterprise discourse is not a well-defined closed entity, but rather a set of tendencies – transformations within fields that, at least at the level of transformations across discourse types in the order of discourse, are of a diffuse nature. One implication of this position is that enterprise discourse cannot be located in any text. The focus needs to be rather on processes across time and social space of text production, and the wider strategies that text production enters into.

But one also needs a complementary focus upon the reading of texts, and from this perspective the analyses I have offered in this chapter are too one-sided. Texts are open to multiple readings, and the ways in which they are read depend upon the purposes, commitments and strategies of readers − upon the reading positions the texts are exposed to. This, in turn, is a function of the distribution of a text − the set of contexts of reception it enters. The texts of face-to-face discourse have a relatively simple distribution, though even here there may be a context of overhearing as well as a context of address, and various contexts of reporting. Public discourse such as political speeches tends to have a complex distribution − perhaps an immediate audience of political supporters, but beyond that multiple audiences of political allies and opponents, multiple mass-media audiences, international audiences and so forth. Anticipation of the potential polyvalence of the texts that such complex distributions imply is a major factor in their design.

What the multiplicity of readings underscores is that strategies are inevitably pursued in circumstances of contestation and struggle. I have argued in papers 4 and 5 that the Gramscian concept of hegemony is a rich one for conceptualizing such processes of struggle and their discoursal dimensions. Hegemony is a useful matrix and model for discourse. It is a matrix, in the sense that processes of discoursal change such as those around enterprise culture can be satisfactorily explicated if they are referred to wider hegemonic struggles to establish, maintain, undermine and restructure hegemonies on the part of alliances of social forces − the struggle of the Thatcherites for hegemony has been described, for instance, by Hall (1988). It is a model, in that there are homologies between hegemonies as unstable equilibria constantly open to contestation and restructuring, and linguistic and discoursal conventions. The view of meaning and meaning change I have outlined in terms of shifting salience hierarchies of senses invites such a comparison. So, too, do the shifting configurations of subject positions I have pointed to in the case of the DTI publicity.

A discourse type from this perspective is just a configuration of elements with greater or lesser durability − or rather a network of related (and perhaps quite loosely related) configurations across discoursal domains. What this implies in terms of the place of discourse in cultural change is a rather diffuse set of changes affecting orders of discourse that might be quite difficult to pin down, and might be overlooked if one is anticipating a well-defined code or formation triumphantly colonizing one bastion of cultural ascendancy after another. The investment of an order of discourse by a newly salient cultural dominant is perhaps a more subtle and even insidious process.

If this is so, there are important political and ideological implications for those who wish to resist the achievement of cultural and discoursal hegemonies.

There are also implications for one's view of discourse analysis. 'Discourse' and 'discourse analysis' are fashionable in various disciplines and open to many interpretations. For some analysts, discourses are conceptual structures such as narratives, myths or schemata. Others are more oriented to language form, though with contrasting focuses on, for example, vocabulary and metaphor, or grammatical features of various sorts (e.g. pronouns, modality, voice, intersentential cohesion), or dialogical structures (e.g. turn-taking, formulating). Van Dijk (1987) shows some of the bewildering variety of analytical focuses, as well as the theoretical and disciplinary variations that cut across it.

A danger in this situation is that analysts will divide too quickly into separate camps. Of course this stifles intellectual exchange and is objectionable for that reason. But the unstable and diffuse character I have attributed to enterprise discourse in this chapter also suggests that it is objectionable on the grounds that a single type of discourse can 'show up' variously as aspects of either the content or the form of texts: as narratives, vocabularies, metaphors, particular selections in grammar, particular ways of conducting dialogue and so forth. It would, therefore, be unhelpful to see these various dimensions of content and form as alternatives that the discourse analyst has to choose between.

NOTES

1. I am grateful to Paul Morris for providing this material for analysis.
2. The Enterprise Initiative Consultancy Scheme (EICS) - Design Consultancy finally closed for applications on 15 September 1994.

SIX

Critical discourse analysis and the marketization of public discourse: the universities

The objective of this paper is, first, to set out my own view of critical discourse analysis, and, second, to illustrate the practice of critical discourse analysis through a discussion of marketization of public discourse in contemporary Britain. The first section of the paper, 'Towards a Social Theory of Discourse', is a condensed theoretical account of critical discourse analysis. The second section, 'Analytical Framework', sets out a three-dimensional framework for analysing discursive events. Readers will find the view of the field sketched out in these sections more fully elaborated in Fairclough (1989, 1992a). The third section makes a transition between the rather abstract account of the first two sections and the illustrative example: it is a reflection on language and discursive practices in contemporary ('late capitalist') society, which it is claimed make a critical, social and historical orientation to language and discourse socially and morally imperative. The fourth section is a text-based examination of the marketization of discursive practices as a process which is pervasively transforming public discourse in contemporary Britain, with particular reference to higher education. The paper concludes with a discussion of the value of critical discourse analysis, as a method to be used alongside others in social scientific research on social and cultural change, and as a resource in struggles against exploitation and domination.

TOWARDS A SOCIAL THEORY OF DISCOURSE

Recent social theory has produced important insights into the social nature of language and its functioning in contemporary societies which have not so far been extensively taken on board in language studies (and certainly not in mainstream linguistics). Social theorists themselves have generally articulated such insights abstractly, without analysis of specific language texts.[1] What is needed is a synthesis between these insights and text-analytical traditions within language studies. The approach developed in this section of the paper is aiming in that direction.

'Discourse' is a category used by both social theorists and analysts (e.g. Foucault, 1972; Fraser, 1989) and linguists (e.g. Stubbs, 1983; van Dijk, 1987). Like many linguists, I shall use discourse to refer primarily to spoken or written language use, though I would also wish to extend it to include semiotic practice in other semiotic modalities such as photography and non-verbal (e.g. gestural) communication. But in referring to language use as discourse, I am signalling a wish to investigate it in a social-theoretically informed way, as a form of social practice.

Viewing language use as social practice implies, first, that it is a mode of action (Austin, 1962; Levinson, 1983) and, secondly, that it is always a socially and historically situated mode of action, in a dialectical relationship with other facets of 'the social' (its 'social context') – it is socially shaped, but it is also socially shaping, or *constitutive*. It is vital that critical discourse analysis explore the tension between these two sides of language use, the socially shaped and socially constitutive, rather than opting one-sidedly for a structuralist (as, for example, Pêcheux (1982) did) or 'actionalist' (as, for example, pragmatics tends to do) position. Language use is always simultaneously constitutive of (i) social identities, (ii) social relations and (iii) systems of knowledge and belief – though with different degrees of salience in different cases. We therefore need a theory of language, such as Halliday's (1978, 1985), which stresses its multifunctionality, which sees any text (in the sense of note 1) as simultaneously enacting what Halliday calls the 'ideational', 'interpersonal' and 'textual' functions of language. Language use is, moreover, constitutive in both conventional, socially reproductive ways, and creative, socially transformative ways, with the emphasis upon the one or the other in particular cases depending upon their social circumstances (e.g. whether they are generated within, broadly, stable and rigid, or flexible and open, power relations).

If language use is socially shaped, it is not shaped in monolithic or mechanical ways. On the one hand, societies and particular institutions and domains within them sustain a variety of coexisting, contrasting and often competing discursive practices ('discourses', in the terminology of many social analysts). On the other hand, there is a complex relationship between particular discursive events (particular 'instances' of language use) and underlying conventions or norms of language use. Language may on occasion be used 'appropriately', with a straightforward application of and adherence to conventions, but it is not always or even generally so used as theories of appropriateness would suggest (see paper 10 for a critique of such theories).

It is important to conceptualize conventions which underlie discursive events in terms of *orders of discourse* (Fairclough, 1989, 1992a), what French discourse analysts call 'interdiscourse' (Pêcheux, 1982; Maingueneau, 1987). One reason for this is precisely the complexity of the relationship between discursive event and convention, where discursive events commonly combine two or more conventional types of discourse (for instance, 'chat' on television is part conversation and part performance: Tolson, 1991), and where texts are routinely heterogeneous in their forms and meanings. The order of discourse of some social domain is the totality of its discursive practices, and the relationships (of complementarity, inclusion/exclusion, opposition) between them — for instance in schools, the discursive practices of the classroom, of assessed written work, of the playground, and of the staff-room. And the order of discourse of a society is the set of these more 'local' orders of discourse, and relationships between them (e.g. the relationship between the order of discourse of the school and those of the home or neighbourhood). The boundaries and insulations between and within orders of discourse may be points of conflict and contestation (Bernstein, 1990), open to being weakened or strengthened, as a part of wider social conflicts and struggles (the boundary between the classroom and the home or neighbourhood would be an example). The categorization of types of discursive practice — the elements of orders of discourse — is difficult and controversial: for present purposes I shall simply distinguish between *discourses* (*discourse* as a count noun), ways of signifying areas of experience from a particular perspective (e.g. patriarchal versus feminist discourses of sexuality), and *genres*, uses of language associated with particular socially ratified activity types such as job interview or scientific papers (see, further, Kress, 1988, on the distinction between discourses and genres).

By 'critical' discourse analysis I mean discourse analysis which aims to systematically explore often opaque relationships of causality and determination between (a) discursive practices, events and texts, and (b) wider social and cultural structures, relations and processes; to investigate how such practices, events and texts arise out of and are ideologically shaped by relations of power and struggles over power; and to explore how the opacity of these relationships between discourse and society is itself a factor securing power and hegemony (see below). In referring to opacity, I am suggesting that such linkages between discourse, ideology and power may well be unclear to those involved, and more generally that our social practice is bound up with causes and effects which may not be at all apparent (Bourdieu, 1977).[2]

ANALYTICAL FRAMEWORK

I use a three-dimensional framework of analysis for exploring such linkages in particular discursive events (see paper 5). Each discursive event has three dimensions or facets: it is a spoken or written language *text*, it is an instance of *discourse practice* involving the production and interpretation of text, and it is a piece of *social practice*. These are three perspectives one can take upon, three complementary ways of reading, a complex social event. In analysis within the social practice dimension, my focus is political, upon the discursive event within relations of power and domination. A feature of my framework of analysis is that it tries to combine a theory of power based upon Gramsci's concept of *hegemony* with a theory of discourse practice based upon the concept of intertextuality (more exactly, *interdiscursivity* − see further below). The connection between text and social practice is seen as being mediated by discourse practice: on the one hand, processes of text production and interpretation are shaped by (and help shape) the nature of the social practice, and on the other hand the production process shapes (and leaves 'traces' in) the text, and the interpretative process operates upon 'cues' in the text.

The analysis of text is form-and-meaning analysis − I formulate it in this way to stress their necessary interdependency. As I indicated above, any text can be regarded as interweaving 'ideational', 'interpersonal' and 'textual' meanings. Their domains are respectively the representation and signification of the world and experience, the constitution (establishment, reproduction, negotiation) of identities of participants and social and personal relationships between them, and the distribution of given versus new and foregrounded versus backgrounded information (in the widest sense). I find it helpful to distinguish two subfunctions of the interpersonal function: the 'identity' function − text in the constitution of personal and social identities − and the 'relational' function − text in the constitution of relationships. The analysis of these interwoven meanings in texts necessarily comes down to the analysis of the forms of texts, including their generic forms (the overall structure of, for instance, a narrative), their dialogic organization (in terms, for instance, of turn-taking), cohesive relations between sentences and relations between clauses in complex sentences, the grammar of the clause (including questions of transitivity, mood and modality), and vocabulary. Much of what goes under the name of pragmatic analysis (e.g. analysis of the force of utterances) lies on the borderline between text and discourse practice. (See Fairclough (1992a) for a more detailed analytical framework, and see below for examples.)

The analysis of discourse practice is concerned with sociocognitive (Fairclough (1989) and paper 1) aspects of text production and interpretation, as opposed to social-institutional aspects (discussed below). Analysis involves both the detailed moment-by-moment explication of how participants produce and interpret texts, which conversation analysis and pragmatics excel at, and analysis which focuses upon the relationship of the discursive event to the order of discourse, and upon the question of which discursive practices are being drawn upon and in what combinations. My main interest, and main concern in this paper, is the latter.[3] The concept of *interdiscursivity* highlights the normal heterogeneity of texts in being constituted by combinations of diverse genres and discourses. The concept of interdiscursivity is modelled upon and closely related to *intertextuality* (Kristeva, 1980), and like intertextuality it highlights a historical view of texts as transforming the past — existing conventions, or prior texts — into the present.

The analysis of the discursive event as social practice may refer to different levels of social organization — the context of situation, the institutional context, and the wider societal context or 'context of culture' (Malinowski, 1923; Halliday and Hasan, 1985). Questions of power and ideology (on ideology, see Thompson (1990)) may arise at each of the three levels. As indicated in paper 5, I find it useful to think about discourse and power in terms of hegemony (Gramsci, 1971; Fairclough, 1992a). The seemingly limitless possibilities of creativity in discursive practice suggested by the concept of interdiscursivity — an endless combination and recombination of genres and discourses — are in practice limited and constrained by the state of hegemonic relations and hegemonic struggle. Where, for instance, there is a relatively stable hegemony, the possibilities for creativity are likely to be tightly constrained. For example, one might draw a rather gross contrast between dominance of cross-gender interaction by normative practices in the 1950s, and the creative explosion of discursive practices associated with the feminist contestation of male hegemony in the 1970s and 1980s.

This combination of hegemony and interdiscursivity in my framework for critical discourse analysis is concomitant with a strong orientation to historical change (see paper 5).

It may be helpful to readers to have available a summary of some of the main terms introduced in the last two sections:

discourse (abstract noun)	language use conceived as social practice.
discursive event	instance of language use, analysed as text, discursive practice, social practice.
text	the written or spoken language produced in a discursive event.
discourse practice	the production, distribution and consumption of a text.
interdiscursivity	the constitution of a text from diverse discourses and genres.
discourse (count noun)	way of signifying experience from a particular perspective.
genre	use of language associated with a particular social activity.
order of discourse	totality of discursive practices of an institution, and relations between them.

LANGUAGE AND DISCOURSE IN LATE CAPITALIST SOCIETY

Critical discourse analysis tends to be seen, certainly in many linguistics departments, as a marginal (and, for many, suspect) area of language study. Yet it ought, in my view, to be at the centre of a reconstructed discipline of linguistics, the properly social theory of language recently appealed for by Kress (1992). My first objective in this section is to suggest that strong support for this position comes from an analysis of the 'state' of language and discourse (i.e. of 'orders of discourse') in contemporary societies: if language studies are to connect with the actualities of contemporary language use, there must be a social, critical and historical turn. A second objective is to fill in the wider context of the processes of marketization of public discourse discussed in the next section.

My premise in this section is that the relationship between discourse and other facets of the social is not a transhistorical constant but a historical variable, so that there are qualitative differences between different historical epochs in the social functioning of discourse. There are also inevitably continuities: I am suggesting not radical disjuncture between, let us say, pre-modern, modern and 'postmodern' society, but qualitative shifts in the 'cultural dominant' (Williams, 1981)[4] in respect of discursive practices, i.e. in the nature of the discursive practices which have most salience and impact in a particular epoch. I shall refer below particularly to Britain, but a *global* order of discourse is emerging, and many characteristics and changes have a quasi-international character.

Foucault's (1979) investigations into the qualitative shift in the nature and functioning of power between pre-modern and modern societies are suggestive of some of the distinctive features of discourse and language in modern societies. Foucault has shown how modern 'biopower' rests upon technologies and techniques of power which are embedded within the mundane practices of social institutions (e.g. schools or prisons), and are productive of social subjects. The technique of 'examination', for example, is not exclusively linguistic but it is substantially defined by discursive practices – genres – such as those of medical consultation/examination and various other varieties of interview (Fairclough, 1992a). Certain key institutional genres, such as interview, but also more recently counselling, are among the most salient characteristics of modern societal orders of discourse. Discourse in modern as opposed to pre-modern societies is characterized by having the distinctive and more important role in the constitution and reproduction of power relations and social identities which this entails.

This Foucaultian account of power in modernity also makes sense of the emphasis in 20th-century social theory upon ideology as the key means through which social relations of power and domination are sustained (Gramsci, 1971; Althusser, 1971; Hall, 1982), the common-sense normalcy of mundane practices as the basis for the continuity and reproduction of relations of power. And Habermas (1984) gives a dynamic and historical twist to the analysis of the discourse of modernity through his postulation of a progressive colonization of the 'lifeworld' by the economy and the state, entailing a displacement of 'communicative' practices by 'strategic' practices, which embody a purely instrumental (modern) rationality. The process is well illustrated, for example, in the ways in which advertising and promotional dis-course have colonized many new domains of life in contemporary societies (see further below and the next section).

I ought not to omit from this brief review of language and discourse in modernity phenomena of language standardization, which are closely tied in with modernization; one feature of the modern is the unification of the order of discourse, of the 'linguistic market' (Bourdieu, 1991), through the imposition of standard languages at the level of the nation-state.

Many of these characteristics of modern society are still evident in contemporary 'late capitalist' (Mandel, 1978) societies, but there are also certain significant changes affecting contemporary orders of discourse; they thus manifest a mixture of modernist and what some commentators (Jameson, 1984; Lash, 1990) characterize as 'postmodernist' features. The identification of 'postmodernist' features of culture is difficult and necessarily controversial in the sphere of discourse as in others. In what follows, I shall draw, very selectively, upon two recent accounts of contemporary culture, as 'late modernity' (see Giddens (1991) and the related discussion of the 'risk society' in Beck (1992)) and as 'promotional culture' (see Wernick (1991) and Featherstone (1991) on 'consumer culture'), to tentatively identify three sets of interconnected developments in contemporary discursive practices.

1. *Contemporary society is 'post-traditional'* (Giddens, 1991). This means that traditions have to be justified against alternative possibilities rather than being taken for granted; that relationships in public based automatically upon authority are in decline, as are personal relationships based upon the rights and duties of, for example, kinship; and that people's self-identity, rather than being a feature of given positions and roles, is reflexively built up through a process of negotiation (see also (3) below). Relationships and identities therefore increasingly need to be negotiated through dialogue, an openness which entails greater possibilities than the fixed relationships and identities of traditional society, but also greater risks.

A consequence of the increasingly negotiated nature of relationships is that contemporary social life demands highly developed dialogical capacities. This is so in work, where there has been a great increase in the demand for 'emotional labour' (Hochschild, 1983), and consequently communicative labour, as part of the expansion and transformation of the service sector. It is also true in contacts between professionals and publics ('clients'), and in relationships with partners, kin and friends. These demands can be a major source of difficulty, for not everyone can easily meet them; there is a notable new focus on training in the 'communicative skills' of face-to-face and group interaction in language education.

This provides a frame within which we can make sense of the process of 'informalization' (Wouters, 1986; Featherstone, 1991) which has taken place since the 1960s in its specifically discursive aspect, which I have called the 'conversationalization' of public discourse (Fairclough, 1992a, 1994 and paper 5).[5] Conversationalization is a striking and pervasive feature of contemporary orders of discourse. On the one hand, it can be seen as a colonization of the public domain by the practices of the private domain, an opening up of public orders of discourse to discursive practices which we can all attain rather than the elite and exclusive traditional practices of the public domain, and thus a matter of more open access. On the other hand, it can be seen as an *appropriation* of private domain practices by the public domain: the infusion of practices which are needed in post-traditional public settings for the complex processes of negotiating relationships and identities alluded to above. The ambivalence of conversationalization goes further: it is often a 'synthetic personalization' associated with promotional objectives in discourse (see (3) below) and linked to a 'technologization' of discourse (see (2) below).

2. *Reflexivity, in the sense of the systematic use of knowledge about social life for organizing and transforming it, is a fundamental feature of contemporary society* (Giddens). In its distinctive contemporary form, reflexivity is tied to what Giddens calls *expert systems*: systems constituted by experts (such as doctors, therapists, lawyers, scientists and technicians) with highly specialized technical knowledge which we are all increasingly dependent upon. Reflexivity and expert systems even 'extend into the core of the self' (Giddens, 1991: 32): with the demise of the given roles and positions laid down within traditional practices, the construction of self-identity is a reflexive project, involving recourse to expert systems (e.g. therapy or counselling). Discursive practices themselves are a domain of expertise and reflexivity: the technologization of discourse described in paper 5 can be understood in Giddens' terms as the constitution of expert systems whose domain is the discursive practices of, particularly, public institutions.

3. *Contemporary culture has been characterized as 'promotional' or 'consumer' culture* (Wernick, 1991; Featherstone, 1991).[6] These designations point to the cultural consequences of marketization and commodification – the incorporation of new domains into the commodity market (e.g. the 'culture industries') and the general reconstruction of social life on a market basis – and of a relative shift in emphasis within the economy from production to consumption (see paper 2). The concept of promotional culture can be understood in discursive terms as the generalization of promotion as a communicative function (Wernick, 1991: 181) – discourse as a vehicle for 'selling' goods, services, organizations, ideas or people – across orders of discourse.

The consequences of the generalization of promotion for contemporary orders of discourse are quite radical. First, there is an extensive restructuring of boundaries between orders of discourse and between discursive practices; for example, the genre of consumer advertising has been colonizing professional and public service orders of discourse on a massive scale, generating many new hybrid partly promotional genres (such as the genre of contemporary university prospectuses discussed in the next section). Second, there is a widespread instrumentalization of discursive practices, involving the subordination of meaning to, and the manipulation of meaning for, instrumental effect. In Fairclough (1989), for instance, I discussed 'synthetic personalization', the simulation in institutional settings of the person-to-person communication of ordinary conversation (recall the discussion of conversationalization in (1) above). This is a case of the manipulation of interpersonal meaning for strategic, instrumental effect.

Thirdly, and most profoundly, and also most contentiously, there is a change in what Lash (1990) calls the 'mode of signification', the relationship between signifier, signified and referent. One aspect of this is a shift in the relative salience of different semiotic modalities: advertising, for example, had undergone a well-documented shift towards greater dependence upon visual images at the relative expense of verbal semiosis. But there is also, I suggest, a significant shift from what one might call signification-with-reference to signification-without-reference: in the former, there is a three-way relation between the two 'sides' of the sign (signifier, signified) and a real object (event, property, etc.) in the world; in the latter there is no real object, only the constitution of an 'object' (signified) in discourse. Of course, the possibility of both forms of signification is inherent in language, but one can nevertheless trace their comparative relative salience in different times and places.

The colonization of discourse by promotion may also have major pathological effects upon subjects, and major ethical implications. We are, of course, all constantly subjected to promotional discourse, to the point that there is a serious problem of trust: given that much of our discursive environment is characterized by more or less overt promotional intent, how can we be sure what's authentic? How, for example, do we know when friendly conversational talk is not just simulated for instrumental effect?[7] This problem of trust is compounded by the significance for reflexive building of self-identity of choices made among the 'lifestyles' projected in association with the promotion of goods. But the pathological consequences go deeper; it is increasingly difficult not to be involved oneself in promoting, because many people have to as part of their jobs, but also because self-promotion is becoming part-and-parcel of self-identity (see (1) above) in contemporary societies. The colonizing spread of promotional discourse thus throws up major problems for what we might reasonably call the ethics of language and discourse.

This is, let me repeat, a tentative identification of changes in discursive practices and their relationship to wider social and cultural changes. Nevertheless, this sketch does, I hope, give some sense of aspects of 'the language question' as it is experienced in contemporary society. If this account carries conviction, then it would seem to be vital that people should become more aware and more self-aware about language and discourse. Yet levels of awareness are actually very low. Few people have even an elementary metalanguage for talking about and thinking about such issues. A critical awareness of language and discursive practices is, I suggest, becoming a prerequisite for democratic citizenship, and an urgent priority for language education in that the majority of the population (certainly of Britain) are so far from having achieved it (see Clark *et al.* 1990, 1991; paper 11). There is a major role and opportunity here for applied language studies, yet it will not be capable of undertaking it unless there is the critical, social and historical turn I am calling for.

MARKETIZATION OF PUBLIC DISCOURSE: THE UNIVERSITIES

In this section I refer to a particular case and specific texts in order to illustrate the theoretical position and analytical framework set out in the first two sections, at the same time making more concrete the rather abstract account of contemporary discursive practices in the previous section. The case I shall focus upon is the marketization of discursive practices in contemporary British universities,[8] by which I mean the restructuring of the order of discourse on the model of more central market organizations. It may on the face of it appear to be unduly introspective for an academic to analyse universities as an example of marketization, but I do not believe it is; recent changes affecting higher education are a typical case and rather a good example of processes of marketization and commodification in the public sector more generally.

The marketization of the discursive practices of universities is one dimension of the marketization of higher education in a more general sense. Institutions of higher education come increasingly to operate (under government pressure) as if they were ordinary businesses competing to sell their products to consumers.[9] This is not just a simulation. For example, universities are required to raise an increasing proportion of their funds from private sources, and increasingly to put in competitive tenders for funding (e.g. for taking on additional groups of students in particular subject areas). But there are many ways in which universities are unlike real business – much of their income, for instance, is still derived from government grants. Nevertheless, institutions are making major organizational changes which accord with a market mode of operation, such as introducing an 'internal' market by making departments more financially autonomous, using 'managerial' approaches in, for example, staff appraisal and training, introducing institutional planning, and giving much more attention to marketing. There has also been pressure for academics to see students as 'customers' and to devote more of their energies to teaching and to developing learner-centred methods of teaching. These changes have been seen as requiring new qualities and skills from academics and indeed a transformation in their sense of professional identity. They are instantiated in and constituted through changed practices and behaviour at various levels, including changed discursive practices, though these have very much been 'top-down' changes imposed upon academic staff and students and the extent to which they have actually taken effect is open to question (see further below).

In what follows I wish to take up the discussion of 'promotional' culture in (3) in the last section. I suggest that the discursive practices (order of discourse) of higher education are in the process of being transformed through the increasing salience within higher education of promotion as a communicative function. This development is closely intertwined with the emergence of post-traditional features (see (1) in the last section), and I investigate in particular, focusing upon discursive practices, the following two interconnected questions: (a) What is happening to the authority of academic institutions and academics and to authority relations between academics and students, academic institutions and the public, etc? (b) What is happening to the professional identities of academics and to the collective identities of institutions?[10] This entails an emphasis on interpretational dimensions of textual form/meaning (recall the discussion of the multifuntionality of language and discourse in the first section), and I refer in particular to four examples that are partially and of course highly selectively representative of the order of discourse of the contemporary university: press advertisements for academic posts (*Example 1*), programme materials for an academic conference (*Example 2*), an academic curriculum vitae (*Example 3*), and entries in undergraduate prospectuses (*Example 4*). I shall draw upon the analytical framework sketched out earlier.

Example 1: Advertisements

My first example consists of three advertisements for academic posts which appeared in the *Times Higher Education Supplement* on 22 May 1992. Advertisements by the newer universities (until the summer of 1992, polytechnics) and the older universities in general follow sharply different patterns at the time of writing. Sample 1 is a typical newer-university advertisement; Sample 2 a typical older university advertisement, though, as Sample 3 shows, there are intermediate types and incursions of the newer-university model into the more traditional one. (It will be interesting to see how practices evolve during the first few years of the post-binary system.) The analysis focuses upon Sample 1 and to a lesser extent Sample 2. I present my analysis here in accordance with the three-dimensional framework introduced earlier, but (for reasons of space) I am less systematic in discussing my other examples.

Discourse practice

Sample 1 is interdiscursively complex, articulating together a variety of genres and discourses, including elements of advertising and other promotional genres. It is an illustration of one of the features of promotionalized discursive practices I identified in the previous section – the generation of new hybrid, partly promotional genres. An obvious promotional element is the presence of features of commodity advertising genre, realized textually for instance in the 'catchy' headline (*Make an Impact on the Next Generation*) and in personalization of the reader (*you*) and the institution (*we*). In the latter respect, advertising simulates conversational genre, which is also therefore a part of the interdiscursive 'mix'. In addition to general commodity advertising elements, there are elements from the genre of prestige or corporate advertising, including the self-promotional claims at the beginning (*With our reputation . . .*) and the logo. Some of the self-promotional material draws upon narrative genre; the section under the heading *School of Engineering*, for example, can be construed as a (simple) story about the institution's

SCHOOL OF ENGINEERING

With our reputation as one of the UK's leading centres of teaching excellence and research innovation, we're making a lasting impact on the next generation of innovators and business leaders in the field of Engineering – and you can help.

With your ambition, energy and expertise, you will be committed to teaching at both undergraduate and post-graduate level, while enjoying the advantage of our close links with Industry and applied research initiatives to add to both your own reputation and ours.

SENIOR ACADEMIC POST
VEHICLE EMISSION TECHNOLOGY

Up to £31,500 p.a. plus substantial enhancement available by negotiation.

The School of Engineering is renowned for its innovative work in the area of Vehicle Emission Technology and is a leader in the field of Automotive Research. A team leader is now required to join this active team to help build on our success.

This leading post requires an outstanding Engineer who can bring expertise in at least one of the following:- Vehicle Pollution, Hybrid Vehicles, Air Quality Systems. You'll also need to be dedicated to progressing research and consultancy whilst lecturing to undergraduate and postgraduate students.

Along with appropriate qualifications, technological expertise and industrial experience, you will need to have energy, enthusiasm and communication skills to motivate your team.

We offer an excellent salary and benefits package, but more importantly the ideal environment and opportunity to really make a contribution to the future of automotive engineering.

You may be awarded the title of Professor if the relevant criteria are met.

For an informal discussion about the post please ring Professor David Tidmarsh, Director of School of Engineering on (0742) 533389.

Application forms and further details are available from the address below. Ref. 40/92.

LECTURERS /SENIOR LECTURERS
PRINCIPAL LECTURERS

£10,949 – £28,851 p.a.

COMPUTER AIDED ENGINEERING

With expertise in one or more of the following: CAD, CAM, FEA, Expert Systems, AMT. Ref. 41/92.

QUALITY SYSTEMS

Applications to both Design and Manufacturing Engineering, offering expertise in one or more of the following areas: TQM, SPC, BS5750, BS7000, Taguchi Methods. A capability to contribute to the teaching of operations management will be an advantage. Ref. 42/92.

MAKE AN IMPACT ON THE NEXT GENERATION

MANUFACTURING TECHNOLOGY

With expertise in one or more of the following: Metal and Polymer Forming, Non-conventional Manufacturing, AMT, Environmental Impact of Manufacturing. Ref. 43/92.

OPERATIONS MANAGEMENT

With expertise in one or more of the following: Expert Systems, Database Systems, Simulation, Manufacturing Planning and Control, CIM, CAPP, MRP. Ref. 44/92.

ENVIRONMENTAL ENGINEERING

(Two Posts)

Post 1: With expertise in one or more of the following: The chemistry of air/water pollution, the impact of geology, hydrology and ecology on environmental issues, impact of transport on the environment. Ref. 45/92.

Post 2: With expertise in Electro-hydraulic Control Systems, Automation, PLCs, Environmental Noise, Noise Control, Acoustics, Vibrations. Ref. 46/92.

MATERIALS ENGINEERING : MATERIALS RESEARCH INSTITUTE

An experienced graduate Materials Scientist or Metallurgist, ideally with an appropriate higher degree, to undertake research and development work in the Metals and Ceramics Research Group. The research work will involve the use of extensive SEM/STEM/XRD and surface analysis facilities applied to a range of metallurgical problems with a particular emphasis on surface engineering. Ref. 47/92.

For all the above posts you will ideally have industry-related experience to add to your degree and a record of achievement in research and/or consultancy activities. You will be committed to teaching excellence at both undergraduate and postgraduate levels and also have the enthusiasm and ability to be part of an active group and to initiate and supervise research, consultancy and short course programmes.

If you feel you have the ideas and expertise to make an impact in a dynamic, forward-looking environment, then please send for an application form and further details to the Personnel Department, Floor 3, 5 Storey Block, Pond Street, Sheffield S1 1WB. Telephone (0742) 533950. Closing date 8th June 1992.

We are actively implementing equality of opportunity policies and seek people who
share our commitment. Job share applicants welcome. Women are under represented
in this area and applications from this group are particularly welcomed.

The University working in partnership with industry and the professions.

Sheffield City Polytechnic   Promising Futures

EXAMPLE 1: Sample 1

University of Newcastle upon Tyne

Department of English Literature

LECTURER

Applications are invited for a Lectureship in the Department of English Literature from candidates who have expertise in any Post-Medieval field. The post is available to be filled from 1st October, 1992, or as soon as possible thereafter.

Salary will be at an appropriate point on the Lecturer Grade A scale: £12,860 - £17,827 p.a. according to qualifications and experience.

Further particulars may be obtained from the Director of Personnel, Registrar's Office, University of Newcastle upon Tyne, 6 Kensington Terrace, Newcastle upon Tyne NE1 7RU, with whom applications (3 copies), together with the names and addresses of three referees, should be lodged not later than 29th May, 1992.

Please quote ref: 0726/THES.
(18704)   B9905

University of Nottingham

The Department of Law is a thriving department committed to excellence in teaching and research across a broad range of legal disciplines. The successful applicant will share this commitment. Applications are invited from candidates with an interest in any field of Law, but the Department has a particular need in the area of Property Law.

The appointment will be made at the appropriate point on the Lecturer A and B scales according to age, qualifications and experience. Professor M.G. Bridge, the Head of the Law Department is happy to answer any enquiries (Ext. 3376).

Further details and application forms, returnable not later than 26th May, from the Personnel Office, University of Nottingham, University Park, Nottingham NG7 2RD (Tel: 0602 484848, Ext. 2696). Ref. No. 1529. (18699)   B9905

EXAMPLE 1: Sample 2   EXAMPLE 1: Sample 3

impact on the next generation. A discourse of personal qualities is also an element of the interdiscursive mix (e.g. *with your ambition, energy*), as is a discourse of (educational) management, realized textually most notably in nominalizations such as *teaching excellence, expertise, a dynamic, forward-looking environment.* There are also, of course, elements of the more traditional genre and discourse of university job advertisements (e.g. *Application forms and further details are available from the address below. Ref. 40/92*).

Text

I begin with more general comments on contrasting interpersonal meanings in Samples 1 and 2, then move on to a more detailed discussion of their textual realizations.

The institutional identity projected in Sample 2 is impersonal, distant, settled (in a sense I explain below) and conservative. The institutional voice is that of a traditional university. The institution claims authority only with respect to the post and its conditions and procedures of application. There is no attempt to project a specific professional identity for the potential applicant. Very similar interpersonal meanings are present in those parts of Sample 1 which draw upon the traditional genre and discourse of academic advertisements (e.g. *Application forms and further details are available from the address below*), but the sample is characterized by contradictory interpersonal meanings in accordance with its complex interdiscursive mix, and its most salient interpersonal meanings are drawn from the dominant, promotional and self-promotional elements in that mix. The predominant institutional identity projected is personalized and assertive (self-promotional). While the identity of the institution in Sample 2 is taken as settled and given, there is an obvious sense in which Sample 1 is actively constructing an institutional identity. Again, not only is a professional identity for the potential applicant set up in the text in contrast with Sample 2, but also it is actively constructed in parts of the text which are about the qualities of a successful applicant (e.g. *With your ambition, energy and expertise, you will be committed to teaching . . .*). In these sections, the institution is claiming authority over the identity of applicants (including in terms of what are traditionally seen as personal qualities), as well as elsewhere (like Sample 2) over the post, its conditions and application procedures. The personalization of both institution (*we*) and addressees (*you*), and the individualized address of potential applicants (it is a singular not a plural *you*), simulate a conversational and therefore relatively personal, informal, solidary and equal relationship between institution and potential applicant, and other features (see below) reinforce this.

Realization of these interpersonal meanings involves analysis of the text in several dimensions. The *generic structure* of Sample 2 follows traditional advertising for academic posts: a heading identifying the institution, then the main heading giving the title of the post, then details of the post and salary, then procedure for applying. Sample 1 is hybrid, showing evidence of three elements in its interdiscursive mix: commodity advertising, and prestige advertising, as well as traditional advertising for academic posts. The traditional headings are missing, and there is a catchy advertising-style headline (though not actually at the head of the advertisement) and a signature line which identifies the institution with a logo and slogan as well as its title. The body of the advertisement begins with a promotional characterization of the institution, and a characterization of the suitable applicant for the **posts** advertised. These advertising and promotional elements foreground the predominant interpersonal meanings identified above.

Parts of Sample 1 are generically structured as narratives – the section beneath the heading *School of Engineering* is an example. The rather simple story is of the reader as a possible future employee working within the institution. Such narrative is not a feature of traditional university job advertisements (nor of Sample 2), and its presence here is linked to the shift identified above towards a more active discursive construction of professional identity. Notice in this connection an otherwise rather odd feature of modality and tense, exemplified here in *you will be committed to teaching*, which occurs several times in the sample; this is a potentially face-threatening prediction about the professional ethics as well as behaviour of the potential employee, with the modal verb (*will*) marking a high level of commitment to the proposition, which, however, loses its face-threatening character in the imaginary scenario portrayed in the narrative. Although the story is, as I have said, a rather simple one, it is more elaborate than its meagre two sentences would suggest. These narrative sentences have a form of complexity which one does not find in traditional academic advertisements. Both sentences contain a number of subordinate clauses and both have prepositional phrases introduced by *with* which contain presupposed propositions. In all, there are seven propositions in this narrative (in abbreviated form: we have a reputation, we are making an impact, you can help, you have ambition, etc., you will be committed to teaching, you will enjoy the advantage of our links, you will add to your reputation and ours). Notice that the paratactic clause linked with a dash to sentence 1 (*–and you can help*) evokes a conversational style which gives a touch of informality to the personalized relationship between institution and potential applicant.

Turning to the *grammar* of the *clause*, I want to comment in turn on features of *modality, mood* and *transitivity* (Halliday, 1985). The authority of the institution with respect to the post, its conditions and the procedure of application in Sample 2 is partly realized in mood and modality features. Clauses are, of course, declarative, with high-affinity epistemic (or 'probability') modalities such as *the post is available* or *salary will be* ... There is also one instance of deontic ('obligational') modality (*applications ... should be lodged*), and one case (*further particulars may be obtained*) with an ambivalence between epistemic and deontic modality (mixing 'possibility' with 'permission') which is characteristic for this discourse. Sample 1 has several instances of imperative mood (*make an impact on the next generation, please send for an application form*) which accord with the personalized institution–audience relationship noted above. As in Sample 2, the authority of the institution is marked through high-affinity epistemic modalities. However, explicit obligational modalities are absent. I noted above the frequency of clauses with modal auxiliary *will* marking futurity plus high-affinity epistemic modality. These are, in some cases, set within developed if simple narratives, as I have indicated, but this is not always so: the advertisement seems generally to cast the potential applicant in the imaginary role of future employee. But notice that these clauses (e.g. *for all the above posts you will ideally have industry-related experience*) provide *alternatives* to obligational clauses (such as *you should have industry-related experience*), in which obligational meanings can be backgrounded. This accords with the personalized, solidary and equal relationship claimed between institution and potential applicant which I described above. So also does the foregrounding of the activity of the potential applicant in these clauses (and also, for instance, in *you can help*, with a modal verb ambivalent between 'possibility' and 'ability'). Although it takes us beyond mood to pragmatics and speech acts, let me also note here the frequency of clauses which make claims about the institution (e.g. *The School of Engineering is renowned for its innovative work* . . .), which realize the self-constructive and self-promotional institutional identity I have referred to.

In terms of transitivity, there are two features of Sample 2 which contribute to its qualities of impersonality: passives and nominalizations. Both are illustrated in its opening sentence: *Applications are invited for a Lectureship*. The passive verb is agentless, so that the institution is not present in the surface grammar, and the nominalization (*applications*) also lacks an agent, so that the potential applicant is also absent. There are elements of this impersonal style in Sample 1 (e.g. *applications from this group are particularly welcomed*) but they are not salient.

There are a number of points which might be made about the vocabulary of these samples, but I shall make just two. First, the formal-sounding and slightly archaic vocabulary of Sample 2 (such as *thereafter, particulars, lodged*) accords with the impersonality and distance of the institutional identity set up. Vocabulary of this sort is not present in Sample 1. By contrast (and this is the second point), Sample 1 uses a vocabulary and collocations of educational management (*teaching excellence, expertise, a dynamic, forward-looking environment, progressing research, research and consultancy*), as well as a vocabulary of personal qualities and skills. From the perspective of discursive practice, these vocabularies belong to separate discourses which I identified earlier as belonging to the interdiscursive mix. The appropriation of these discourses is, I think, part of the process of constructing a new corporate identity for the higher education institution.

Social practice

The observations on marketization of universities at the beginning of this section are part of the wider social practice within which these discourse samples are located. It is also relevant that these samples appeared in a period of transition between announcement of the abolition of the binary divide between polytechnics (referred to as the 'newer' universities above) and (older) universities, and its full implementation. There are many relevant historical factors here. For example, there have been particularly strong links between the newer universities and business, and polytechnics were in conception more vocationally oriented than universities, though they have also evolved many courses which are like traditional university courses. Sample 1 illustrates a type of job advertisement found widely for posts in business. For instance, a rapid survey of the *Guardian* at the time of writing shows that the great majority of advertisements for posts in marketing resemble Sample 1 rather than Sample 2 in terms of the sorts of features discussed above. One development that is at issue here, therefore, seems to be the fracturing of the boundary between the orders of discourse of higher education and business as regards advertising, and a colonization of the former by the latter. This can be construed as one rather particular discursive manifestation of the processes of marketization of higher education referred to above. As Sample 3 shows, this colonization of academic discourse affects older universities as well, though there is generally at the time of writing a rather clear correlation between the two types of advertisement and the older and newer universities. This case is, I think, an interesting one in terms of struggles to restructure hegemony within the order of discourse of higher education. At present, there are in this specific area of discursive practice two orders of discourse which have not been unified. I would predict that, with the breakdown of divisions between institutional types, that situation is highly unlikely to persist. It will be interesting to see whether and how the two orders of discourse begin to unify, and whether and how a struggle develops around the traditional advertising practice illustrated by Sample 2 and the new, interdiscursively complex practice illustrated by Sample 1. A significant issue in monitoring developments will be to monitor changes in processes and routines of drafting and production of advertisements, and it will also be interesting to monitor the responses of potential applicants to different advertising styles.

Example 2: Programme materials; Example 3: Curriculum vitae

I want to refer rather more briefly, and without systematically using the three-dimensional framework of analysis, to two of my other examples, as further instances of the incursion of promotion and self-promotion into the order of discourse of higher education, and of the reconstruction of, respectively, corporate and individual professional identities.

Example 2

The first is the 'pack' given to participants in a one-day academic conference held recently at Lancaster University.[11] The conference was a highly prestigious event with two of the foremost sociologists in Europe as its main speakers. The 'pack' consisted of

(a) a brief account of the topic of, participation in and organization of the conference;
(b) a programme;
(c) a page of notes on 'platform participants', their academic positions, publications and other distinctions;
(d) a page on the research centre which co-organized the conference, its history, personnel, research activities, relationships with other organizations;
(e) a rather spaciously laid-out seven-page list of participants with their institutions, divided into external participants and Lancaster participants;
(f) an evaluation form for the conference.

Conferences of this sort are increasingly used as a means of promoting academic organizations, as well as being motivated for more conventional academic reasons, and this example is, I think, fairly typical of the tendency. While (a) and (d) are the most obviously promotional elements, one could argue that even (e) has a promotional function in using a rather spacious layout to underline the distinguished array of participants in the conference. Here is (a):

This one-day conference links the growing body of sociological thought on Risk in Society (as in recent studies by social theorists such as Giddens, Beck, Baumann and others), with the phenomenon of world-wide environmental concern and cultural change. It is timed to relate to the imminent first publication in English of Ulrich Beck's celebrated book *Risikogesellschaft* (*The Risk Society*), one of the most influential and best-selling works of post-war European sociology.

The conference will bring together sociologists from the UK and continental Europe on these questions for the first time. It is organised jointly by Lancaster's Centre for the Study of Environmental Change (CSEC) and Sociology Department, with the support of the Economic and Social Research Council (ESRC).

It is quite a good example of a widespread contemporary ambivalence; is this information, or is it promotion? The promotional function seems to have become more salient in ('colonized') a whole range of types of informative discourse. Does meaning (here, the giving of background information relevant to the conference) have primacy, or is it subordinated to effect (constructing the conference as a highly significant event in the minds of its participants)? For example, the information in sentence 2 is on one level certainly accurate (Beck's book has had a rapturous reception and has just been published in English). Yet why *imminent* (with its portentous associative meaning) rather than *forthcoming*? Why *first* publication (implying, but only on the basis of a guess, that there will be more)? Why *Ulrich* Beck (it was simply *Beck* in sentence 1)? Why not stop at *celebrated book* (which gives the information about the book's reception), why add the reduced relative clause (*one of the . . . European sociology*), especially since the addressees are those who have elected to attend the conference, who are mostly 'in the know'? Is this sentence on balance *referring* to the book and its imminent publication, or rather *constructing* the book and the event? In short, is this sentence mainly informative or mainly to do with promoting the book (notice the vague — one might even say euphemistic — verb *relate to*) and thereby implicitly the conference (if the book is that significant, so by implication is a conference where the author is talking about the topic of the book)? As so often in contemporary society, the giving of information is taking place in a context where there is a premium on winning people to see things in a particular way (see the discussion of 'telling' and 'selling' in paper 2). Notice the closed nature of this promotional work; the conference is being promoted amongst its own participants, who constitute a significant section of the constituency empowered to give the institution the recognition it is seeking. I should perhaps add that I suspect that these promotional objectives would be no mystery to most of those who participated; people who attend such conferences seem generally pre-pared to live with promotional objectives, limiting themselves to ironic, distancing comments in private which suggest that for some academics at least such apparently necessary work on institutional identity does not sit easily with their sense of their own professional self-identity.

Example 3

The next example I want to look at specifically in terms of promotion – and more exactly self-promotion – is an extract from a curriculum vitae (CV). Such data are sensitive for obvious reasons, and I have therefore used an extract from a CV I prepared myself in 1991 for an academic promotions committee. The form of submissions to this committee is controlled by procedural rules which specify the maximum length of a CV and the categories of information it should contain, and require a 'supporting statement' of no more than 'two sides of A4 paper'. The extract I have chosen is a paragraph from the supporting statement. Unlike the CV proper, the content of the supporting statement is not specified in the procedural rules. I had to make informal enquiries to find out what was expected. I was able to look at previous submissions by colleagues, and I received advice from a colleague with experience of the committee. From these sources, I gathered that the supporting statement had to be a compelling account of one's contribution to, if possible, all the categories of activity in two overlapping schemes of categorization: to research, teaching and administration; and to the department, the university, and the wider community (these categorization schemes are actually spelt out in the procedural rules, though not specifically with reference to the supporting statement). The advice I received was that one had to 'sell' oneself to stand any chance of success. The following extract from an internal memorandum, produced shortly after I had prepared the submission, gives a sense of the prevailing wisdom at the time:

> To succeed, departments have to 'sell' their candidates. One cannot expect merit to gleam with its own halo; the halo has been assiduously polished up! Put differently, this means that one has to hone one's application to give an impression of all-round excellence, preferably over a period of time, with feedback from others.

This easily extends to an emphasis on the need for extended

preparation for the well-honed application – for instance, it is helpful to have favourable student feedback on one's courses, ideally over several years. One's future promotability may become a significant factor in the planning of one's current activities. Here is the extract:

> *Contributions to the Department*
> I have I believe played a significant role in the academic and administrative leadership of the Department over the past eight years or so. I was Head of Department from 1984 to 1987 and again for one term in 1990, and I have carried a range of other responsibilities including MA and undergraduate programme coordination and admissions. I helped to set up and now help to run the Centre for Language in Social Life. Through my coordination of the Language, Ideology and Power research group and in other activities, I have stimulated research (e.g. on critical language awareness) among colleagues and postgraduate students, and helped form what is now being recognized nationally and internationally as a distinctive Lancaster position on and contribution to study of language and language problems in contemporary British society. I am currently helping to edit a collection of Centre for Language in Social Life papers for publication.

Some of the self-promotional properties of the extract are obvious enough. There is a series of claims realized as clauses with past tense, present perfective and present continuous verbs and *I* as subject and theme. These are mainly claims which are categorical in their modality, positive assertions without explicit modalizing elements, though there is a subjective modality marker in the first clause (*I believe*) which (a) foregrounds the subjective basis of judgement in the whole paragraph in that the first clause is a summary/formulation of the paragraph, but also (b) foregrounds (one might say rather brazenly) the self-promotional nature of the activity. (For the analytical terminology used here see Halliday, 1985, and Fairclough, 1992a.) Except for one relational process (*I was Head of Department*), all clauses in the extract contain action processes. It would seem that material actional process verbs are consistently being selected even where other process types would be just as congruent with or more congruent with the happenings and relationships reported – for instance, although I am indeed one of the five co-directors of the Centre for Language in Social Life, it receives practically no 'running' from anyone, and I might well (indeed better) have worded this *am now an active member of.* Similarly *played a significant role in* might have been *been a significant part of, carried a range of other responsibilities* might have been *had a range of other responsibilities, helped to set up* might have been *was a founding member of,* and so forth. These changes would, I think, reduce the sense of dynamic activity conveyed in the extract. A noteworthy lexical choice is *leadership* in the first sentence. The wording of academic relationships in terms of *leadership* belongs, in my view, to a managerial discourse which has come to colonize the academic order of discourse recently, and which I actually find deeply antipathetic. In terms of the characteristics of promotional discourse discussed earlier, the extract is very much a signification/construction of its subject/object rather than just referentially based description, and meaning would seem to be subordinated to effect.

I suppose I saw the preparation of the submission as a rhetorical exercise. By which I mean that I was consciously using language in a way I dislike, playing with and parodying an alien discourse, in order to 'play the game' and convince the committee of my merits. That is rather a comforting account of events, and a common enough one; the self stands outside or behind at least some forms of discursive practice, simply assuming them for strategic effects. I felt embarrassed about the submission, but that is, I think, compatible with the rhetorical account. There are, however, problems with this account. In the first place, it assumes a greater consciousness of and control over one's practice than is actually likely to be the case. For instance, while I was quite conscious of what was at stake in using *leadership*, I was not aware at the time of how systematically I was 'converting' all processes to actions, although I *could* have been (and perhaps I ought to have been) – unlike most people I have the analytical apparatus. More seriously, the rhetorical account underestimates the incorporative capacity of institutional logics and procedures. Whereas the average academic rarely has contact with promotions committees, contact with other organizational forms whose procedures are based upon the same logics are necessary and constant. Doing one's job entails 'playing the game' (or various connected games), and what may feel like a mere rhetoric to get things done quickly and easily becomes a part of one's professional identity. Self-promotion is perhaps becoming a routine, naturalized strand of various academic activities, and of academic identities.

Example 4: Prospectuses

My final example consists of extracts from Lancaster University's undergraduate prospectuses for the years 1967–8 (Example 4.1), 1986–7 (Example 4.2), and 1993 (Example 4.3) see pp. 161-6. (See also the prospectus sample in paper 4.) I have used part of the English entry from the first, and part of the Linguistics entries from the second and third (Linguistics was taught within English in 1967–8). I focus upon differences between the 1993 and 1967–8 samples, the 1986–7 sample being included to show an intermediate stage in the development of the prospectus genre. A first observation is that the earliest and most recent entries are sharply different in their content. The 1967–8 entry (Example 4.1) consists of: (a) approximately half a page on the English BA degree, specifically on the view of the study of English it embodies; (b) an itemized list of the 'special interests' of the department; (c) approximately one page on the detailed content of the English BA degree. The 1993 entry (Example 4.3) consists of (a) a box detailing entry policy and requirements; (b) three paragraphs on the department – its staff, courses, academic links, academic achievements, and ethos; (c) a headed section on assessment; (d) a headed section on graduate careers; (e) a one-page diagrammatic summary of the undergraduate Linguistics degree. I shall focus my comments again on aspects of authority and identity.

I shall begin with textual analysis, considering specifically meanings of requirement and obligation and their formal realizations. Sections (a), (c) and (e) of the 1993 entry (entry requirements, assessment, and the undergraduate degree structure) involve requirements placed by the institution upon students or applicants. Most of the 1967–8 entry deals with degree structure, with entry requirements and assessment being dealt with elsewhere in the prospectus. Meanings of obligation and permission are extensively and overtly present in the 1967–8 entry. There are quite a few obligational and permissive modal auxiliary verbs (e.g. *subjects may be offered, each undergraduate will choose, third-year undergraduates must choose, any one course . . . may be offered*) and other modal expressions (*second-year undergraduates . . . are required to take*; compare *must take*). Obligation is expressed lexically as well as modally (in *no specialization . . . is permitted, a very limited concentration . . . is allowed*). By contrast, although meanings of requirement and obligation are implicit in the 1993 entry, they are not explicitly worded. This is facilitated by the use of tabular and diagrammatic layout for the entry requirements and the degree structure, which allow requirements to be left implicit. For instance, while **A/AS-level grades:** *BCC or equivalent* implies that applicants are required to achieve these grades, explicit obligational meanings are conspicuously absent. The degree structure section consists mainly of phrases (or 'minor clauses' – see Halliday, 1985), but where a full clause is used the wording again backgrounds requirement (e.g. *You take at least three,* rather than, for example, *You must take at least three*). The assessment section again uses minor clauses and lacks overt obligational meanings.

A related contrast is between the impersonal style of the 1967–8 entry and the personalized style of the 1993 entry. Notice, for example, that the three passive verbs in the 1967–8 entry referred to above as instances of obligational meaning (*are required to take, is permitted, is allowed*) are 'agentless', that is, they lack an explicit agent, though in each case the institution is the implicit agent (it is the department, or the university, that requires, permits and allows). There are also other agentless passives in the entry where the institution is implicit (e.g. *the Language course is so constructed as to be*). The opening sentence uses a different syntactic–semantic means to maintain impersonality; selecting *the undergraduate courses* as subject and agent of *treat*. This is, in Halliday's terms, a 'grammatical metaphor' for a 'congruent' (non-metaphorical) grammaticization with, for example, *we* as subject/ agent of *treat* and *undergraduate courses* within an adjunct (*we treat English as a whole subject in our undergraduate courses*). Another impersonalizing device is nominalization; *the special interests of the Department include the following*, with the nominalization (*the special interests of the Department*) as clause subject, avoids more personalized alternatives like *members of the Department* (or *we*) *are particularly interested in. . . .* It is also worth noting that what appear to be merely descriptive statements about the course could be reworded and regrammaticized in personalized ways: compare (the actual) *the course consists of three parts* with *the department/we organize(s) the course in three parts*.

Actually, there are two issues involved here. First, there is the issue of to what extent participants (here the institution and the potential applicant/student) in the processes referred to are made explicit or left implicit. Secondly, there is the issue of the grammatical person of these participants when they *are* explicit: third person, or first (*we*) and second person (*you*). (A further question is whether first and second person are singular or plural – in fact, where they are used, the institutional first person is plural [*we*] whereas the second person is singular – addressees are addressed individually.) With regard to the institution as participant, the 1967–8 entry is impersonal in both senses – not only is the institution referred to in the third person where it is explicit, it is often not explicit at all – whereas the 1993 entry is personalized in both senses as far as the institution is concerned – it is frequently explicit in the text, and it is first person.

But the picture is somewhat more complex for the addressees. There is some second-person direct address in the 1993 entry (*Linguistics does*

not commit you to any one career, you take at least three of). But applicants
are referred to in the third person in the opening entry requirements
section (e.g. *all accepted candidates are invited to open days* – notice also
the passive verb and missing institutional agent), and applicants/stu-
dents are not referred to in the next section until its third paragraph
(beginning *We are a friendly . . .*), and then in the third person (e.g. *the
people we teach, students*). On the other hand, the 1967–8 entry is again
impersonal in both senses with respect to adressees. For example:

> . . . *no specialization in either language or literature separately is permitted until the
> third year of study when a very limited concentration on either is allowed.*

While the agentless passives avoid personalization of the institution
as noted above, the nominalizations acting as their subjects (*no specialization, a very limited concentration*) avoid personalization of addressees
(compare *you cannot specialize until the third year of study*). An agentless
passive is used to the same effect: *in Part II, various periods are studied.*
Where the student participants are explicitly textualized, in the third
person, it is generally particular groups of students who need to be
explicitly identified (e.g. second-year undergraduates), though notice
cases of individualized third person reference with *each* (*each undergraduate will choose*) and generic reference with the indefinite article (*may be
offered by an undergraduate*).

Turning to some broader issues of social practice, these contrasting
textual features mark a major historical shift in the nature and objectives
of university prospectuses, in line with the wider changes in higher
education I discussed earlier. The 1967–8 entry gives information
about what is provided on a take-it-or-leave-it basis. In the 1993
prospectus, by contrast, the promotional function is primary; it is
designed to 'sell' the university and its courses to potential applicants,
in the context of a competitive market where the capacity of a
university to attract good applicants is seen as one indicator of its
success, and a factor which can affect how well it is funded. A revision
of the prospectus can lead to a dramatic increase in applications; for
instance, when Lancaster University revised its prospectus in the late
1980s, the number of applicants went up by 15 per cent for two
successive years. The content and form of the contemporary prospectuses are informed by market research – evidence of what applicants
most want to know (hence the prominence of careers information in
the 1993 entry), an understanding of the literacy culture of young
people (e.g. the salience within it of 'glossy' printed material of various
sorts), an understanding of the conditions of reading documents of this

sort (they are likely to be flicked through rather than carefully read), and so forth.

These changes entail a shift in discourse practice, and specifically in the processes of prospectus production, of which the textual features noted above are realizations. The primacy of the promotional function in contemporary prospectuses entails drawing upon genres associated with advertising and other forms of promotional activity as well as the more traditional informationally oriented genre of university prospectuses, so that the 1993 entry, for example, is an interdiscursively hybrid quasi-advertising genre. The two entries are strikingly different in physical appearance: the earlier entry is based upon the conventional printed page, whereas the 1993 entry uses a brochure-style page size and layout with three print-columns per page, colour (the first page of the entry uses five colours), tabular layout and a photograph. The document is drawing upon visual and design features widely used in advertising and promotional material. As to the features noted earlier, promotional considerations are certainly behind the marked change in content between 1967–8 and 1993, especially the introduction of the three paragraphs about the department, which bring in a genre of prestige or corporate promotion. The personalization of the institution (as *we*), which occurs heavily in this part of the entry, is a part of this. Like individualized direct address with *you*, it is widely used in advertising. The avoidance of explicit obligational meanings is also in line with the elevation of the promotional function. The avoidance of explicit obligational meanings marks a significant shift in authority relations. Promotional material addresses readerships as consumers or clients, and when someone is selling to a client, the client is positioned as having authority. This is generally true in advertising. It is in contradiction with the traditional authority of the university over applicants/students, and it places the institution in something of a dilemma, for it will obviously still wish to impose requirements and conditions upon entry, course structure and assessment. This dilemma over authority is given a textual resolution (though not necessarily a very satisfactory one): these requirements *are* included in the text, but *not* in overtly obligational forms. The text effects a compromise between the demands of two different situations and the conventions of two different genres. The text also effects a compromise as regards self-identity. The series of claims about the department which make up the first three paragraphs point to a promotional genre, but the claims are quite restrained (in comparison with, for example, Sample 1 of the job advertisements). A final note is that the interdiscursive mix I have suggested here appears to be achieving a hegemonic status in higher education publicity, as part of a more general dominance of a marketing ethos in this area of higher educational activity.

Summary

The four examples I have used above can hardly be said to be properly representative of the complex order of discourse of a modern university, but they do provide four contrasting 'takes' on the discursive practices of such institutions. They have, I hope, suggested how analysis of the discourse of organizations such as universities (in the terms of analytical framework introduced earlier) in their 'text' and 'discourse practice' dimensions can illuminate such matters as shifting authority relations and shifts in self-identity within organizations. The particular shifts I have identified can be summed up as (i) the decline of stable institutional identities which could be taken for granted, and a much greater investment of effort into the construction of more entrepreneurial institutional identities, (ii) a corresponding decline in the implicit (unspoken) authority of the institution over its applicants, potential students and potential staff, (iii) a reconstruction of professional identities of academics on a more entrepreneurial (self-promotional) basis, with the foregrounding of personal qualities.

The discursive instantiation of these shifts illustrates, I think, all three of the sets of developments in contemporary discursive practices identified in the previous section. I have already sufficiently highlighted the third of these, the elevation and generalization of the promotional function in discursive practices, and its consequences in terms of the hybridization of discourse practice, the subordination of meaning to effect, and the mode of signification. But the shifts I have identified can also be read (with respect to the first of my sets of developments) in terms of Giddens' account of the post-traditional nature of contemporary society, and the corresponding informalization of society which is partly constituted through a conversationalization of discursive practices, which is also evident in my examples. The second set of developments, associated with the increased reflexivity of contemporary life and my concept of technologization of discourse, is also relevant here: one dimension of the much increased emphasis on staff development and training in higher education is the training of staff in the discursive practices of, for instance, marketing or preparation of research proposals for research councils (itself a heavily promotional form of discourse these days).

It would be premature to draw sweeping conclusions with respect to the 'social practice' dimension of my analytical framework on the basis of such a limited range of illustrative examples. But as I indicated in note 9, this paper is linked to a longer-term study of change in higher education. One of the questions which that study will address is whether developments in higher education amount to the emergence of a new, reconstituted hegemony, and whether one can talk of a restructured hegemony in the domain of the order of discourse in particular. It would be unwise to leap too quickly to such a conclusion before there has been some investigation of the reception of and response to the sort of changes I have illustrated amongst various categories of members of higher educational institutions. It may well be, for example, that largely 'top down' changes in discursive practices are widely marginalized, ignored or resisted by certain categories of staff and/or students in a significant range of their activities.

CONCLUSION

I conclude this paper with some brief reflections upon the social use and utility of a critical discourse analysis (see also papers 5 and 8). I have tried to indicate how critical discourse analysis might contribute to more broadly conceived social research into processes of social and cultural change affecting contemporary organizations. Discourse analysis is, I believe, an important though hitherto relatively neglected resource for such research. It has the capacity to put other sorts of social analysis into connection with the fine detail of particular instances of institutional practice in a way which is simultaneously oriented to textual detail, the production, distribution and interpretation/consumption of texts, and wider social and cultural contexts.

However, discourse analysis also has the capacity to be a resource for those engaged in struggle within institutions. For many members of higher educational institutions, for example, the dramatic changes of the last decade or so have been profoundly alienating, yet their capacity to resist them has been weakened by their reluctance to fall back upon traditional practices and structures which have been widely criticized from the Left and the Right and which have been the target for change. Many have experienced a sense of helplessness, which critical discourse analysis can, I believe, help to illuminate. Part of the difficulty, which emerges from an investigation of discursive practices,

English

The undergraduate courses treat English as a whole subject and not as two divergent specializations. Accordingly, when English is taken as a major subject for the degree of B.A., no specialization in either language or literature separately is permitted until the third year of study when a very limited concentration on either is allowed. For higher degrees, specialization in either language or literature may be complete or subjects may be offered which connect these two branches of study.

In the study of *language* for the B.A. degree, modern English is central and is combined with some general linguistics and phonetics, and in Part II with history of the language. Language specializations in the third year include optional courses on older forms of English, and also on various aspects of the modern language and of linguistics. The study of English language throughout the first degree course will include fieldwork, special studies of varieties of modern English and the use of language laboratory techniques. The Language course is so constructed as to be of value to those who wish to specialize in English as a second or as a foreign language. As much as possible of the material used for literary study is also used for the study of language.

In the study of *literature* the syllabus is divided into periods, each taught with emphasis on a different aspect of literary study. The first-year course, based mainly on modern literature, deals with problems of reading and with the forms and functions of literature in contemporary society. In Part II, various periods are studied, two in two-year courses and the remainder in one-year courses.

The special interests of the Department include the following:

1. Project work in the drama courses using the facilities which will be available in the Theatre Workshop, at present being designed.
2. Special studies of the relationship between language and literature, including work on literary structures from a linguistic point of view.
3. Poetry as a performed art and its links with song.
4. Relations between the study of literature and of philosophy.
5. Relations between literature and scientific thought.
6. Relations between literary and historical study.

Undergraduate studies

PART I (FIRST YEAR) COURSE

The course consists of three parts:

(a) Language: a general introduction, including some elementary phonetics and linguistics.

(b) Literature: a course on problems of reading, and the forms and functions of literature, based on modern English poetry and prose fiction and on texts from three different types of drama (Classical, Renaissance, Modern).

(c) Special courses: each undergraduate will choose one of the special courses referred to below, the choice being determined by his other first-year subjects.

EXAMPLE 4.1

(i) For those taking groups involving History or Economics or Politics or French Studies or Classical Background, a study of certain historical aspects of literature in the seventeenth century.

(ii) For those taking groups involving Economics or Politics or Philosophy, a study of some of the relationships of literature and philosophy, centred on the works of William Blake.

(iii) For those taking groups involving Environmental Studies, Mathematics or Philosophy, a study of certain scientific texts from a literary and linguistic point of view.

The Part I course, or selected parts of it, will also (timetable permitting) be available as a one-year minor course for certain second-year undergraduates majoring in Boards of Studies A, B and C who did not take English in their first year.

PART II (SECOND AND THIRD YEAR) COURSES

Major course

Second-year undergraduates majoring in English are required to take four lecture courses – two in literature and two in language, from the following:

(a) Literature 1780-1860
Literature 1660-1780
Elizabethan Drama, including some project work in the theatre

(b) Varieties of Modern English I (study of the varieties of modern English outside the United Kingdom)
History of the English Language I
Principles and Techniques of General Linguistics, with special reference to English

Third-year undergraduates must choose four courses: *either* three language and one literature, *or* three literature and one language, *or* two of each. Any one course in language or literature may be offered by an undergraduate as a special option to be examined as such in the Final Examination. Third-year courses listed for 1966-67 (subject to the availability of staff) are as follows:

(a) Literature 1860-1966, Literature 1550-1660, Mediaeval Literature, Jacobean Drama.

(b) Old English, Middle English, Old Norse, Writing Systems, Linguistic Study of Style, Varieties of Modern English II, History of the Language II, Principles and Techniques of General Linguistics II.

Combined major course in English and French Studies – see page 118

Combined major course in English and Philosophy – see page 118

Combined major course in Latin and English – see page 118

EXAMPLE 4.1 continued

LINGUISTICS

Linguistics (BA) Q100 Ling
Human Communication (BA) P300 Hum
    Comm
Classical Studies and Linguistics (BA) QQ98
    Class/Ling
Computer Science and Linguistics (BA) GQ51
    Comp/Ling
English and Linguistics (BA) QQ13 Eng/Ling
French Studies and Linguistics (BA) QR11
    Fr/Ling
German Studies and Linguistics (BA) RR32
    Germ/Ling
Italian Studies and Linguistics (BA) QR13
    Ital/Ling
Language and Education (BA) Y656 Lang/Educ
Linguistics and Philosophy (BA) QV17
    Ling/Phil
Linguistics and Psychology (BA) LQ71 Ling/Psy
Modern English Language (BA) Q312 MEL

L ancaster is a major centre in the United
Kingdom for study in Linguistics, the
science of human language. There are
about five thousand languages, and their
enormous diversity and complexity supply the
raw data for Linguistics. Language is Man's
most remarkable achievement, and its
systematic study provides insights into Man's
psychological and social nature. The study of
language tells us something about the nature
of the human mind, since languages are
abstract systems of peculiar and labyrinthine
structure and yet men are capable of
communication in them very easily and
speedily. Language is of interest sociologically,
since it is the stuff that binds complex
societies together: without language no
sophisticated social organisation is possible.
The Department of Linguistics and Modern
English Language, which has a staff of 12, is
unique among departments of Linguistics in
the country in the way its degree schemes
offer students *three* alternative but complementary perspectives: on the structure and
functions of human language; on the use of
symbols by humans as a means of under-

standing themselves and their place in society;
on English, as one of the world's most
important means of communication and the
language of one of its most significant
literatures. Degree schemes in Linguistics,
Human Communication, English and
Linguistics and Modern English Language, as
well as combined schemes with other
departments, provide the perspectives.

The department makes use of a variety of
modes of teaching in its undergraduate
programme. Typically, teaching is by lecture
and small group seminars of up to 12
students, where the seminars are used to
discuss readings related to the lecture topic.
Many courses, especially those concerned with
the collection of language data, concentrate
on seminars and workshops and often involve
more than one member of staff.

Linguistics and Human Communication offer
useful training and expertise that are of special
professional relevance to many working in
education, public services and administration,
industry and management, the mass media
and creative arts, for example as language
teachers, speech therapists, as social workers,
as counsellors and as translators. Indeed an
understanding of how language works and the
structure and purposes of human communication is available in a whole range of careers
in which there is a need for clear communication, sensitive to people's interests and
needs.

A detailed departmental prospectus can be
obtained from the Departmental Secretary.

Admission requirements and policy
Linguistics is not a subject taught at
school,and prospective applicants should try
to get some idea of the subject before
committing themselves to it. (They may read,
for example, one or more of the following
introductory books: *The Articulate Mammal*
and *Language Change: Progress and Decay* by
Jean Aitchison, *Linguistics* by D Crystal,

EXAMPLE 4.2

Phonetics by D J O'Connor, *Grammar* and *Semantics* by F R Palmer.) The Department usually makes conditional offers on the basis of the UCCA form. We look for evidence of a keen interest in the structure of language *per se* and a willingness to analyse it objectively. When such evidence cannot be found in the UCCA form, we interview candidates. GCE attainments in Languages and Mathematics are taken as indications of likely talent in Linguistics, but there are no specific formal prerequisites. (For the general requirements see page 178.) *We welcome applications from mature candidates.*

About 25 candidates gain admission each year to the degree scheme in Human Communication and to single and combined major degree schemes in Linguistics.

Part 1 course in Linguistics
The purpose of this course is to provide a foundation for the Part II studies of students who intend to major in Linguistics or in Human Communication and to provide a balanced and self-contained introduction for those undergraduates who go on to major in another subject.

Part I Linguistics comprises Introduction to General Linguistics (151) which is compulsory and which introduces students to core areas of the subject (Phonetics, Phonology, Syntax, Semantics, Pragmatics and Sociolinguistics), together with a set of options (152) in which students choose two of a range of more specialised topics each studied for half the year. The available options vary from year to year: they currently include Structure of a non-Indo-European Language (e.g. Chinese, Arabic or Hebrew), Writing systems, History of Modern Linguistic Thought, Field Methods, the Linguistics of Literacy.

Linguistics (3-year scheme)
Part I
Students are free to choose any two courses from the list on page 175 in addition to Linguistics at Part I, subject to timetable restrictions and departmental advice; but it is

wise to select courses that will permit at least one alternative choice of Part II degree scheme (since you might wish to change your mind). Subjects that combine well with Linguistics include English and the other language subjects, Computer Studies, Educational Studies, Philosophy, Psychology, and Sociology, and the Department of Linguistics has close links with those departments.

Part II
(Six units in Linguistics, two units in a minor and a free ninth unit course: see page 18.)

Students take six units in Linguistics from a wide range of courses on various aspects of the subject. A unit can comprise either two half-unit courses or one full course. They cover the core areas studied in Part I and specialisms that include Sociolinguistics, Psycholinguistics, Stylistics, and Anthropological, Computational, Philosophical and Applied Linguistics. Some of the courses are designed specifically for the needs of the students combining Linguistics with a particular subject, while others are appropriate for all students of Linguistics. For detailed information on the courses available see the departmental prospectus.

Students also take two courses in a minor, chosen freely (subject to departmental advice and prerequisites: see page 175), and a free ninth unit course.

Human Communication (3-year scheme)
The degree scheme in Human Communication, jointly offered by the departments of Linguistics, Psychology and Sociology, places language in a broader context; it investigates human communication as a unified field of academic enquiry through the interrelated perspectives of the three subjects. Its aim is to bring the student to an awareness of the centrality of communication in human behaviour and consciousness. The only specific entry requirement is that undergraduates who take Psychology in Part I must have a pass in Mathematics at Ordinary level.

EXAMPLE 4.2 continued

LINGUISTICS AND HUMAN COMMUNICATION   SOCIAL SCIENCES

Places available: 30
Admissions tutors: Jenny Thomas
(Linguistics courses); Greg Myers
(Human Communication)

A/AS-level grades: BCC or
equivalent; AS-levels accepted
GCSE: Maths and normally a
language for Linguistics courses
Scottish Highers: BBBBB
International Baccalaureate:
30pts
BTEC: at least merits in BTEC
National
Mature students: we are keen
to recruit mature students.

All accepted candidates are
invited to open days; interviews
in special cases.

The Department of
Linguistics and Modern
English Language is one of
the largest in the UK with a
teaching staff of fourteen.
We offer a series of flexible
degrees with a wide range of
courses in 'core' areas like
phonetics, grammar and
discourse analysis; areas
which connect strongly with
other disciplines, like
sociolinguistics and
psycholinguistics; and more
'applied' areas like adult
literacy, language teaching
and the linguistic study of
literature. We have strong
links through collaborative
degrees with English,
Computer Science, the social
sciences (especially
Psychology and Sociology)
and Modern Languages.

We received a grade 4
(national excellence in most
areas of Linguistics and
international excellence in
some) in the 1989 research
ratings carried out by the
Universities Funding
Council. We are especially
well known for our research
work in Linguistics in
relation to language
teaching, for the study of
language in social settings
(e.g. school classrooms and
interaction between cancer
patients and their carers), for
the automatic analysis of
texts by computer, and for
the linguistic study of
literature.

We are a friendly and
flexible group of teachers
who like to have social
contact with the people we
teach. Every year, students
are invited to join staff for a
walking weekend in the
nearby Lake District. There
are also opportunities for
students to spend part of
their second year in
Copenhagen as part of an
ERASMUS student
exchange arrangement. We
are currently exploring
similar links with universities
in other European countries.

Assessment

For Linguistic and Human
Communication courses:
coursework (at least 60%)

and exams. For courses run
by the English Department:
coursework (50% in the first
year, usually 40% in later
years) and exams.

What our graduates do

Linguistics and Human
Communication offer useful
training and expertise that
are of special professional
relevance to many working
in education, language
teaching, speech therapy,
translation, industry and
commerce, management, the
mass media, creative arts,
social work and counselling.

Recent graduates have gone
to work or train as teachers
of English overseas, teachers
of English as a mother
tongue, computer
programmers and
consultants, bankers,
chartered accountants, O &
M analysts, air traffic
planners, managers in the
retail industry, personnel
managers, journalists, social
workers, nurses and so on. A
sizeable proportion of our
Linguistics graduates take up
employment overseas.

A degree in Human
Communication or
Linguistics does not commit
you to any one career, but
can open many doors.

EXAMPLE 4.3

is a polarization between unacceptable traditional practices and equally
distasteful, highly promotional, marketized new practices. Advertisements for academic posts are a very small but interesting case in point:
they do appear to be rather starkly polarized, as I showed earlier, with
no real alternative to the two main types. The situation can be
conceived of in terms of an *absence* within the order of discourse: the
absence of a language – of discursive practices – through which

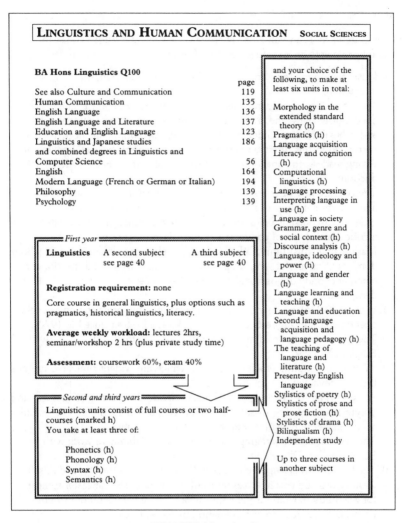

EXAMPLE 4.3 continued

authority relations and institutional and professional identities different from either traditional or marketized forms can be constituted. Critical discourse analysis cannot solve this problem, but it can perhaps point to the need for a struggle to develop such a new 'language' as a key element in building resistance to marketization without simply falling back on tradition, and perhaps give a better understanding of what might be involved in doing so.

NOTES

I am grateful to Teun van Dijk, Theo van Leeuwen and Ruth Wodak for their helpful comments on an earlier version of this paper.

1. I use the term 'text' for both written texts and transcripts of spoken interaction.
2. The pendulum of academic fashion seems to be swinging against such an 'ideological' view and in favour of a greater stress on self-consciousness and reflexivity (see Giddens, 1991). While accepting the need for some correction in this direction (see further on reflexivity below), I believe it is wrongheaded to abandon the ideological view. See General Introduction.
3. The two are not, of course, independent. The nature of detailed production and interpretation processes in particular cases depends upon how the order of discourse is being drawn upon. See Fairclough (1992a: 18–19) for a critical discussion of conversation analysis in these terms.
4. I am using this term rather more loosely than Williams, for whom dominant, emergent and oppositional culture were tied to dominant, emergent and oppositional classes. See Wernick (1991: 183–4) for discussion.
5. Wouters (1986), however, sees informalization and formalization as cyclical phenomena, and suggests a new wave of formalization since the 1970s.
6. The discussion here draws heavily upon Wernick (1991) as well as Fairclough (1989).
7. Another question is whether practices which are widely simulated are not thereby devalued in a general way.
8. At the time of writing, the binary divide between universities and polytechnics is being dissolved. I shall refer below to the ex-polytechnics as the 'newer universities' and to the 'older universities'.
9. The account in this paragraph is drawn from collaborative work with Susan Condor, Oliver Fulton and Celia Lury.
10. The threefold focus upon changes in the market, in authority, and in self-identity broadly characterizes much of the work of the Lancaster Centre for the Study of Cultural Values, of which I am a member. I draw here particularly upon a recent formulation by Russell Keat.
11. Conference on 'The Risk Society: Modernity and the Environment', 29 May 1992, Lancaster University.

SEVEN

Ideology and identity change in political television[1]

This paper is an analysis of part of a late-night political television programme entitled *Midnight Special* which was broadcast during the April 1992 British General Election campaign on Channel 4. The reporter is a well-known TV presenter and 'personality' Vincent Hanna, and this part of the programme features a panel of MPs, one from each of the three main parties (Conservative, Labour, Liberal-Democrat). I shall be using the framework for CDA described in paper 7. Let me summarize the argument of the paper. I want to suggest that the *Midnight Special* programme is complex, creative and productive inter-discursively, that is, in its discourse practice. This is manifested through a mixing of genres and discourses, including the mixing of elements of (i) conventional political interview, (ii) simulated conversation, and (iii) entertainment – performance, 'act', even including comedy routine. Following Tolson (1991), we might group together the second and third of these as constituents of 'chat', understood by Tolson as an institutionalized version of conversation which serves as a form of entertainment (see further below). The generic and discoursal mixture of the discourse practice is realized textually in heterogeneity: the text is heterogeneous in its meanings (ideational and interpersonal, and both identity and relational aspects of the latter) and in their realizations in the forms of the text. The complexity and creativity of the discourse practice accords with the complex, unstable and innovative sociocultural practice it is a part of. Putting the same points in different terms, the contradictions of the sociocultural and discourse practice are manifest in the heterogeneities of the text. The discourse practice here is representative of a more general tendency for the order of discourse of political broadcasting to be restructured, specifically through a redrawing of boundaries between the discursive practices (and orders of discourse) of the traditional political public sphere, the private sphere of the 'lifeworld', and the media as institution of entertainment. This restructuring of orders of discourse is one facet of a more general restructuring of relationships between these domains of life. One might see this in terms of the possible emergence of a new hegemonic structure in the domain of politics and political broadcasting, and associated ideological changes affecting social identities, social relations, and knowledges (see further below).

My analysis will focus upon a point in the programme immediately following a report on a Conservative Party Election Broadcast which was centred upon the origins and personality of the Prime Minister, John Major. The extract is a discussion of the report between Vincent Hanna, the presenter, and MPs Jonathan Aitken (Conservative), Robin Corbett (Labour) and Simon Hughes (Liberal Democrat).[2] I shall supplement this extract with others later. My main aims in the analysis of the first extract are to illustrate the genre mixing referred to above; show how it is realized in heterogeneous textual meanings and forms, which constitute identities, social relations, and knowledges in complex and contradictory ways; and suggest that ambivalence and disfluency are two notable and significant features of this mixed-genre discourse.

(talk and laughter)

    VH: /splendid piece there by Fiona Murch# the arts corre-   /smiling#
         spondent . of Channel 4 news. now ... you struck me
         during that as if you weren't sure whether to laugh or
         throw up
  5 JA: /well I'll give him an Oscar *(laughter)* . in a loyal way.   /smiling#
         (laughs) it looked to me rather attractive I mean it is a
         good story you have to admit that
    VH: ⌈yeah
    JA: ⌊the boy from Brixton who's made it to Number 10 e:
 10.   left school at 16 it's a ⌈good yarn a good script. um
    VH: ⌊(unclear)
    JA: I⌈should think John Schlessinger's probably (voiced
    VH: ⌊(but unclear)
    JA: hesitation) e:m done a first class job I I'm looking for-
 15.   ward to it. looking forward to seeing the real thing# =
    VH: = backing   nervously   away   from   this   question
         Jonathan
         ⌈(unclear)
    JA: ⌊what is the question sorry *(laughter)*.

20.   ⌈ I said I'd give him an Oscar (*laughter*)
   VH: ⌊ do you find it (*laughs*)
               /do you# find it embarrassing that the . party   /laughing#
               leaders descend to this kind of .
   JA: /no   I   think   it's ⌈ showbusiness   it's   poli   /smiling#
                                        ⌊ thing
25. VH:
   JA   ⌈   modern politics#
   VH   ⌊ right   fine OK
   JA: um . and (voiced pause) I mean I I wonder how many
               votes are in it I mean . I think in the last election we
30.   just saw a s-soupcon of it there . Neil Kinnock's
               broadcast with the Beethoven's 9th. it was an
   VH: ⌈ right
   JA: ⌊ outstanding ⌈ piece of
   VH: ⌊ Brahms Brahms 1st
35. JA: /no it was Beethoven's 9th   /smiling#
   VH: no
   JA: anyway . let's not argue about the music# but it was
               the um the rather stunning um presentation of Kinnock
               /in a much better light than certainly I'd ever seen him   /smiling#
40.   before# and . it didn't make a tupenny ha'penny worth
               of votes in the end . I mean the so I think it's part of
               the razzamatazz of electioneering but . /the British   /sober#
               people are not fooled by . any . director's presentation
               I think in the end . uh it is the issues an and the
45.   substantive things that count   #
   VH: well from one practising journalist to another . /Ro#   /laughing#
               Robin Corbett

I want to begin with the discourse practice and the mixing of genres.
A preliminary point is that genres drawn upon within a text may be
related to each other in various ways. In this extract, we have both
'sequential' and 'mixed interdiscursivity' (Fairclough 1992a: 118): to
some extent there is a sequential alternation between parts of the text
which seem to be primarily political interview or primarily 'chat', but
many particular parts of the text (even down to individual clauses) are
also interdiscursively mixed.

The most obvious presence of conventional political interview genre
in the section of the programme from which the extract is taken is the
control exercised by VH over turn-taking and topic. In this part of the
programme, which is located between two reports, VH interacts with

each of the politicians in turn. Although VH does not always ask *questions*, his talk does count as elicitations which require (and receive) an on-topic response; so while there is a direct question in lines 22–25 (*do you find it embarrassing that party leaders descend to this kind of thing*), VH's contributions in lines 2–4 (*you struck me as if you weren't sure whether to laugh or throw up*) and lines 16-17 (*backing nervously away from this question Jonathan*) are not questions, but are still elicitations requiring responses. The elicitation in lines 16-17 might also be taken as fulfilling the conventional interviewer's responsibility to sanction an interviewee who fails to answer 'the question'. But if it is a sanction it is heavily mitigated, by humour and by first-name address: the difficulty for the interpreter is to know whether the interpretative procedures associated with conventional political interview apply in this case, given a general ambivalence of genre (see further below on ambivalence).

There are also elements of political *discourse* (on the distinction between genre and discourse, see paper 7), notably in lines 42–45, which consist of two hackneyed formulae of political speech-making ('the British people are not fooled by . . .'; 'in the end it is the issues . . . that count'). The shift into political discourse is marked by *but* in line 42, and is accompanied by a shift to a more measured delivery, and a sober facial expression which JA sustains while the camera is on him even after he has finished speaking. Although I do not have the space to pursue this dimension of the analysis here, different discourses and genres imply *bodily* as well as linguistic differences, and a text which mixes genres and discourses may entail complex and hybrid corporealities (Threadgold 1989).

Turning to conversational elements in the generic mix, before VH speaks there is a snatch of talk and laughter (from RC, I think) presumably directed at the report, and VH's first word (*splendid*) is audibly said 'smilingly', and in fact he is smirking through the first part of this contribution. Such features would be unproblematic in conversation but would not be expected in conventional political interview, and the same is true of the elicitation directed by VH at JA (*you struck me during that as if you weren't sure whether to laugh or throw up*), in terms of its force (it is a comment on JA's apparent response to the report), its use of a conversational formula for reporting someone taken aback by events ('x looked as if s/he didn't know whether to y or z'), and style (note the lexical selection of *throw up*), as well as perhaps the absence of an explicit nomination of JA to respond. It is also conversational in the sense that it elicits a personal response from JA 'as an individual' rather than as occupier of an official political role (representative of the Conservative Party): a politician would not standardly feel a need to answer such a comment in a personal way even if it was made. Both VH in making the comment and JA in answering it in a personal way show an orientation to their co-involvement, conversationally, as individuals here rather than role-holders. A noteworthy feature of this exchange and the extract generally, which is indicative of this conversational orientation to person rather than position, is the density of 'mental process' clauses (Halliday 1985). Some of the mental process verbal groups are: *struck* (2), *weren't sure* (3), *looked* (6), *I should think* (12), *I'm looking forward* (14), *do (you) find* (22), *; (I) think* (24), *(I) wonder* (27). A number of these operate modally as what Halliday calls 'subjective' modality markers, highlighting the subjective basis of commitment to propositions (there is an example even of the political discourse of lines 42–45 – recall my earlier suggestion that there is extensive mixed interdiscursivity). A further conversational feature of VH's talk are the responses he makes during JA's contributions, in lines 8 (*yeah*), 27 (*right, fine OK*), and 32 (*right*). Notice also how VH's elicitation in lines 16-17 'latches' onto the end of JA's contribution, giving it the force of a rejoinder. In the disagreement about the music (lines 34–37), both VH's interruption of JA to correct him and JA's assertive and mock-outraged response are again more typical of conversation than of conventional political interview.

VH's opening elicitation/comment (*you struck me as if you weren't sure whether to laugh or throw up*) is also a humorous one, delivered in a deadpan, ironic way which is part of VH's style (and 'personality'), and perhaps part of the communicative ethos of the programme. (This is perhaps an example of how 'personality' can be transformed into 'product image' in the leisure market, indicating that the preoccupation with personality in the contemporary media may not be the substantive concern for individuals that it is often represented as being). Humour is a major element of this section of the programme, and it is systematically registered by the participants through their smiles and laughter. Although there is of course humour in conventional political programmes such as *Question Time*, it is incidental, whereas here it is a basic and sustained feature of the talk. There is an element of 'chat' in the programme, a form of witty conversation which is at the same time entertainment, performance. In line 19, JA's humorous response to VH's (humorous) elicitation (*what is the question*) has the split-second timing of a line in a comedy double-act. Even some of the apparently serious parts of the programme have an undercurrent of humour. For instance, in JA's serious answer to VH's (serious) question in lines 24–45, there are elements of ironic humour (e.g., *we saw just a soupcon of it*, lines 29-30). The groundrules of the programme seem to require serious political talk not to be sustained for more than a few seconds without being 'lightened' by humour (see further below). There is a general correspondence in 'key' between VH's elicitations and the responses they elicit. In this case, for example, a humorous elicitation elicits a humorous response, and its humour is also marked by JA's smiling delivery. I shall have more to say about the humour of the programme shortly in discussing its high level of ambivalence.

Another aspect of the presence of elements of conversation and entertainment/performance in the generic mix is the way in which viewers are addressed and constructed in the programme. VH begins with direct address on camera to the audience, before (*now . . . you struck me*) swivelling his chair sideways to face and address JA. It is a general feature of this part of the programme that, except for VH at points of transition between report and studio discussion, the audience is not addressed, and indeed there is little surface evidence at all of orientation to audience or of contributions being designed for viewers rather than co-participants. The talk is designed ostensibly as if the studio were a private place and as if this were a private conversation. This is, of course, just an intricate pretence: like all broadcast talk, the programme is in reality carefully designed for its audience. Interestingly, the pretence is at one point explicitly alluded to by Robin Corbett when he jokingly reveals a professional secret, 'just . . . inside this studio because I know it won't go anywhere else'. Vincent Hanna joins in the joke by agreeing with him ('no'). The programme is constructed as a spectacle for, rather than interaction with, the viewer, and viewers are positioned as voyeurs surreptitiously observing the 'conversation' (including a substantial amount of close observation of participants through camera close-ups). Yet at the same time viewers are constructed in the Corbett–Hanna joke as 'knowing' with respect to the pretence and the act.

The generic mix I have sketched out above leads to a text with complex and contradictory meanings, in terms of the identities set up by/for participants and audience, the relationships between participants, and between participants and audience, and the 'knowledges' which are constituted in the text. Let me summarize some aspects of this as they show up in the extract. VH has a composite identity as part political interviewer, part entertainer, and part conversationalist, and JA's identity includes the two latter elements plus of course that of politician, and the relationship between them is correspondingly complex (interviewer–politician, double act, co-conversationalists). These complex identities and relations articulate together the three domains of public (political) life, the media as a domain of leisure and entertainment, and private life. And that articulation is anchored in, and condensed into, specific personalities. These complex identities and relations are realized in the language used, in the co-occurrence of heterogeneous meanings and styles, some details of which I have referred to above. Although I am stressing contradictoriness and heterogeneity, such language, identities and relations can come in time to be naturalized (and indeed to an extent probably is now). Audience members are as I have suggested positioned as voyeurs watching the conversation as an entertaining spectacle, but also through the elements of more conventional political discourse in the programme as political subjects, as citizens.

AMBIVALENCE

One consequence of genre mixing which I have already referred to is that it produces a great deal of ambivalence. Genres are associated with particular principles of interpretation, so that the interpretation of any given linguistic text will depend upon how it is contextualized generically. Where two or more genres are operative, the question arises as to how they are hierarchized. For example, interpreters might ask whether the extract above or a part of it is still 'at bottom' political interview so that interpretative principles associated with interview should apply.

JA's response to VH's first elicitation (lines 5–15) will serve as an illustration. I am not sure whether to take it 'at bottom' as a conventional political response, a defence of his leader, mitigated in a way which accommodates it to the groundrules of this programme, or as a performance, an entertainment, where the audience is invited to share the joke of JA dutifully going through the motions of defending Major. Let me pursue first a reading according to the interpretative principles of conventional political interview. As a politician in an election campaign JA is bound to defend his leader against attack, yet in the cultivated intimacy of studio conversation he cannot solemnly defend what is commonsensically agreed to be indefensible – electoral 'razzamatazz'. Being positive about Major's performance in the indirect, metaphorical and humorous way of *well I'll give him an Oscar . . . in a loyal way* allows him to reconcile these conflicting demands. The rest of JA's contribution (from *it looked to me* to *looking forward to seeing the real thing*) seems on the face of it a more serious defence of Major. It is very defensive (notice the 'low affinity' modalities *it looked to me, I should think, probably,* the 'hedges'[3] *rather, I mean,* and *you have to admit*). There is also as VH points out a nervous quality to it, in the repetitiveness and in its rhythm of delivery. But the apparent shift to a more serious key is offset by the fact that JA continues to smile throughout, and by lexical markers of continuing humorousness (*the boys from Brixton, yarn*). The nervousness upon this reading might indicate the balancing act JA is trying to bring off, aggravated perhaps by the potentially derailing interruptions which VH seems to embark upon at two points (line 10) and the disaffiliation which VH expresses in the way he says *yeah* in line 7. Alternatively, however, one could read JA's answer according to the interpretative principles of entertainment: as a joke which depends upon our recognition of JA going through the political motions of defending his leader, where the conspicuous defensiveness and nervousness (as well as *in a loyal way*) are so many cues to help us 'see' the joke.

There is a similar ambivalence about VH's second elicitation (*backing nervously away from this question Jonathan,* lines 16-17). Like the first, it is not a question but a comment on JA's answer. On one reading, VH is 'at bottom' operating in his role as interviewer and sanctioning JA's failure to answer the 'question', but mitigating the sanction with humour, with an indirect formulation of it, and with first-name address, in accordance with the ethos of the programme. On another reading, there is no real sanctioning going on, it is just a joking way of giving the floor back to JA.

DISFLUENCY

The programme is characterized by a rather high incidence of disfluency. Disfluencies seem to register the difficulties which participants are faced with in trying to negotiate the mixed genres of the programme. The following contribution by RC follows an interaction between VH and SH about a sharp rebuke administered by Paddy Ashdown to a journalist, which ends in a long and seemingly uncomfortable pause. It is not clear whether RC takes it upon himself to come to the rescue or whether VH nominates him non-verbally to do so – VH does appear to turn towards RC during the pause.

RC: well prickly Paddy Ashdown there eh . uh I mean I have uh
some sneaking sympathy for him except of course that . um .
we: . need to feed this monster . . television . in order to try
and . grub around for the extra handful of votes and you're
5. you're quite right . uh most of us will do : m— most things .
the most improbable things outside of an election period .
to: snatch a headline or better still get ten seconds . on film .
but . um . . I I agree to this extent I think that . um . . I don't
think uh . Paddy should have put in exactly those words but
10. I think there is a line to be drawn somewhere a judgement
to be made it is . . is this wrong when I say this is our
election and not yours . ours and the electors' rather than
television's.
VH: well I— I mean you're not wrong to say anything on this
15. programme (*laughter*) you can say what you want I mean I
would I hope it's the voters' election

The transcription only captures a part of what is going on, but
nevertheless RC's disfluency is evident in the number and positioning
of voiced (*uh, um*) and unvoiced pauses, the false starts, and the
anacolutha (constructions which are started then abandoned, e.g., *it is*
in line 11). RC's opening (*well prickly Paddy Ashdown there eh* seems to
be a joke which does not come off, and thereafter he is manifestly
struggling to put together a coherent contribution, his discomfort even
being registered at one point by a flustered and anxious look from VH.
It is an indication of RC's lack of control that he effectively asks for
VH's judgement on whether what appears to be his main point is
legitimate (*is this wrong when I say this is our election and not yours*). This
is perhaps an appeal for help, asking VH to rescue him from his
discursive discomfort (which he does not do).

Apart from instances of disfluency, there are points in the programme
where participants apparently fail to conform with its groundrules and
ethos. I include these with disfluencies because they also are indicative
of difficulties that participants have in negotiating the complex expectations of the programme. On such occasions there is sometimes evidence
of sanctioning devices for keeping participants in order. The following
extract includes RC's reaction to Major's 'performance' in the Conservative election broadcast:

RC: I don't th— I shall be very surprised if that movie on the
basis of the snatch I've seen gets a any Oscar nominations .

the thing is a joke .. it's an absolute joke .. a bloke in the
back of a chauffeur-driven car .. uh . trying to send out the
5. message you too can do this sweetheart if you vote Tory . I
don't believe it .
VH: Simon Hughes
SH: that . particular . clip of film looked pretty dire . I have to / /laughing#
say#

RC makes a rather sharp attack on the election broadcast which seems
to be treated as 'over the top' in terms of the programme's groundrules
and ethos. Perhaps the camped-up 'message' *you too can do this
sweetheart if you vote Tory* is an attempt to mitigate the attack with
humour, but it doesn't appear to come off, there is no audible or visible
recognition of this as a joke. There is no response to RC's attack from
VH — perhaps an indication that it is embarrassing or reprehensible in
the context of the programme — and VH, after a pause which is
perhaps just long enough to be uncomfortable, shifts squarely into the
conventions of political panel interview in simply nominating SH as
next speaker. SH's contribution begins with a strikingly measured (in
terms of rhythm of delivery) and mitigated (through hedging — *pretty
dire*, modalization — *I have to say*, and his laughing delivery of *say*)
critique of the broadcast which ostensibly does adhere to what I think
are the groundrules of the programme — that political point-scoring
should be mitigated. This seems to be a way for SH to dissociate
himself from RC's immoderate attack and get the programme back on
track. The example illustrates how participants can come unstuck in
trying to negotiate the complex demands of this mixed-genre format,
and also the availability of sanctioning devices for keeping participants
in line with the groundrules and ethos of the programme.

A further illustration of sanctioning devices but also of ways in
which a participant can try to pre-empt sanctioning is the following:

SH: but the- there's an interesting thing I mean I think that
. certainly the Labour Party last time and I understand
this time . and it looks like the Tory Party last time
and this time . are staging most of their leaders' .
5.   appearances
VH: (unclear) what do you mean staging
JA: don't pretend Paddy Ashdown isn't
⌈ staging things (unclear)
SH: ⌊ well well no it in a slightly different way what I

```
10.         mean is the Labour Party had . ticket only rallies
            ⌈membership only⌈ra⌉llies . and and Neil Kinnock was
      JA:   ⌊hm              ⌊  ⌊hm
      VH:                       ⌊yes
      SH:   only seen in front of his ⌈own people . and it gave the
15.   RC:                             ⌊yes yes
      SH:   impression of solidarity and support . and Mrs
            Thatcher again generally had a prearranged careful
            oppor⌈tunity
      VH:        ⌊that's (indeed) for security ⌈reasons
20.   JA:                                      ⌊hm
      SH:   in in her case . much more than the leader of the
            opposition . fair to say . it looks as if John Major in
            the round . members again supporters . people who
            are not going to be hostile throw wobbly questions . I
25.         I have to say I think Paddy doesn't put himself in that
            position . the meetings certainly the venues that I'm
            aware of . anybody could turn up
            ⌈I mean it's a risky it's risky
      VH:   ⌊well it's possible but then he is the only one of the
30.         three party leaders who's trained to kill
      SH:   ✓well yes ⌈and maybe that#                    /smiling#
      JA:             ⌊he's the only one who has trouble getting
            a crowd
```

SH seems to take a great deal of trouble preparing the ground for what can be construed as the political point-scoring which occurs towards the end of this contribution. Firstly in claiming the floor for the point he wants to make he types it as 'an interesting thing', which implies he is about to make an analytical rather than a point-scoring contribution. Secondly, SH's claims are carefully and cautiously modalized: *I understand* in line 2, *it looks like* in line 3 with the meaning of appearance foregrounded through *look* being heavily stressed and carrying a falling intonation contour, *it looks as if* in line 22, and *I have to say* and *I think* (a sort of double modalization) in line 25. Thirdly, SH downtones his claims with hedges: *slightly* in line 9, *generally* in line 17. Nevertheless, his claim about 'staging' is sharply challenged in lines 6–8 by VH and JA. Thereafter, all the participants seem to be working at re-establishing a tone of reasonable discussion: the other participants' audible responses (lines 12, 13, 15) to SH's conciliatory explanation in lines 9–18 signal agreement and acceptance; VH's intervention in 18–19 is a supportive clarification rather than a challenge, and again SH is conciliatory in his response and accepts VH's point ('fair to say'). There are no audible responses from the other participants for the rest of SH's contribution until VH interrupts SH with a joke, followed by another from JA which also interrupts SH, which deflate SH's political point-scoring. All of the participants – SH in his cautious design of his contribution, the others in their response – in this exchange are demonstrating an orientation to the programme's groundrules and to the delicate balance which they require between serious (and especially partisan) politics and chat: the former is tolerated if at all only in short bursts, and preferably mitigated by humour. The implicit message is that reasonable, fair-minded non-partisan discussion is acceptable (in moderation), but partisan point-scoring is not, especially when it is not mitigated, and is a fair target for humorous attack.

MEDIATIZED POLITICAL DISCOURSE: A NEW HEGEMONY?

Let me summarize the analysis so far in the terms of the CDA framework introduced in paper 7. I have suggested that the *Midnight Special* programme is characterized by a complex discourse practice involving the mixing of genres and discourses of politics, conversation and entertainment; that this complexity is realized in heterogeneous and contradictory textual meanings (identities, relations, and knowledges) and forms; and that it leads, on the text production side of the discourse practice, to disfluences and other difficulties in managing the complex demands of this hybrid format, and, on the text reception side, to considerable ambivalence.

I now want to comment upon how these properties relate to the sociocultural practice which the discourse practice and the text are embedded within. There are some difficulties in doing so, especially within the confines of a short article. Firstly, an account of aspects of the social context at various levels of generality which may be relevant to reaching an understanding of the discursive and textual features of the programme risks being a many-sided and highly complex account in its own right. I can do no more than identify broad themes here. Secondly, a full analysis would need to generalize over contemporary political discourse as an order of discourse and political broadcasting within that, whereas all this paper does is refer to one programme which is illustrative of one trend within that order of discourse. I think it is a particularly significant trend in the emergence of a new hegemony in political discourse, but that can obviously be no more than a hypothesis.

I want to suggest that the discourse practice illustrated in this programme is a significant part in a shift in social practice which involves, in the terms of Habermas (1989), a 'structural transformation of the public sphere' of politics. One aspect of this transformation is a restructuring of the relationship between the traditional sphere of politics, the media as a domain of entertainment, and private life. Public life, including important elements in the political process such as conferences, elections and proceedings of Parliament, has become increasingly open to media coverage. However, there is a contradiction and a gap between the public nature of media production and media sources, and the private nature of media reception, which is embedded within a home and family life. The gap has been bridged, as work by Cardiff and Scannell has recently shown (Cardiff 1980, Scannell 1992) by a progressive (if not always even) accommodation of public practices and discourses towards the private conditions of reception. One aspect of this movement has been a 'domestication' (Cardiff) or 'conversationali-sation' (Fairclough 1994) of mediated public discourse – though as I suggested earlier there are also more general cultural conditions favour-ing conversationalization, which is by no means confined to media (Fairclough 1994). At the same time, media consumption has evolved as an important element of leisure activity, in which audiences expect relaxation and entertainment, and in which audiences are increasingly constructed as consumers rather than citizens. 'Chat' has emerged as a genre in which an institutionalized version of private discursive practice, conversation, becomes a form of entertainment.

The mediatization of politics has entailed a shift from the media merely transmitting political events happening elsewhere whose nature was determined autonomously, to the media generating its own politi-cal events (interviews, debates, programmes such as *Midnight Special*) and political events which happen elsewhere being reshaped to enhance their media worthiness. The revaluing of ordinary life and its practices in the media goes along with a devaluing of public, formal, impersonal, demagogic and so forth practices. Correspondingly, we can perhaps see a restructuring of hegemony in the sphere of political practice and political discourse which is placing the chatty, conversational, entertain-ing political discourse illustrated by *Midnight Special* in an increasingly dominant position in the order of broadcast political discourse, and the order of political discourse more generally. There is in this connection a paradoxical quality to the programme: one of its main themes is dismissing the 'razzamatazz' of electioneering and party political broad-casts, what JA in the extract calls 'showbusiness'; one thing that the participants share is a cynical view of politics in that form. And yet the programme itself is manifestly a form of 'showbusiness', an act, a performance. It is I think highly significant of the shift in dominance within the political order of discourse that more traditionsl forms of political performance attract general derision, whereas other emergent forms are apparently acceptable.

What is at issue in the restructuring of the order of political discourse is the nature of politics in a fundamental sense, including: political beliefs, knowledges, practices and representations; political identities; and political relations. In terms of the beliefs and knowledges, there is little space for serious debate of political issues, which is present only in a fleeting and ambivalent form; in terms of identities, politicians are reconstituted as 'real' individuals and personalities (a concept which, like 'chat', bridges the public realm of entertainment and the private realm) and the political public is reconstituted as voyeurs and consumers of spectacle, yet at the same time 'knowing' about the conventions and illusions of the new political game; in terms of political relations, politicians and public are constructed as co-mem-bers of a private domain culture whose dominant values are ordinari-ness, informality, authenticity and sincerity. Issues of truthfulness and authenticity have perhaps become more salient here than issues of truth.[4]

The features of the programme I noted above in the discussion of disfluencies are of interest in the latter connection: on the one hand they indicate perhaps the tolerability of disfluences and misjudgements in the new sphere of political discourse, but on the other hand they perhaps suggest the risks for politicians which go hand-in-hand with the opportunities offered by their new accessibility and visibility (Thompson 1990: 247). Politicians are certainly losing their traditional mystique and authority, though this is not perhaps a development which is explained only by the evolution of broadcast politics: there has been a more general shift, or apparent shift, of authority away from professional groups such as teachers, doctors and lawyers as well as politicians, which some have taken to be entailed by a shift of authority *towards* consumers in 'consumer society' (Keat, Whiteley and Abercrombie 1994).

The changes I am pointing to, and which are illustrated in *Midnight Special*, have I believe an ideological nature. Much ideological analysis of media has focused upon stability and reproduction, but analysis of change in media output and of relatively innovative types of programme such as this one provides an opportunity for investigating the emergence of ideologies. In suggesting that, for instance, the representations of traditional politics and the identities and relations set up for politicians and for the political public in this programme are ideological, I am assuming that (a) there is a difference between the actuality of political practice and its representations in the media, and (b) its representations in the media are enabling for real political practice, specifically in (c) helping to sustain relations of domination which structure real practice. I have some sympathy with the account in Pilger (1992) of apparently ever-increasing openness and visibility of the political process being underlaid by an increasingly secretive state engaged in more and more covert operations, and an increasingly disciplinary society. In this light, the restructured order of political discourse has more of a legitimizing function than a democratizing function, though the ambivalence of conversationalization which I referred to earlier precludes simple black-and-white interpretations.

NOTES

1. This paper is based upon a presentation at a conference on media discourse at Strathclyde University in September 1992. I am grateful for comments of other participants on the presentation.
2. Pauses are indicated as dots, one for a short pause and two for a longer pause. Overlaps are shown by square brackets. Talk which is unclear is indicated in round brackets, as are vocalizations such as laughter. Aspects of non-verbal communication simultaneous with talk (including laughter) are shown in the margin, and their onset and termination in the text are marked respectively as '/' and '#'.
3. Modalities can be differentiated in terms of the degree of speaker affinity with (commitment to) a proposition (or a person) that they express – see Hodge and Kress (1988). A hedge is a device for qualifying, toning down or mitigating an utterance– see Brown and Levinson 1978.
4. In the terms of Habermas 1984, some parts of the media are perhaps manifesting a shift in the relative salience of implicit validity claims, in favour of truthfulness and sincerity, and at the expense of truth. I am grateful for this point to Martin Montgomery and Sandra Harris, in their contributions to the conference mentioned in note 1.

TEXTUAL ANALYSIS IN SOCIAL RESEARCH

Introduction

'Discourse and text: linguistic and intertextual analysis within discourse analysis' is a methodological paper targeted especially at discourse analysts whose disciplinary base is outside language studies. It argues that substantive forms of textual analysis – analysis of what I refer to as the 'texture' of the text as opposed to commentary upon its 'content' – can increase the value of discourse analysis as a method for researching a range of social science and cultural studies questions. Textual analysis is seen as comprising two different, and complementary, forms of analysis: linguistic analysis and intertextual analysis. My strategy in this paper is to show how close attention to text can enhance the analysis and results achieved in papers published in the first four issues of the journal *Discourse and Society*. In some cases, this is a matter of closer linguistic analysis, in others it is a matter of adding intertextual analysis to the linguistic analysis that the papers offer. The paper concludes with arguments for textual analysis being more widely accepted, within discourse analysis, as part of the array of methods available for social and cultural analysis.

The case for the analysis of text and texture is not just a technical argument within discourse analysis. Critical discourse analysis claims that close analysis of texts should be a significant part of social scientific analysis of a whole range of social and cultural practices and processes. Many social scientists are ready to accept in principle that social life is built in and around language, but it is often more difficult to persuade them on a more practical level that text analysis needs to be one of their methods. One problem here is that frameworks for text analysis have been forbiddingly technical and formalistic. Another is that some discourse analysts (especially those working outside language studies) try to reduce all of social life to discourse, and all of social science to discourse analysis. In formulating the case reductively, they overstate and undermine it. The best way of convincing social scientists is by doing socially and culturally sensitive discourse analysis, using analytical frameworks which are accessible, clearly suited to social research, and complement other forms of (e.g. ethnographic, or organizational) analysis. What will clinch the argument is showing that textual analysis is better able than other methods to capture sociocultural processes in the course of their occurrence, in all their complex, contradictory, incomplete and often messy materiality.

But CDA is not just another form of academic analysis. It also has aspirations to take the part of those who suffer from linguistic–discursive forms of domination and exploitation. Part of the task is to contribute to the development and spread of a critical awareness of language as a factor in domination (see paper 9). This requires the case for text and texture to be made among the general population in educational institutions, especially schools and other types of social institutions (e.g. medical and legal). In that sense, the arguments of this paper have a much broader relevance.

EIGHT

Discourse and text: linguistic and intertextual analysis within discourse analysis

In his editorial statement for the first issue of *Discourse & Society*, Teun van Dijk declares that the journal aims to 'bridge the well-known gap between micro- and macroanalyses of social phenomena', that 'research published in *D&S* focuses especially on the complex relationships between structures or strategies of discourse and both the local and global, social and political context', and that 'both text and context need explicit and systematic analysis, and this analysis must be based on serious methods and theories' (1990: 8, 14). A later statement on 'preferred papers' for the journal states that 'analysis should be as detailed, explicit and systematic as possible, that is, be guided by theoretical concepts, and not be limited to mere paraphrases or quotations' (supplement to *D&S* 2(2) 1991).

This paper is about the analysis of text as a part of discourse analysis. It is broadly premised upon the sort of view of discourse analysis set out by van Dijk in his editorial statement, and particularly on the need for discourse analysis to map systematic analyses of spoken or written texts onto systematic analyses of social contexts (my version of this position is given in Fairclough (1989) and (1992a). The main objective of the paper is to try to stimulate a dialogue amongst discourse analysts about the nature and value of textual analysis in the interdisciplinary project which *D&S* is most notably associated with. I endeavour to do this by arguing that detailed textual analysis will always strengthen discourse analysis, notwithstanding the considerable range of objectives and theories and methods in the field, and the diversity of the academic disciplines which draw upon it and contribute to it.

Specifically, I show how more systematic and detailed textual analysis can add to a variety of current approaches to discourse analysis, without of course wishing to minimize what these approaches achieve without it. Closer attention to texts sometimes helps to give firmer grounding to the conclusions arrived at without it, sometimes suggests how they might be elaborated or modified, and occasionally suggests that they are misguided. I have taken as a sample of current approaches to discourse analysis the twenty papers which appeared in the first four numbers of *D&S* – 1(1), 1(2), 2(1) and 2(2), 1990–1.

Textual analysis is distinguished in this instance from other ways of treating texts, some of which are exemplified in the *D&S* papers. For example, in some papers (e.g. West, 1990) textual samples are adduced to illustrate a pre-established coding system, while in other papers (e.g. Hacker *et al.*, 1991) there is commentary on the content of textual samples but not on their form. I understand textual analysis to necessarily involve analysis of the form or organization of texts – of what one might call, after Halliday and Hasan (1976), their 'texture'. This is not simply analysis of form as opposed to analysis of content or meaning: I would argue that one cannot properly analyse content without simultaneously analysing form, because contents are always necessarily realized in forms, and different contents entail different forms and vice versa. In brief, form is a part of content. I elaborate and illustrate this claim below.

I regard textual analysis as subsuming two complementary types of analysis: linguistic analysis and intertextual analysis. And I understand linguistic analysis in an extended sense to cover not only the traditional levels of analysis within linguistics (phonology, grammar up to the level of the sentence, and vocabulary and semantics) but also analysis of textual organization above the sentence, including intersentential cohesion and various aspects of the structure of texts which have been investigated by discourse analysts and conversation analysts (including properties of dialogue such as the organization of turn-taking).

Whereas linguistic analysis shows how texts selectively draw upon linguistic systems (again, in an extended sense), intertextual analysis shows how texts selectively draw upon *orders of discourse* – the particular configurations of conventionalized practices (genres, discourses, narratives, etc.[1]) which are available to text producers and interpreters in particular social circumstances (on orders of discourse in this sense, see Fairclough, 1989, 1992a). Bakhtin's writings on text and genre (especially Bakhtin, (1986)) contain a sustained argument for intertextual analysis as a necessary complement to linguistic analysis, and that argument has recently been vigorously supported by, amongst others, social semioticians such as Kress and Threadgold (1988) and Thibault (1991). Intertextual analysis draws attention to the dependence of texts upon society and history in the form of the resources made available within the order of discourse (genres, discourses, etc.); genres according to Bakhtin are 'the drive belts from the history of society to the history of language' (1986: 65). Intertextual analysis consequently presupposes accounts of individual genres and types of discourse (e.g. the accounts of conversation which have been produced by conversation analysts, or accounts of what are sometimes called 'registers', such as scientific German or the English of advertising). But intertextual analysis as it is dynamically and dialectically conceived by Bakhtin also draws attention to how texts may transform these social and historical resources, how texts may 're-accentuate' genres, how genres (discourses, narratives, registers) may be mixed in texts. In the words of Kristeva, it is a matter of 'the insertion of history (society) into a text and of this text into history' (1986: 39). From this perspective, accounts of individual genres and discourse types appear to be largely accounts of ideal types, for actual texts are generally to a greater or lesser degree constituted through mixing these types. I also argue, in the final section of the paper, that intertextual analysis crucially mediates the connection between language and social context, and facilitates more satisfactory bridging of the gap between texts and contexts, referring to my three-dimensional framework for discourse analysis in which intertextual analysis occupies this mediating position (Fairclough, 1989, 1992a).

The intertextual properties of a text are realized in its linguistic features. Given the dynamic view of genre above, according to which a particular text may draw upon a plurality of genres, discourses or narratives, there is an expectation that texts may be linguistically heterogeneous, i.e. made up of elements which have varying and sometimes contradictory stylistic and semantic values (see Maingueneau, 1987; Kress and Threadgold, 1988; Fairclough 1992a). This contrasts with a common assumption in textual analysis that texts are (normally) linguistically homogeneous. In fact, real texts may be relatively homogeneous or relatively heterogeneous, and I would wish to historicize claims about the linguistic and intertextual heterogeneity of texts: it is a particular feature of periods and areas of intense social and cultural change, which perhaps accounts for the current popularity of theories stressing intertextuality and heterogeneity (see Fairclough, 1990).[2]

What has moved me to write this paper is the feeling that if discourse analysis is to establish itself as a method in social scientific research it must move beyond a situation of multidisciplinarity and pluralism towards interdisciplinarity, which entails a higher level of debate between proponents of different approaches, methods and theories. The aim is not of course uniformity of practice, but a roughly common agenda – the establishment of at least some consensus over what are the main theoretical and methodological issues in the field. The nature of texts and textual analysis should surely be one significant cluster of issues of common concern.

Of the 20 papers in the four issues of *D&S*, 15 include substantial textual samples and therefore fall within the scope of this paper. Of these, 7 analyse a specific discourse event or linked series of events (e.g. a political speech, two contrasting medical interviews, contributions to a public dialogue over US nuclear weapons policy), 4 analyse a corpus of collected data, and 4 analyse interviews generated in the course of the research. In 3 of the 15 papers (West, 1990; WAUDAG, 1990; Yankah, 1991), textual samples are mainly used to illustrate coding categories rather than being subjected to detailed textual analysis.

The papers can roughly be divided into five groups on the basis of what properties of discourse are the main focus of systematic analysis. Four papers focus upon linguistic features of texts (Fisher, 1991; West, 1990; WAUDAG, 1990; Yankah, 1991); 2 focus upon discourse strategies in dialogue between institutions or nations (Chilton, 1990; Mehan *et al.*, 1990); and 2 upon a version of what I call intertextual analysis (Michael, 1991; Seidel, 1990); 3 analyse narrative structures (Billig, 1990; Downing, 1990; Sorensen, 1991); and finally 4 analyse argumentation (Hacker *et al.*, 1991; Liebes and Ribak, 1991; Ullah, 1990; Wodak, 1991). Beyond these differences of emphasis, there is quite a lot of common ground. Thus most of the papers include some textual analysis, and indeed some (e.g. Chilton, 1990) include a great deal, though in most cases analysis is neither systematic nor detailed. I refer in some detail to 5 papers (in order of discussion: Fisher, 1991; Downing, 1990; Hacker *et al.*, 1991; Mehan *et al.*, 1990; Ullah, 1990), and more briefly to 4 others (Billig, 1990; Chilton, 1990; Liebes and Ribak, 1991; Wodak, 1991), using and reanalysing textual samples from them all.

One source of difficulty for textual analysis is the use of translated data (as for Chilton, 1990; Wodak, 1991; Yankah, 1991). To include textual analysis of translated data as part of the analysis of a discursive event, as these papers do, strikes me as a procedure which is open to serious objections. What light can analysis of the researcher's English translation of a Gorbachev speech cast upon the political and discursive analysis of a Soviet, and Russian-language, discursive event? In my opinion, discourse analysis papers should reproduce and analyse textual samples in the original language, despite the added difficulty for readers.

LINGUISTIC ANALYSIS IN SEARCH OF INTERTEXTUAL ANALYSIS

The first paper, Fisher (1991), contains a great deal of linguistic analysis, but no intertextual analysis. I argue that the latter would enhance Fisher's analysis of the data, and I extend that argument to Billig (1990). Carrying out intertextual analysis also entails further linguistic analysis, as I show.

Fisher's paper is a comparison between two medical interviews, one conducted by a doctor, and another by a 'nurse practitioner', a new category of health professional in the USA characterized by an emphasis on 'adding caring to curing' and on prevention and education. Fisher's analysis focuses upon the organization of interaction: differences in how the two types of medical staff control patients' contributions to the interaction. Thus, for example, the doctor asks closed questions which limit patient accounts, whereas the nurse practitioner asks open questions which encourage them; and the doctor filters patient responses to focus upon medical issues, whereas the nurse practitioner follows up clues in the patient's responses about her social circumstances and style of life. This counts as linguistic analysis in terms of the distinctions I set up above; more specifically, it is what many linguists would see as discourse analysis.

According to Fisher, one difference between the doctor and the nurse practitioner is that the latter 'supports' the patient and 'legitimizes her explanations' (p. 170). For example (p. 167), the patient in the nurse practitioner interview (Prudence) gives an account of her day from early morning to evening, concluding her description as follows:

> You know, just the normal things that I've always been doing. I don't know, I'm just tired. I don't now if I need vitamins or what?

and the nurse practitioner (Katherine) responds:

And then you fall face forward on the floor.

The response 'legitimizes the patient's experience', according to Fisher, and she describes Katherine's responses in the exchange below in the same terms (p. 169):

> *Prudence*: I've always been a mother, a wife and a housecleaner. I want to do something else (laughs). You know?
> *Katherine*: You know that's absolutely understandable. That's, that doesn't (P.: Good, laughs) make you a bad person.
> *Prudence*: Good (laughs) that's one reason I went out and got a job in September cause I couldn't handle it being home all the time, you know, I was, just no adult conversation . . .
> *Katherine*: You know that's a real growth step for you, to realize those needs and then to go take some action, to do something about them. Do you see that as a growth step?

And, again, when Prudence says (p. 167):

> He thinks his sex life is crazy. He thinks, 'what do you want to read books', when you know it . . .

Her voice trails off and Katherine 'finishes her sentence':

> When you could be having sex.

Fisher describes her analysis as a search for 'recurrent patterns in form – the discourse structure – and content' (p. 161). Whereas some of the earlier comparisons between the discourse of the doctor and that of the nurse practitioner are comparisons of form, the way Katherine 'legitimizes the patient's experience' in these extracts is dealt with as a matter of content. I want to suggest that it is also a matter of the texture of her texts, and therefore of form: in particular, Katherine's contributions repay an intertextual analysis. Her way of conducting interviews seems to be a mixture of medical interview genre and counselling interview genre. One feature of counselling interview genre is that the interviewer sometimes shows empathy with the interviewee by completing or capping her contributions (see Fairclough, 1989: 222–5, for an example). This happens where Katherine 'finishes Prudence's sentence', and is realized linguistically by Katherine's turn consisting only of a grammatically subordinate clause (a temporal adverbial clause). It also happens in the first extract above where Katherine's turn (*And then you fall face forward on the floor*) completes Prudence's story of a normal day with a sort of punch line, the completive function of the turn being linguistically marked by the cohesive element *and then*. (Notice how intertextual analysis in these cases leads into additional linguistic analysis.)

Another element of counselling interview genre is that the speech-exchange system is in part conversational rather than simply that of the canonical interview. In the four-turn interaction reproduced above, for example, Katherine and Prudence are engaged in what is recognizably a conversational exchange, responding to and building upon each other's contributions in a symmetrical way: Katherine's first turn is a comment on and evaluation of Prudence's first turn (*that* refers anaphorically to Prudence's statement that she wants to do something else), Prudence's second turn begins with an acknowledgement of Katherine's evaluation (*Good*), and then elaborates the statements of her first turn with a brief personal narrative, which Katherine then evaluates (and classifies, as 'a growth step'), again using *that* anaphorically to refer to Prudence's account. Responses are also elicited, most clearly by *you know* at the end of Prudence's first turn, presumably with question intonation, but *you know* arguably has a more covert eliciting function in all the turns. *You know* can be interpreted in these terms as a marker of conversational style, but it perhaps also points to a third feature of this genre: accommodation by the nurse practitioner to the communicative style of the patient, both of whose turns include *you know*. It would be interesting to listen to the recording for phonetic or prosodic evidence of accommodation. In addition to elements of counselling interview genre, Katherine's contributions also feature a counselling *discourse* (see note 1 on the distinction between discourse and genre), specifically the signification of individual biography in terms of personal 'growth'. The discourse is linguistically realized in a distinctive lexicalization of the self, exemplified and evoked here by the collocation *growth step*.

The focus for systematic analysis in Billig's (1991) paper, in contrast with Fisher's, is narrative structures, but the two have in common relatively close attention to linguistic features of texts which can be enhanced by intertextual analysis. Billig's paper is a study of a *Souvenir Royal Album* published by the *Sun* in 1988 to mark the birth of the daughter of the Duke and Duchess of York, compared with a similar series of 'cigarette cards' on the Kings and Queens of England published by John Player in 1935.

Billig notes that the two differ in their representations of historical time, and that in particular the *Sun's Royal Album* 'expresses an assumption about the essential role of personality in the diachronic movement of history' (p. 28). He also notes that the *Album* is in keeping with the daily style of its parent newspaper in certain respects. Taking these two observations together, an intertextual analysis of Billig's textual samples does, I think, point to a development of his analysis of them. Here is one of them:

Charles I
(1600–1649) was a sickly child who had difficulty walking. He became a
short, shy, lonely man with a stammer and high voice. He was a good
husband and father and loved beautiful things, but he had no sense of
humour and was pig-headed. He was not afraid to die, and when his head
was cut off the assembled crowd gave a groan of despair.

Much of this portrait is very similar to portraits in the John Player
series and belongs, as Billig points out, to a common historical culture
which those of my generation in the UK easily recognize. But I suspect
that one clause (*he had no sense of humour and was very pig-headed*)
contains a new element, belonging to a different culture and a different
discourse. Whereas the common historical culture Billig identifies is a
culture of the public sphere associated with the written language,
lacking a sense of humour and being pig-headed are standard personality attributions in the private sphere, and in casual conversation. What
we have is not, I think, as Billig suggests, a text which is 'internally
consistent', 'smooth' and 'undilemmatic' (pp. 18–19), but a text which
shows the sort of intertextual and linguistic heterogeneity which is
typical of the journalism of the *Sun* and similar newspapers, being a
hybridization of public, written discourse and private, conversational
discourse (Fowler, 1991; Fairclough, 1992a). The development of Billig's
analysis which the example suggests is that the personalities which
play such an essential role in the *Sun*'s representation of history are
partly drawn from models in the (predominantly private sphere) world
of common experience, the 'lifeworld' in the sense of Habermas, the
world of 'more or less diffuse, always unproblematic, background
convictions' (1984: 70), which increase their potency. It is noteworthy
that the heterogeneity of the text is linguistically realized through a
conjunctive 'listing' structure in which the clause I have mentioned is
conjoined with a discursively contrasting clause (*He was a good husband
and father and loved beautiful things*). Notice that the clauses have
parallel internal structures involving conjunction of predicates. See
Fairclough (1989, chapter 7) for a further example of listing structures
as vehicles for creating configurations of contrasting discourses.

SCRIPTS IN SEARCH OF TEXTUAL ANALYSIS

Downing (1990) is concerned with the role of media in the constitution
of 'political memory' and their effect upon public participation in the
formation of US foreign policy on South Africa in the post-Second

World War period. The media help build up 'mnemonic frameworks of definition' in terms of which news stories are subsequently interpreted. These frameworks comprise (following van Dijk, 1988) 'frames', 'scripts' and 'situation models'. The paper traces how these frameworks are drawn upon and developed, what they exclude as well as what they include, in articles published in *Time* and *Newsweek* over the period. The paper actually includes quite a lot of textual analysis, specifically linguistic analysis. However, there is a gap between the textual analysis and the identification of constructs such as scripts. I want to suggest that the gap could be filled by more detailed textual analysis including intertextual analysis. Here is one of the textual samples from the paper (Downing, 1990: 56):

> Exactly how and why a student protest became a killer riot may not be known until the conclusion of an elaborate inquiry that will be carried out by Justice Petrus Cillie, Judge President of the Transvaal.

and Downing's analysis of it:

> The text does not pronounce on the reason for this proclaimed transition from student protest to 'killer riot', but it is implied that the most sombre aspect of the event is to be found here, not in the behaviour of the regime's police and army in rioting against unarmed schoolchildren. 'African barbarism' seems to be lurking in the wings once more. Nothing, moreover, underpinned a 'law and order' definition of the situation more strongly than the bestowal of judicial authority, supreme in its impartiality, on Mr Cillie, Judge President of the Transvaal. Somehow *Time*'s writers could not disentangle themselves from the assumption that a judge in a legal system cannot but be detached from prejudice and bias. The character of the regime's legal system and policies of most of the judges prepared to work within it posed a very serious question-mark against this glib inference.

Downing's reference to a 'proclaimed transition' from student protest to 'killer riot' hints at the ambivalence of voice[3] in this extract without actually going into that issue. Whose formulation (Heritage and Watson, 1979) of events *is* 'a student protest became a killer riot'? There is a weak implication that this is the formulation which defines the scope of the legal inquiry, but there is no clear legal authority behind the formulation. The proposition is presupposed (Levinson, 1983) rather than asserted, and therefore taken as 'given' and in principle attributable, but it is not possible to identify (at least from this short extract) other external voices to attribute it to. So is this the voice of the journal(ist) masquerading, through presupposition, as the voice of some unspecified external authority? These issues of speech reportage and multiplicity of voice in texts are a concern for intertextual analysis (see Fairclough, 1992a and paper 6; Thibault, 1991).

The key expression is, of course, *killer riot.* Since what Downing calls our 'mnemonic frameworks of definition' tell us that police and army don't riot but students do, *riot* implicitly puts the responsibility onto the students. But how is it that the script of 'African barbarism' seems to be 'lurking in the wings', as Downing puts it? If it is lurking in the wings, that is because it is evoked by some feature of the text, and textual analysis should attempt to specify what it is that evokes this script. It is, I think, the unusual collocation of *killer + riot. Riot,* as I have suggested, places the responsibility on the students, and *killer* implies not just the production of fatalities on this occasion (*fatal riot* would have done that), but the involvement in the riot (and therefore the existence among the students) of those whose nature is to kill (which is the reputation of 'killer whales', and which is implied in locutions like 'he's a killer', 'killer on the loose').[4] Linguistic analysis identifies a creative collocation, and intertextual analysis points to the provenance of its elements in different discourses of race and the social, indicating how readers might be pointed in an interpretative direction which evokes the 'African barbarism' script.

A further point to make about this example is that the 'bestowal of judicial authority' which Downing notes emerges more clearly with a little closer linguistic analysis. Passivization places *Justice Petrus Cillie, Judge President of the Transvaal* in the informationally salient final position (as 'information focus', see Halliday, 1985). This is enhanced by the weight of the identifying expression (it consists of two nominal groups), and the unusual nominal compound structure of *Judge President* which dignifies the status of the judge.

Closer linguistic analysis again supports Downing's comments on the following extract from *Newsweek's* report of the Sharpeville massacre (1990: 53), but also suggests that they could be developed:

> Frightened and perhaps in very real danger of their lives, the police simply leveled their carbines and Sten guns and fired at point-blank range. . . .

Downing notes that police fear is strongly emphasized, which 'could not but mitigate the regime's responsibility'. The emphasis on police fear is achieved textually by topicalizing *frightened,* i.e. putting it at the beginning of the sentence as one of a pair of 'minor' clauses without finite verbs. The other minor clause, *perhaps in very real danger of their lives,* is striking in its modality: there are two contradictory reporter assessments of the danger, *perhaps* constructing it as no more than a possibility, whereas *very real* in effect cancels out this nod in the direction of journalistic circumspection. (On topicalization, minor clauses and modality, see Halliday, 1985.) This indicates how, in mitigating the regime's responsibility, the report manages to nevertheless appear to be cautious and circumspect. A third linguistic feature worth noting is the word *simply*, a 'hedge' which implies absence of malicious intent or premeditation, and comprehensible human error. What, indeed, is the significance of choosing *the police simply leveled their carbines and Sten guns and fired at point-bland range* rather than the semantically adequate *the police fired at point-blank range*? It strikes me that the former, along with the initial minor clauses, embeds the shooting in a police-centred narrative, which mitigates it.

INTERACTIONAL ANALYSIS IN STUDIES OF MEDIA RECEPTION

Hacker *et al.* (1991) is an analysis of deconstruction of news (i.e. the identification and criticism of ideology in news) by television viewers in cognitive response and interview data collected by the authors. The method employed is, according to the authors, 'content analysis'. The following extract (p. 193) illustrates again my claim earlier in the paper that form is a part of content, and that textual analysis is a part of content analysis:

> *Barb*: There was one on, there was that story about the Muslims and about how they were holding neighbourhood watches or something . . . and people do that all the time and they're telling about how these people, they turn violent, but they're really stressing that these people are Muslim, and it was like because these people are Muslim they were doing this and I don't know, I didn't see the connection about, like, what liberty do they have in making the connection that these people were violent because they were Muslim? Or that these people are wrong because they are Muslim.
> *Res*: Okay, did you see the news making that connection?
> *Barb*: Yeah.
> *Res*: Okay, how were they making that connection?
> *Barb*: Well, it was like in, every time they referred to these people, and what they did it was because they were, it was just like, Muslim, and these Muslim people live in, it just seemed like they were making that connection. Like between that people group, and the, everyone that, is like that act that way.

According to Hacker *et al.*, this extract illustrates that although viewers could often identify news bias, they 'had difficulty' in explaining on what basis they arrived at a judgement of bias. But what Hacker *et al.* do not show is that the 'difficulty' Barb experiences is manifest in the text: her reply to the researcher's last question is noticeably disfluent, with a number of anacolutha (grammatical constructions abandoned before completion in favour of other grammatical constructions), in contrast to the greater fluency of her first turn in the extract. The following are some of the incomplete constructions: *it was like in, these Muslim people live in, between that people group, and the*. The 'difficulty' is part of the content *and the form* of what Barb says.

However, what I want to focus on in the case of this paper is what intertextual analysis has to contribute specifically to studies of media reception. Here is another textual sample from the paper (p. 194), which occurred in an interview just after the researcher had given the interviewee (Beth) an account of media economics:

> *Beth*: Well, they would have to, there probably'd be some relationship
> between the two because they have a responsibility to the companies
> that are backing them. And if something's going on with a company in
> another country, you know it, you can't, they wouldn't be able to show
> a bad side. I wouldn't think. Because that company'd yell, like loud. You
> know, pull away their backing.
> *Res*: So you think there could be some sort of relationship there.
> *Beth*: Mmmm hmmm.
> *Res*: Between who owns the news companies and perhaps what they do
> with the content.
> *Beth*: Yeah, it's almost like the company owns the news, so like they're the
> boss and you have to follow what the boss says. That's kind of a
> general way to put it.

Hacker *et al.* comment as follows on this sample (p. 195):

> The viewer does not elaborate on her bias statement until the researcher
> clarifies for her what she might, in effect, be stating. Beth's clarification in
> this case may or may not be a result of her own deconstruction of the
> news. It is arguable, of course, that she may be adjusting her discourse to
> the researcher. On the other hand, it may be that Beth has perceived some
> form of ideology in the news, but has never had this type of context for
> articulating these perceptions.

Intertextual analysis helps, I think, to shed light on whether Beth's deconstruction of the news is indeed her own, or an adjustment to the discourse of the researcher. Specifically, Beth draws for the deconstructive statements upon a range of lifeworld discourses, that is, discourses which circulate in the commonplace interactions of the private domain rather than in public, institutional spheres. *You can't, they wouldn't be able to show the bad side* draws upon a popular discourse of bias and equity according to which equity means 'showing all sides' (an expression used by Beth in another textual sample); the rewording of *you can't* as *they wouldn't* seems to index the process of shifting this discourse from a matrix of experiential lifeworld talk of a matrix of analytical public talk (*you* as an indefinite pronoun being predominantly a lifeworld form). *That company'd yell, like loud* assimilates inter-institutional relations to the discourse of interpersonal relations; notice, however, that Beth reformulates it in public domain discourse (*you know, pull away their backing*), as if she were providing the researcher with a translation. *So like they're the boss and you have to follow what the boss says* assimilates the position of the media organization in relation to the media corporation to the position of the worker in relation to the boss, in the discourse of work relations. Notice again the presence of the lifeworld indefinite pronoun *you*. There is no evidence that Beth is adjusting her discourse to the researcher if that means using the researcher as a model in her deconstructive statements (though there is the instance where she adjusts in the sense of offering the researcher a translation of lifeworld discourse). On the contrary, she is drawing upon her own resources, her own discursive experience.

Here is another of the textual samples discussed by Hacker *et al.* (p. 195):

> I guess my view is that the way I view is, deconstruction is to look at the issue and think about it from your own perspective. And I, that's what I like to do anyways. I like to watch a story and, and just kind of take in what's broadcast and what's told to me and then just to kind of think about it. And come up with my own viewpoints. And I think that's how I would, in general, relate to deconstruction.

Hacker *et al.* see this extract in terms of a modification by the viewer of their definition of deconstruction. The viewer does indeed give an explicit definition in the first sentence, but I think a more fruitful way of interpreting the extract is in intertextual terms. The viewer is appropriating the concept of deconstruction through a lifeworld narrative of media use and opinion formation. The viewer tells a story about his own viewing practices: he watches and assimilates a news story, then thinks about it from his own perspective, and arrives at a point of view about it. This is by no means just his own account of the viewing process; it is a widely used, and ideologically potent, social narrative.

What intertextual analysis offers media reception studies is a textual basis for answering questions about what social resources and experiences are drawn upon in the reception and interpretation of media, and what other domains of life media messages are linked or assimilated to in interpretation. Such an approach would seem to be a helpful one in the context of recent arguments that media reception studies should extend their concerns beyond the moment of reception to consider how media messages are taken up, used and transformed in various spheres of life – the family, work, political activities, leisure activities, religion, etc. According to Thompson (1990), such investigations should involve studies of the 'discursive elaboration' of media messages, of how they figure and how they are transformed in a variety of discursive practices and across a variety of orders of discourse. Intertextual analysis would clearly be an important resource for such studies.

The same case for intertextual analysis applies to the other media reception paper (Liebes and Ribak, 1991), which is a study of different decoding strategies, on the part of political 'hawks' and 'doves' within the same family, for Israeli television news reports about the Palestinian *intifada*. The authors point out, for instance, that whereas the hawkish daughter of the family draws upon 'social scientific terms' in asserting that television represents the dominant reality, the mother, a 'dove', criticizes television coverage in the light of her own experience. This indication of the establishment in reception of contrasting connections between the media message and other domains of social practice (social science on the one hand, lifeworld experience on the other) can again be strengthened through intertextual analysis. Thus a striking feature of the mother's discourse is the extent to which it draws upon oral narrative genre, constantly telling stories to support a critical reading of the news. The following sample (p. 214), for instance, is made up almost entirely of a complex tissue of stories (I have numbered the lines of the transcription for ease of reference below):

> As I was saying, no Arab ever threw a stone at me, but some Jew did. On a *Shabbat* I got hit by a stone, on my car, and they threw a garbage bin at me, and they almost jumped at us; she's [i.e. the daughter] my witness; here, just next to the house. I believe more in
> 5   the Arabs than in the religious Jews. I am more afraid of them. I don't know, this is my opinion. In the morning I sit in the kitchen and I hear under my window, 'shabbes!' [Sabbath!] and 'pritzes!' [whoring!]; here under this window is the problematic street Yam

Suf, and they want to close it [to traffic on Saturdays]. If I got into
10   my car I don't know what they would do to me. They would come
in the tens and hundreds, and would anybody pay attention? So
they arrest them, and in the evening they let them go. On *Lag
Ba'omer* [a holiday when bonfires are lit]: I was at a friend's today,
and she told me that she went to see a bonfire in the center of town,
15   not in Mea She'arim, not Mea She'arim but closer to the center of
town, and she said that the religious started a bonfire there, and
burned the Israeli flag.

The passage contains different types of narrative which are closely
integrated with the non-narrative sections of the passage, which argue
that the 'religious Jews' are more reprehensible than the Arabs. Line 1
sets up the contrast between Arabs and Jews in terms of the mother's
personal experience of violence, and pre-formulates the story of lines
2–3, which is a personal experience narrative. Notice the rhetorical
structure of this story, in particular how the outrageous nature of the
incident is underscored through the double locative adverbial of *here,
just next to the house*, and the positioning of it after *she's my witness* as a
post-completion to the story. This strikes me as very much a form of
conversational narrative rhetoric. Like the other stories in the passage,
this one has the primarily indexical function (Barthes, 1977: 91–7) of
connoting the character of the 'religious Jews', which is the basis for
coherent linkage between the story and the main argumentative part of
the passage in lines 4–6: the former provides a reason for the latter,
though their logical relationship is left implicit. The same relationship
exists between the argument of lines 4–6 and the next story, in lines
5–8, which is also a narrative of personal experience but of a different
type, what one might call a narrative of ritual personal experience (the
mother's story of what she regularly hears). This is followed immediately by a thematically linked hypothetical narrative in lines 9–11,
about what would happen if she drove her car in Yam Suf street on a
Saturday. Within the same sentence, from the end of line 11, there is
an interpolated argument (to the effect that nobody controls the
violence of the 'religious Jews') which is itself implicitly grounded in
the non-personal ritual narrative of lines 11–12. Finally, in lines 12–17
there is another personal experience narrative about the mother's visit
to a friend into which is embedded the friend's personal experience
narrative about the burning of the Israeli flag (lines 14–17). The
brevity and pointedness of these narratives is striking. They are typical
of the conversational narratives which constitute an important element
of the social repertoires of the lifeworld, and the way in which they are

knitted together for purposes of argument here is typically conversational. What I think is potentially useful in this sort of analysis for studies of media reception is that it can show in some detail how conversational resources are mobilized in the reception of media, and how therefore the practices and experience of the lifeworld come to be integrated with the mass media.

DISCOURSE STRATEGIES AND INTERTEXTUAL ANALYSIS

Mehan *et al.* suggest that 'the relations between voices in public political discourse take the form of a conversation' (1990: 135), a dialogue, in which discourse strategies or moves on the part of one organization (government, churches, other governments, etc.) provoke responses from others. This perspective is applied to the evolution of the 'nuclear conversation', discourse appertaining to nuclear arms policy, in the USA in the 1980s. The authors see this conversation in terms of a loss of control by the Reagan Administration of the discourse system associated with deterrence, and the consequential opening up of a new discourse space which domestic and foreign opponents of the regime used to undermine deterrence. Discourse strategies were identified through a content analysis of texts. I want to suggest that intertextual and linguistic analysis of texts provides a solid and more tangible analytical grounding for the identification of moves and strategies.

Let me briefly review the moves and counter-moves identified by the authors within the nuclear conversation. The first move is talk on the part of the Reagan Administration about the need for a war-winning capacity, a significant departure from the discourse system of deterrence which assumed that the deployment of nuclear weapons was about avoiding rather than winning wars. This provoked many responses, including one from the National Council of Catholic Bishops, whose discourse strategy was to shift the argument from technical to moral ground. This in turn sparked off a battle for control of the moral highground involving supporters of deterrence and of the Reagan Administration, other protest groups, etc. A further move was the proposal for a nuclear freeze, which involved a 'populist appeal' (p. 148) for wider participation in the debate, provoking further counter-moves which effectively buried the freeze proposal. A dramatic new move was the Reagan Administration's proposal for the Strategic

Defense Initiative (popularly known as 'Star Wars'), which 'began as a way to silence moral voices and the nuclear forces of the peace movement' by seizing the moral ground, but 'achieved success . . . at the cost of further undermining the conventions of deterrence' (p. 152). When the Strategic Defense Initiative began to run into trouble, Gorbachev 'entered the American strategic conversation by proposing the elimination of nuclear weapons' (pp. 156–7).

Implicit in the authors' account of the nuclear conversation is a series of shifting articulations between the technical/strategic, political and moral public domains, and the private domain of the lifeworld. The authors' formulations also suggest a struggle to produce configurations of these domains capable of dominating the discursive field. What is missing, however, is detailed analysis of how the strategic moves within this struggle are textually enacted. This is where intertextual analysis can be of help. Let me illustrate this for two of the moves in the conversation.

The bishops' response to the Reagan Administration's initial move took the form of a pastoral letter addressed to the Catholic faithful. Here is an extract (pp. 139–40):

> Under no circumstances may nuclear weapons or other instruments of mass
> slaughter be used for purposes of destroying population or other
> predominantly civilian targets. We also cannot reconcile our principles
> with the use of any weapons aimed at military targets, however defined,
> where the targets lie so close to concentrations of populations that
> destruction of the targets would likely devastate those nearby populations.
> . . . No Christian can carry out orders or policies deliberately aimed at
> killing non-combatants.

What is striking about this extract from an intertextual point of view is the hybridization of military/strategic discourse and theological discourse, the latter involving both the regulative ('edict enunciating') genre of the first and last sentences (both of which are categorical prohibitions realized linguistically by the placement of negative particles not on their modal verbs but in their initial prepositional and nominal phrases) and the genre of moral debate and analysis in the second. This hybridization is most starkly illustrated in another sentence which the authors quote, by the sharp transition from the strategic discourse of the grammatical subject to the moral discourse of the predicate complement: 'the deterrence relationship between the United States, the Soviet Union and other powers is an objectively sinful situation' (p. 140). Metaphor is used here as a vehicle for achieving reclassification (deterrence is reclassified as a form of sin, with the simple present tense form of the verb (*is*) giving the new classificatory relationship the modal status of categorical fact: on the relationship between tense and modality, see Kress and Hodge, 1979; Halliday, 1985). The bishops would need to choose between alternative means of making their intervention, and the choice of a pastoral letter genre is significant: because of the ostensibly 'internal' nature of the document (i.e. internal to the Church) they can draw upon an authoritative and unmitigated moral discourse which might be difficult for them to use if they were overtly addressing themselves to the outside (including the government).

The nuclear freeze proposal was the focus for a political movement, and included a critique of institutionalized expertise and a call for wider popular participation in the nuclear conversation. This populism is manifest in textual samples in the presence of elements from the discursive repertoires of the lifeworld (e.g. p. 148):

> The real problem is that our governments have gone insane worldwide and the people are the only ones who have the sense that they're crazy. The governments don't think so. And so somehow or other we've got to find a way to get through to governments to say 'we know what's going on and what's going on is you're crazy'.

People talking to governments is represented in the direct speech at the end of the extract on the model of how you might talk to a troublesome neighbour. Moreover, not only is insanity lexicalized in a lifeworld way as *crazy*, *you're crazy* also has a meaning which belongs to lifeworld discourse: it is an accusation of departure from good sense, not a judgement about mental health. Again, the following explanation of 'mutual assured deterrence' is not just, as Mehan *et al.* say, 'a folksy metaphor' (p. 149), but a lifeworld way of making an argumentative point by telling a story:

> I see this as two old adversaries locked in a room knee-deep in gasoline. One has nine matches and the other has seven matches, and it really does not matter who strikes the first match because the consequence for both would be the same – total annihilation.

In both these cases, and more generally, the intertextual constitution of texts is connected with audience. As the authors point out, the bishops' pastoral letter 'was heard by multiple audiences simultaneously' (p. 144). We can also assume that it was designed in anticipation of multiple audiences: that, as I suggested above, a consideration in the choice of pastoral genre would be its effectiveness as a vehicle for directing moral discourse and the bishops' moral authority at the wider governmental, protest group and other audiences in the public sphere; and that in producing a hybridization of theological/moral and strategic discourses, the bishops would be sensitive to the need to come across as plausible in both, given their multiple intended audiences. The fit between intertextuality and audience is not always a matter of such conscious design as it tends to be in the hands of sophisticated politicians (in the wider sense), but the question of audience anticipation is always relevant to intertextuality.

That question is a focus in Chilton's paper (1990), which analyses the politeness strategies used in speeches by Gorbachev and Reagan in their efforts to address multiple audiences in ways which build consensus, play down 'face-threatening' acts, and so forth. Chilton's analysis of Reagan's 1986 State of the Union Address includes observations on the intertextuality of the text, specifically the mixing of religious and political discourse, as a positive politeness strategy. In this case, the strategy is designed to unify a diverse national audience around the supposed common ground of religion. I would argue, however, for systematic recourse to intertextual analysis, rather than intertextuality just being treated as one of a highly diverse set of means for being positively polite. Indeed, since genres are pragmatically variable, a pragmatic analysis would seem to presuppose an intertextual analysis.

A MULTIFUNCTIONAL VIEW OF TEXT

Ullah (1990) writes within a social psychological approach to discourse analysis about the rhetoric of self-categorization, the arguments used by children born in England of Irish parents in identifying themselves as Irish or English, and the effects of context upon these arguments. I shall suggest that the focus upon argumentation entails a monofunctional orientation to texts, while there are good reasons for adopting a multifunctional orientation to texts, especially when dealing with questions of social identity.

The following extract (pp. 179–80) is taken to illustrate how two different 'interpretative repertoires' can be applied to the political conflict in Northern Ireland by the same person on the same occasion without any sense of inconsistency:

> P.U.: You know the Wolf Tones, and bands like that who sing about the Troubles. . . .

Boy: They put their views over in their songs.

P.U.: And so, do you find you sympathize with the Irish cause?

Boy: Oh yes, you do. You're up there and you're banging the tables, you know.

P.U.: Do you believe in it generally, or is it just when you hear the songs that you feel like that?

Boy: No, not even when you hear the songs. I never believe it when I hear the songs, but . . . I don't mind singing. You've had a few pints and someone says 'Up the IRA!' and you say 'Yes, up the IRA!' You're never bothered really . . . and then like, you know, someone will say to you, like, 'Oh, isn't it great what they're doing?' and I just turn around and say 'No I think it's terrible'.

Ullah's comment that 'this boy saw no inconsistency in first claiming that the music made him feel sympathetic with the Irish cause, and then denying that it ever did so' strikes me as misleading. Firstly, it ignores the difference between *sympathize with* and *believe in* in the interviewer's (P.U.'s) questions, and the fact that the 'boy' says *I never believe in it* and not *I never sympathize with it*. This is not at all inconsistent if one assumes that the boy differentiates between sympathy and belief.

Secondly, Ullah's comment does not take account of the intertextual properties of the interaction. The two interpretative repertoires cannot, I think, be reduced, as Ullah suggests, to two 'vocabularies' (on the model of *terrorists* versus *rebels* as terms for the IRA). There is no contrast of vocabularies in this case, but rather a contrast of narratives: the 'boy's' answers include elements of a narrative about having a good time at a gig, and elements of a narrative about a political conversation. He is evoking two distinct discursive practices occurring within the one social setting, and *Up the IRA* is acceptable in one but not in the other. It's not just a matter of it having two different meanings, as Ullah suggests.

Moreover, and this is my main point, a closer textual analysis suggests that there is more than argumentation at issue in the process of self-identification in this extract. Notice that in reply to the interviewer's second turn, the boy uses not the first person pronoun but indefinite *you*: 'Oh yes, *you* do. *You*'re up there and *you*'re banging the tables . . .' (p. 180, emphasis added). *You* coincides with the first of the two types of narrative, *I* with the second (*I think it's terrible*). *You* deindividualizes the boy's answer: he answers as one of a group, not as an individual. And the form of his answer is cast in terms of the habitual practices and common experiences of a group, using preconstructed meanings and expressions (the meanings are inseparable from the expressions) associated with 'a good night out' from the first type of narrative (e.g. 'you're banging the tables', 'you're never bothered'). All this is germane to the self-identification process, for the boy is here constructing his own identity on the stereotypical model of the group. But it is nothing to do with argumentation or indeed with the 'ideational' function of language (language in the construction of knowledge and experience) which subsumes argumentation. This is the 'interpersonal' function of language, involving what I have called elsewhere the 'relational' and 'identity' subfunctions (Fairclough, 1991): language in the construction of social relationships and language in the construction of social identity. (On 'ideational' and 'interpersonal' functions, see Halliday, 1978.) A fuller analysis of these functions could be made on the basis of a more detailed account and transcription of the data: for example, the total communicative style including phonetic, prosodic and paralinguistic properties of the mode of utterance, and other semiotic modalities such as the kinesic, are relevant to the construction of social identity. The general point is that issues of social identification in texts cannot be fully addressed without a multifunctional view of language such as Halliday's.

A focus on argumentation can of course be very productive, but argumentative strategies themselves are not purely ideational in character, they necessarily go along with the interpersonal 'work' of the text and depend upon it for their effectiveness. The following is an extract from Wodak's analysis of argumentative strategies in antisemitic discourse in an Austrian news broadcast (1991: 74–5):

Kreisky: First of all, I knew nothing about any of the things being asserted about Dr Waldheim as a person. However, if I had known, I would certainly not have withheld my recommendation in this case uh uh, because it all happened a long, long time ago. And he was a young man . . . But that is not what it is all about. The point is, that certain groups, albeit very small ones, are interfering in the Austrian campaign . . . with both candidates in an improper way in my opinion. I am not prepared to tolerate this. But these groups have been fighting me for decades . . .

Interviewer: Dr Kreisky, your party argues that, it is said, that to a certain extent he admits that he was there, that he did not say that from the beginning. How do you see this?

Kreisky: Yes, well, that is none of my business. I don't want to have anything to do with it. Oh, it is all very unpleasant, and I don't want to have anything to do with it.

Commenting on the last turn of Kreisky (the former Austrian chancellor),

Wodak says that he employs a 'macro-strategy of justification ... he simply cuts off the discussion'. Applying a strategy label to the turn actually captures little of what appears to be going on. The translation gives the impression of a shift in genre and voice which carries a shift in interpersonal meanings: Kreisky shifts from political argument to what comes across in the English as a petulant emotional outburst.[5] The accomplishment of the argumentative strategy in this case is clearly dependent upon, and inseparable from, the generic and interpersonal shift.

TEXTUAL ANALYSIS IN SOCIAL SCIENTIFIC RESEARCH

There is a need for linguists and others committed to textual analysis to convince not only the diverse community of discourse analysts but also the wider communities of social scientists that textual analysis has an important role to play in social scientific research. This is not an easy thing to do, despite the widely acclaimed 'linguistic turn' in social science. Many social scientists have concerns and objectives which on the face of it lie in quite different directions, and textual analysis can easily be seen as an irrelevance or a formalist diversion. I shall suggest four reasons why textual analysis ought to be more widely recognized, within a framework for discourse analysis, as part of the methodological armoury of social science: a theoretical reason, a methodological reason, a historical reason and a political reason (see also Thibault, 1991). These arguments need to be taken in conjunction with my contention in the main part of the paper that, if one is dealing with texts, it is always worth analysing them in a serious way.

The theoretical reason is that the social structures which are the focus of attention for many social scientists with 'macro' social interests are in a dialectical relationship with social action (the concern of 'micro' social analysis), such that the former are both conditions and resources for the latter, and constituted by the latter (Giddens, 1984; Callinicos, 1987). Texts constitute one important form of social action. As a consequence, even social scientists who have such apparently macro interests as class relations or gender relations cannot justify entirely ignoring texts. In practice, they necessarily base their analyses upon texts, but often do not acknowledge doing so.

A further important point is that language is widely misperceived as transparent, so that the social and ideological 'work' that language does in producing, reproducing or transforming social structures, relations and identities is routinely 'overlooked'. Social analysts not uncommonly share the misperception of language as transparent, not recognizing that social analysis of discourse entails going beyond this natural attitude towards language in order to reveal the precise mechanisms and modalities of the social and ideological work of language.

The methodological reason is that texts constitute a major source of evidence for grounding claims about social structures, relations and processes. The evidence we have for these constructs comes from the various material forms of social action, including texts. There is, for example, a growing recognition that analysis of ideology must be answerable to the detailed properties of texts (Thompson, 1984, 1990).

The historical reason is that texts are sensitive barometers of social processes, movement and diversity, and textual analysis can provide particularly good indicators of social change. This relates to my comments at the beginning of the paper about how a Bakhtinian form of generic analysis (intertextual analysis in my sense) highlights the role of texts in making history, and moreover links this to generic and linguistic heterogeneity. Texts provide evidence of ongoing processes such as the redefinition of social relationships between professionals and publics, the reconstitution of social identities and forms of self, or the reconstitution of knowledge and ideology (see papers 5 and 6; Selden, 1991; for examples). Textual analysis can therefore act as a counter-balance to overly rigid and schematizing social analyses, and is a valuable method in studies of social and cultural change. For example, there is an absence of textual analysis in Foucault's influential historical studies of discourse which I would link to some of the criticisms which have been made of the schematism of his work and its failure to specify detailed mechanisms of change (see Taylor, 1986; Fairclough, 1992a, ch. 2).

The political reason relates specifically to social science with critical objectives. It is increasingly through texts (notably but by no means only those of the media) that social control and social domination are exercised (and indeed negotiated and resisted). Textual analysis, as part of critical discourse analysis, can therefore be an important political resource, for example in connection with efforts to establish *critical language awareness* (Clark *et al.*, 1991; Fairclough, 1992b) as an indispensable element in language education.

The reluctance of social scientists hitherto to recognize the value of textual analysis is, however, comprehensible given the paucity of usable analytical frameworks. Discourse analysis can help fill this gap. But there is a continuing problem with linguistic analysis because linguistics is still dominated by a formalism which has little time for integrating linguistic analysis into interdisciplinary frameworks. There is a real need for relevant models of language: for frameworks which turn the insights of linguists into comprehensible and usable forms. My own feeling is that the systemic-functional theory of language is particularly helpful in this regard (Halliday, 1978, 1985; Hodge and Kress, 1988; Thibault, 1991), both because its approach to studying grammar and other aspects of language form is a functional one (a property it shares with other approaches such as that of Givón, 1979), and because it is systematically orientated to studying the relationship between the texture of texts and their social contexts.

Systemic-functional linguistics also has a view of texts which is a potentially powerful basis not only for analysis of what is in texts, but also for analysis of what is absent or omitted from texts, which is a major concern for a number of the papers in *D&S* (e.g. Downing, 1990). Textual analysis is often exclusively concerned with what is in the text and has little to say about what is excluded. The systemic view of texts emphasizes choice, the selection of options from systems constituting meaning potentials (and lexicogrammatical potentials and phonic potentials). Choice entails exclusion as well as inclusion. This view of text has already been applied critically in 'critical linguistics' (e.g. Fowler *et al.*, 1979), which highlights, for instance, the potential ideological significance of opting for agentless passive constructions and thereby excluding other constructions in which agents are explicitly present. My discussion of intertextual analysis in this paper suggests a view of text as choice at a different level of analysis, involving selection amongst options within what one might call the intertextual potential of an order of discourse (i.e. available repertoires of genres, discourses and narratives). And the same view of text can usefully be extended to the identification of 'absences' as well as presences at other levels suggested in some of the papers.

Another and even more serious obstacle to social scientists recognizing the value of textual analysis is that analysis of text is perceived as frequently proceeding with scant attention to context. This is a fair criticism of much textual analysis that goes on in linguistics. The emphasis in my own publications in the field (see the list of references) has been upon bringing a stronger orientation to context into textual analysis. This paper has in a sense reversed that emphasis by arguing that discourse analysts with a commitment to social and cultural aspects of discursive practice would benefit from a stronger orientation to textual analysis. This is in no sense a change of position, or an abandonment of the project of making textual analysis more socially relevant and meaningful: discourse analysis needs a developed sense of and systematic approach to *both* context *and* text.

As I indicated earlier, I believe that intertextual analysis has an important mediating role in linking text to context. What intertextual analysis draws attention to is the discourse practice of text producers and interpreters, whose properties depend upon the nature of the sociocultural practice, resulting in texts which are relatively homogeneous or relatively heterogeneous. (See paper 7.) Let me briefly illustrate how this three-dimensional view of discourse and discourse analysis (analysis of context, analysis of processes of text production and interpretation, analysis of text) can help strengthen the linkage of text to context in the case of one of the analyses discussed above, Fisher's analysis of doctor–patient and nurse practitioner–patient medical interviews. I argued that intertextual analysis helps to show how the nurse practitioner, in contrast to the doctor, legitimizes the patient's experiences, suggesting that nurse practitioner interviews are constituted through a mixture of medical interview genre and counselling interview genre, the latter entailing elements of conversational style. In fact the tension between traditional forms of medical interview and forms of conversationalized interview, often drawing upon counselling models, is a pervasive feature of contemporary interaction between medical practitioners and patients (Davis, 1988; Mishler, 1984; Fairclough, 1992a), and an important characteristic of discourse production and interpretation in that domain. This property of discourse production and interpretation is one dimension of the social and cultural flux which characterizes this and other spheres of professional–client relations – the problematization of traditional models of professional practice, pressures towards greater individual autonomy and more democracy in relations between professionals and clients, the impact of marketization and models of consumer choice on the professions, and so forth. Structures and relations have become more unstable, and practices more diverse and open to negotiation, such that there are many hybridizations of traditional medical, counselling, conversational, managerial and marketing genres and discourses. The diversity is manifested in the variability and heterogeneity of texts: it is impossible to arrive at a unitary characterization of the language or register of 'the medical interview' in contemporary social and discursive conditions.

Let me now make a few comments about this paper by way of conclusion. A general observation on linguistic analysis in the *D&S* papers is that it is often conceived in rather narrow terms as analysis of vocabulary and perhaps metaphor with an occasional grammatical example. I have tended to focus upon the case for intertextual analysis, so I have not done as much as I might have done to correct that emphasis. In fact linguistics, especially with more recent enhancements from pragmatics, discourse analysis and conversation analysis, offers a rich array of types of analysis, though much of the richness is tucked away in forbidding technical literature.

As regards intertextual analysis, I have tried to show that its use alongside linguistic analysis can help to break down the 'form versus content' distinction. Constructs such as 'frame', 'script', 'move', 'strategy' and 'argument' can be deployed in discourse analysis without textual analysis, and indeed are so deployed in the papers I have referred to with some interesting results. But I have suggested that the results can be more firmly grounded and further insights can be added if their deployment is tied to textual analysis. Let me put the point more forcefully: the signifier (form) and signified (content) constitute a dialectical and hence inseparable unity in the sign, so that one-sided attention to the signified is blind to the essential material side of meaning, and one-sided attention to the signifier (as in much linguistics) is blind to the essential meaningfulness of forms.

Finally, the position I have taken has its own problems. For example, the identification of configurations of genres and discourses in a text is obviously an interpretative exercise which depends upon the analyst's experience of and sensitivity to relevant orders of discourse, as well as the analyst's interpretative and strategic biases. There are problems in justifying such analysis which are not made easier by the slipperiness of constructs such as genre and discourse, the difficulty sometimes of keeping them apart, and the need to assume a relatively well defined repertoire of discourses and genres in order to use the constructs in analysis. Reanalysis of others' data must have an especially tentative character given that one's knowledge of relevant orders of discourse is likely to be considerably less than that of the authors of the papers, and one might not have chosen for purposes of textual analysis the samples which authors include. What all this amounts to is an acknowledgement that the intertextual analyses which I have suggested for fragments of texts can no more than hint at the potential I have identified for analysis of processes of discourse production and interpretation to establish mediating links between text and context: one really needs to engage in social and ethnographic research over significant periods of time in particular institutional settings, gathering and analysing textual samples and information on social and cognitive aspects of their production and interpretation as part of this more broadly defined research. This is not to backtrack on my claims about the importance of textual analysis in social research, merely to insist upon the need to frame it adequately.

NOTES

I am grateful to the following for their helpful comments on an earlier draft of the paper: Paul Chilton, Geoffrey Leech, Gunther Kress, Teun van Dijk.

1. There is unfortunately no agreement about terms for analytical categories in intertextual analyses. I use 'genre' for a socially ratified type of linguistic activity with specified positions for subjects (e.g. interview, television news), 'discourse' for a practice of signifying a domain of knowledge or experience from a particular perspective (e.g. Marxist political discourse, feminist discourse) and 'narrative' for a socially ratified story type. See further Kress and Threadgold (1988), Fairclough (1992a).
2. The distinction between linguistic and intertextual analysis does not clarify the position of pragmatics. See Fairclough (1989) for a proposal that pragmatics and intertextual analysis should be grouped together with 'text interpretation', while linguistic analysis falls within 'text description'.
3. 'Voice' is adapted from its use in Bakhtin's writings (see, for example, Bakhtin, 1986) to focus specifically upon subject positions associated with particular genres or discourses. For other uses of the terms see Mishler (1984) and Thibault (1991).
4. An examination of collocation of *killer* + lexical item in three million words of computerized corpus data available at Lancaster University (the Lancaster–Oslo–Bergen corpus, the Brown corpus and the Associated Press corpus) seems to bear this out, though the numbers are surprisingly small with only seven collocations in all. There are two instances of *killer dust*, one each of *killer earthquake*, *killer hurricane*, *killer rabbit* and *killer sub*. All of these involve the notion of that whose nature or function is to kill. There is also one instance of *killer instinct*. I am grateful to Geoffrey Leech for supplying me with these data.
5. Kreisky's last turn in the original German is: *Ja, also, das geht mir nichts an. Ich will damit nichts zu tun haben. Ah, das ist alles sehr unerfreulich, und ich will damit nichts zu tun haben.* The shift in genre and voice to a petulant emotional outburst seems to be there in the original (notice sentence initial *Ah*, and the repetition of *ich will damit nichts zu tun haben.* The full German text appears in Wodak *et al.* (1990: ch. 7). I am grateful to Ruth Wodak for providing me with a copy.

CRITICAL LANGUAGE AWARENESS

Introduction

The two papers in this final section of the book represent an educational application of CDA developed with Lancaster colleagues specializing in various aspects of educational linguistics, especially Romy Clark, Roz Ivanic and Marilyn Martin-Jones. A joint paper was presented at the 1987 annual meeting of the British Association for Applied Linguistics, and subsequently published as Clark *et al.* (1990, 1991), and later developments were brought together in a collection of papers (Fairclough 1992). This work was a response to the enthusiasm during the 1980s for 'language awareness' in schools (Hawkins 1984, NCLE 1985). Our concern was that language awareness programmes should be informed by critical views of language and discourse, as well as a conception of language learning which integrated the development of language awareness with the learner's own prior experience and with the development of capacities for practice, including creative and innovative forms of practice.

'Critical language awareness and self-identity in education' locates education within the general social problematic of language and power in contemporary society. Not only is education itself a key domain of linguistically mediated power, it also mediates other key domains for learners, including the adult world of work. But it is additionally at its best a site of reflection upon and analysis of the sociolinguistic order and the order of discourse, and in so far as educational institutions equip learners with a critical language awareness, they equip them with a resource for intervention in and reshaping of discursive practices and the power relations that ground them, both in other domains and within education itself. The paper contrasts the assumptions and objectives of critical and non-critical approaches to language awareness. It then turns to a particular application of critical language awareness work in the reflexive analysis of relations of power which are implicit in the conventions and practices of academic discourse, and in struggles on the part of learners to contest and transform such practices. I use this example for some reflections on the difficulties facing those dealing with issues of language and power in the complex sociocultural circumstances of contemporary societies, and argue that critical language awareness must not go beyond providing a resource for people to use in making their own decisions – it must scrupulously avoid setting out blueprints for emancipatory practice.

'The appropriacy of "appropriateness"' shows that a model of language variation based upon the concept of 'appropriateness' underpins current policy and practice in language education, including noncritical approaches to language awareness. This model is a major obstacle to the development and wider acceptance of critical language awareness work. The first part of the paper discusses the Cox Report (DES 1989) and prevocational education programmes, arguing that an appropriateness model of variation helps rationalize (a) a policy of teaching standard English while claiming to respect other languages and dialects, and (b) the extension to language of a competence-based model of education, highlighting training in 'language skills'. Crucially, the appropriateness model helps, in the Cox Report for instance, to achieve a compromise between these (respectively conservative and modernizing) policy objectives. The second part of the chapter is a critique of the appropriateness model, first on the grounds that it gives a misleading picture of sociolinguistic variation, and second on the grounds that it confuses sociolinguistic realities with ideologies.

NINE

Critical language awareness and self-identity in education[1]

The issue of language and power in education is just a part of the more general social problematic of language and power, and ought not in my view to be isolated from it. At least in developed capitalist countries, we live in an age in which power is predominantly exercised through the generation of consent rather than through coercion, through ideology rather than through physical force, through the inculcation of self-disciplining practices rather than through the breaking of skulls. (Though there is still unfortunately no shortage of the latter, and indeed there has been a reversion to it on the grand scale in certain parts of the world (e.g., the former socialist countries) in the past few years.) It is an age in which the production and reproduction of the social order depend increasingly upon practices and processes of a broadly cultural nature. Part of this development is an enhanced role for language in the exercise of power: it is mainly in discourse that consent is achieved, ideologies are transmitted, and practices, meanings, values and identities are taught and learnt. This is clear from the generally acknowledged role of the mass media as probably the single most important social institution in bringing off these processes in contemporary societies. And it is recognized in the salience given to language and discourse (the 'linguistic turn') in the work of theorists of modern and contemporary society including Heidegger, Foucault, Derrida, Bourdieu and Habermas.

We also live in an age of great change and instability in which the forms of power and domination are being radically reshaped, in which changing cultural practices are a major constituent of social change, which in many cases means to a significant degree changing discursive practices, changing practices of language use. I have discussed for example how the marketization of discursive practices is constitutive of more general processes of institutional marketization, and discursive facets of sociocultural processes of detraditionalization and informalization (paper 7) and the technologization of discourse as a peculiarly contemporary form of intervention in discursive practices to shape sociocultural change (paper 5).

Educational institutions are heavily involved in these general developments affecting language in its relation to power. First, educational practices themselves constitute a core domain of linguistic and discursive power and of the engineering of discursive practices. Much training in education is orientated to a significant degree towards the use and inculcation of particular discursive practices in educational organizations, more or less explicitly interpreted as an important facet of the inculcation of particular cultural meanings and values, social relationships and identities, and pedagogies. Second, many other domains are mediated and transmitted by educational institutions. For example, one general consequence of processes of societal post-traditionalization and informalization for various domains of work (in the context of the emergence of the supposedly dehierarchized, 'flat', organization) is a great increase in expectations of and demands upon the dialogical capacities of workers, which educational institutions are widely expected to meet through a new emphasis on spoken language 'skills'. Third, educational institutions are to a greater or lesser extent involved in educating people about the sociolinguistic order they live in. In some cases they are aiming to equip them with what has in my view become, because of the enhanced social and cultural role of language and because of the technologization of discourse, an essential prerequisite for effective democratic citizenship; the capacity for critique of language. No doubt the critique of language is in the best cases already carried out reflexively, i.e., is directed at the practices of the educational institution itself (and even at the practices of the critical classroom) and towards issues of language and power in education.

Anticipated changes in the linguistic and discoursal needs of work are a major factor in shaping language education in schools. The established shift towards the service sector at the expense of manufacturing is one element, entailing a focus on interaction with publics, customers or clients. Another is the shift from a Fordist, Taylorist mode or organization within manufacturing to a post-Fordist organization, alluded to above. There is an emphasis on the future worker as 'multiskilled', on work as exploiting talents it has not hitherto exploited, including a range of what have hitherto been seen as 'life skills' rather than occupational skills, including conversational forms of talk. Hence in part the new official interest in spoken language education. Barnes (1988) has pointed to the often uncomfortable coexistence of Old

Right and New Right priorities in official educational policy: on the one hand maintenance of traditional language practices and values around standard English with 'back to basics' appeals on spelling and grammar; on the other hand the new emphasis on oracy and spoken language education. The Kingman and Cox reports on the teaching of English in schools (DES 1988, DES 1989) contain elements of both (Fairclough 1990).

I believe that the problematic of language and power is fundamentally a question of democracy. Those affected need to take it on board as a political issue, as feminists have around the issue of language and gender. If problems of language and power are to be seriously tackled, they will be tackled by the people who are directly involved, especially the people who are subject to linguistic forms of domination and manipulation. This is as true in educational organizations as it is elsewhere. Struggle and resistance are in any case a constant reflex of domination and manipulation: the will to impose discursive practices or engineer shifts in discursive practices from above is one thing, but in actuality the conditions in which such a will to power must take its chance may include a diversity of practices, a resistance to change, and even contrary wills to transform practices in different directions. Of course, struggle against domination has varying degrees of success, and one factor in success is the theoretical and analytical resources an opposition has access to. Critical linguists and discourse analysts have an important auxiliary role to play here in providing analyses and, importantly, in providing critical educators with resources for programmes of what I and my colleagues have called 'critical language awareness' (Clark *et al.* 1990b, 1991, Fairclough 1992a) – programmes to develop the capacities of people for language critique, including their capacities for reflexive analysis of the educational process itself.

I have described in other papers an approach to the general societal problematic of language and power, and I want to indicate here its particular applicability to the forms which that problematic takes within educational organizations. The first element in this approach is the development of a critical tradition within language studies and discourse analysis, which has been extensively discussed elsewhere in this book. The second element, which is described in the next section, is the application of this critical theory and method in the development of critical language awareness work within schools and other educational organizations. In the final part of the paper I shall discuss an example, based upon analyses carried out by colleagues at Lancaster University, of how critical language awareness work can lead to reflexive analysis of practices of domination implicit in the transmission and learning of academic discourse, and the engagement of learners in the struggle to contest and change such practices. I shall finally use this example for some reflections on the difficulties facing those dealing with issues of language and power, in education and elsewhere, in the complex and often confusing socio-cultural circumstances of contemporary societies; and the opportunities and dangers faced by CDA as its focus shifts from critique of existing practices to exploration and even advocacy of possible alternatives.

LANGUAGE AWARENESS: CRITICAL AND NON-CRITICAL APPROACHES

In recent years, language awareness, knowledge about language, has been widely advocated as an important part of language education in Britain, by those associated with the 'language awareness' movement (Hawkins 1984, NCLE 1985), independently and in some cases earlier (Doughty *et al.* 1971), and in reports on the teaching of English in schools within the national curriculum (DES 1988, DES 1989). While welcoming this development, I think language awareness work has been insufficiently critical: it has not given sufficient focus to language-related issues of power which ought to be highlighted in language education given the nature of the contemporary sociolinguistic order. What is needed is an approach based upon a critical view of language and language study such as the one described in this book. In this section I shall contrast such a critical language awareness (henceforth CLA) with the non-critical conception just referred to (henceforth LA – I shall refer mainly to Hawkins 1984), in terms of: rationale for language awareness work; conceptions of language awareness work; the relationship envisaged between language awareness and other elements of language education.

A rationale for critical language awareness work emerges from the general contemporary problematic of language and power described at the beginning of the paper: given that power relations work increasingly at an implicit level through language, and given that language practices are increasingly targets for intervention and control, a critical awareness of language is a prerequisite for effective citizenship, and a democratic entitlement. There is some similarity between this rationale for CLA and part of the rationale for LA, in that the latter attempts like the former to use language education as a resource for tackling social problems which centre around language. But the arguments are cast in very different terms. In Hawkins (1984), this dimension of the rationale for LA refers to social aspects of educational failure (which I discuss below), a lack of understanding of language which impedes parents in supporting the language development of their children, and an endemic 'linguistic parochialism and prejudice' affecting minority languages and non-standard varieties. These are indeed problems which language awareness can help to address, but from a CLA perspective they are just particular points of salience within the much broader contemporary problematization of language I have indicated. A fundamental difference between LA and CLA is their assumptions about what language awareness can do for such problems. Within LA, schools seem to be credited with a substantial capacity for contributing to social harmony and integration, and smoothing the workings of the social and sociolinguistic orders. Language awareness work is portrayed as making up for and helping to overcome social problems (e.g. making up for a lack of 'verbal learning tools' in the home, extending access to standard English to children whose homes do not give it to them). In the case of CLA, the argument is that schools dedicated to a critical pedagogy (Freire 1985, Giroux 1983) ought to provide learners with understanding of problems which cannot be resolved just in the schools; and with the resources for engaging if they so wish in the long-term, multifaceted struggles in various social domains (including education) which are necessary to resolve them. I shall suggest below, in discussing the treatment of standard English, that the LA position can in fact have unforeseen detrimental social consequences.

There are a number of other elements in the rationale for LA. I referred above to social aspects of educational failure, and Hawkins refers in this connection to evidence that schools have had the effect of 'widening the gap' between children who get 'verbal learning tools' at home and those who don't (1984: 1). Language awareness work can help all children 'sharpen the tools of verbal learning' (1984: 98). LA is particularly sensitive to the need to improve study skills in the 'difficult transition from primary to secondary school language work, especially the start of foreign language studies and the explosion of concepts and language introduced by the specialist secondary school subjects' (Hawkins 1984: 4). The poor record of British schools in foreign language learning is part of the rationale; there is an emphasis upon developing 'insight into pattern' and 'learning to listen' as conditions for success in foreign language learning. A related educational problem which LA seeks to address is the absence of a coherent approach to language from the child's perspective, including a lack of coordination between different parts of the language curriculum. There is also (NCLE 1985: 23) reference to the particular linguistic demands arising from rapid social change, where 'many more events require interpretation', especially interpretation of linguistic signals.

Although CLA highlights critical awareness of nontransparent aspects of the social functioning of language, that does not imply a lack of concern with issues such as linguistic dimensions of educational failure or inadequacies in foreign language learning. Nor, turning to a comparison of conceptions of language awareness work, does it imply a lack of concern with formal aspects of language, which take up a large proportion of LA materials. I would see the position of CLA rather as claiming that these important issues and dimensions of language awareness ought to be framed within a critical view of language; for example, we must develop the capacity for sensitive attention to formal linguistic features of texts, and the capacity to frame such textual analysis within a critical discourse analysis. Having made these points, I shall focus my comparison of conceptions of language awareness work upon views of linguistic variation, and especially the treatment of standard English.

LA, like the Kingman and Cox Report (DES 1988, DES 1989), takes the position that it is vital for schools to teach pupils standard English, while treating the diversity of languages in the classroom as 'a potential resource of great richness', and recognizing that all languages and varieties of languages 'have their rightful and proper place' in children's repertoires and 'each serves good purposes' (Hawkins 1984: 171–5). Standard English and other varieties and languages are presented as differing in conditions of appropriateness. Vigorous arguments are advanced for the 'entitlement' of children to education in standard English, especially standard written English, as part of the 'apprenticeship in autonomy' which schools should provide (Hawkins 1984: 65). Stigmatization of particular varieties or accents is attributed to parochialism or prejudice.

There is no doubt whatsoever that learning standard English does give some learners life chances they would not otherwise have. On the other hand, this view of standard English and language variation misses important issues and can I think have detrimental effects. Firstly there is an assumption that schools can help iron out the effects of social class and equalize the 'cultural capital' (Bourdieu 1984) of access to prestigious varieties of English. I think this assumption needs cautious handling, because it is easy to exaggerate the capacity of schools for social engineering; the class system is reproduced in many domains, not just education. Secondly, there is no sense in LA work that in passing on prestigious practices and values such as those of standard English *without* developing a critical awareness of them, one is implicitly legitimizing them *and* the asymmetrical distribution of cultural capital I have just referred to. Thirdly, portraying standard English and other languages and varieties as differing in conditions of appropriateness is dressing up inequality as diversity: standard English is 'appropriate' in situations which carry social clout, while other varieties are 'appropriate' at the margins (see paper 11 for a critique of theories of appropriateness). Fourthly, attributing the stigmatization of varieties to individual prejudice papers over the systematic, socially legitimized stigmatization of varieties. Elevating the standard means demoting other varieties. Again, there is likely to be a mismatch between the liberalism and pluralism of the schools, and the children's experience. It is these mismatches, based upon well-meaning white lies about language variation, that carry the risk of detrimental effects; either they will create delusions, or they will create cynicism and a loss of credibility, or most probably a sequence of the former followed by the latter. I think a CLA position on the treatment of standard English is that one should teach written standard English for pragmatic reasons, but one should also expose learners to views about standard English, including the critical views I have alluded to here. And one should raise with the learners the question of whether and why and how dominant rules of 'appropriateness' might be flouted and challenged (see further below).

At the root of the different conceptions of language awareness work are different conceptions of language, and of sociolinguistic variation. LA is based in a tradition which sees a sociolinguistic order as a given and common-sense reality, effectively a natural domain rather than a naturalized domain, which is 'there' to be described. The question of *why* it is there scarcely arises, and there is certainly not the focus upon sociolinguistic orders being shaped and transformed by relations of power and power struggle, which characterizes the critical approach to language study.

Let me come finally to the relationship envisaged between language awareness and other elements of language education. There is agreement between LA and CLA that, as Hawkins puts it (1984: 73–4), 'awareness' affects 'competence' – or as I would prefer to put it, awareness affects language capabilities. LA does not however set out to build into language education explicit connections between develop-

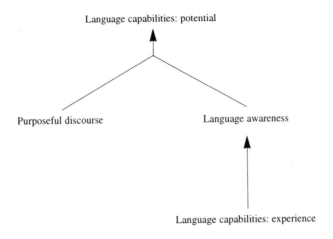

Figure 9.1: A model of language learning

ing awareness and developing capabilities: language awareness work is isolated from other parts of language education as a separate element in the curriculum. By contrast, a central theme in a critical approach is that language awareness should be fully integrated with the development of practice and capabilities.

The diagram above (from Clark *et al.* 1991) gives one representation of this integration. This model incorporates the important principle that critical language awareness should be built from the existing language capabilities and experience of the learner. The experience of the learner can, with the help of the teacher, be made explicit and systematic as a body of knowledge which can be used for discussion and reflection, so that social causes for experiences (e.g. of constraint) can be explored. At the same time, links should constantly be made between work on the development of language awareness and the language practice of the learner. This practice must be 'purposeful'. That is, it must be tied in to the learner's real wishes and needs to communicate with specific real people, because this is the only way for the learner to experience authentically the risks and potential benefits of particular decisions. When critical awareness is linked to such decisions, it broadens their scope to include decisions about whether to flout sociolinguistic conventions or to follow them, whether to conform or not conform (in the use of standard English, for instance, as mentioned above). It also allows such decisions to be seen as in certain circumstances collective rather than individual ones, associated with the political strategies of groups.

CRITICAL LANGUAGE AWARENESS IN PRACTICE: IDENTITY IN ACADEMIC WRITING

Critical language study and critical language awareness work can, as I indicated earlier, be reflexively applied within educational organizations to the practices of such organizations. They constitute a resource for investigating, and intervening in, issues of language and power in education. I have been suggesting that there is an intimate relationship between the development of people's critical awareness of language and the development of their own language capabilities and practices. Accordingly, such reflexive work could involve learners and teachers in analysis of and possibly change in their own practices, as speakers and listeners (and viewers), writers and readers. In this section I want briefly to describe one sort of reflexive application of CLA in work by colleagues at Lancaster (Clark 1992, Ivanic and Simpson 1992), and to use this example for some closing reflections on the difficulty of tackling issues of language and power in complex and often opaque contemporary societies.

The focus of this research is on what I earlier referred to as the identity function of discourse, and specifically the sort of self-identities that are constituted by/for writers in the process of academic writing. Traditional forms of academic discourse, especially in science and social science, demand an impersonal style, and part of the 'apprenticeship' of a student in an academic discipline is the effacing of prior identities in academic writing in order to join the new 'discourse community' (Clark 1992). This can be an uncomfortable and alienating process, perhaps especially for older students with extensive experience or established professional backgrounds. The pressure on students to conform is illustrated in an example given by Clark. An academic made the following comment on an essay written by one of Clark's students: 'Your arguments are undermined by the use of the personal pronoun (meaning the first person pronoun *I*). [Name of student] is not an established authority . . . or not yet, anyway. Avoid the use of personal pronouns and expressions like "in my view" in all academic work'.

Both the Clark paper and the Ivanic and Simpson paper describe experiences of working with a CLA framework with students who are resistant to the constraints of conventional academic writing. In both cases, there are attempts to develop styles of writing which allow students to project self-identities which they feel more comfortable with. Clark's paper reports her work on a study skills course for postgraduates taking Diploma or MA degrees in a department of politics (see also Clark *et al.* 1990). The focus of the course is the written assignments which students have to produce for their politics courses (their practice on the course is thus 'purposeful' in the sense of the last section). The course begins with an exercise designed to raise students' consciousness about the writing process (more fully described in Clark and Ivanic 1992), and the ongoing discussion of the writing process then informs and is fed by collaborative writing workshops and tutorials in which students work on assignments set for their politics courses. Discussion of the writing process leads to work on the development of critical awareness of linguistic resources and conventions, which in turn feeds back into the students' writing. The class used a past student essay to focus a debate on issues of objectivity and impersonalness in academic writing, and these issues are then dealt with in more concrete terms by looking at specific decisions academic writers need to take – whether to use the first person singular pronoun or not, whether to use modality and tense forms which express strong commitment to propositions, or modal forms and hedges which tone down commitment, and so forth. The objective of the study skills course is to 'empower' students by giving them a critical awareness of academic conventions, their social origins and effects. The course provides students with the means for 'emancipation' through the flouting of conventions and the development of nonconventional forms of academic writing, though it is up to students themselves whether they do so (not all do). A major theme of the paper is that students are faced with the dilemma, which they must resolve for themselves, of whether to conform or not conform, whether to lean in the direction of fulfilling obligations or of claiming rights. (On emancipation as a concept in CLA, see also Janks and Ivanic 1992.)

The Ivanic and Simpson paper reports on co-research between an academic (Ivanic) and a mature student (Simpson) who had recently entered higher education, into the latter's development as an academic writer (see also Ivanic and Roach 1990). This paper also focuses upon problems of identity: given the overwhelming prestige of 'impersonal', 'objective' academic style, how can a student – this student – project his own identity in his writing, 'find the "I"', show himself as the sort of person he wants to be? 'Finding the "I"' is a matter of responsibility to oneself and to one's readership: it is a way towards truthfulness and clarity. The authors suggest that writers may be better able to tackle their dilemmas over identity if they become conscious of the 'casts' or 'populations' of identities in the texts they read as well as in their own writing (Talbot 1990). This is a matter of raising their critical awareness of the standard conventions of academic writing, and their effects upon identities. The paper includes an analysis in these terms of three assignments written by Simpson. The 'population' consists of tutors who set the assignments, the people who wrote what he read, the writer himself, the people he writes about, and the people who read what he writes. What emerges is a tense relationship between the pressures upon him to conform to the norms of traditional academic style and his own often cautious and nervous attempts to project his own identity and evolve his own academic style. One noteworthy feature of the paper is that as well as writing about Simpson's attempts to tackle the problem of identity, the authors are explicitly trying to tackle it together in the way in which they write the paper.

The two papers provide useful practical techniques for using CLA in educational organizations to work on one problematic aspect of the interface of language and power in such organizations: the constraints which organizations, and powerholders within them, place upon the discursively constituted self-identities of learners. Evidently, there is a microscopic emphasis in both papers, upon how individual students cope with the tension between a will to resist the impositions of conventional academic writing and requirements to conform, and how critical language awareness programmes can help clarify (if not resolve) such dilemmas. The outcomes of this tension in students' work can be described using the framework for critical discourse analysis discussed elsewhere in this book. One feature of the student work discussed in the two papers is that its 'discourse practice' tends to be complex, involving the mixing of genres and discourses (traditional academic ones and, often, ones drawn from the private domain), and this is realized linguistically in texts which tend to be heterogeneous in style, meanings and forms. I want however to explore a little how this microscopic focus relates to a more macroscopic view of the state of hegemonic relations and hegemonic struggle in the orders of discourse of educational organizations, in order to raise some issues which have a more general relevance to the problematization of language and power in education.

In my view, a microscopic focus upon individual calculations of risk and benefit should always be complemented with and contextualized within a macroscopic view. Student resistance to academic conventions is widespread in contemporary higher education, but the situation is not unified academic institutions stolidly defending traditional practices against reluctant students. Traditional practices have already been extensively undermined from within. For instance, as Ivanic and Simpson point out, academic writing is 'becoming less segregated from informal speech'. There has already been a hegemonic shift which constitutes a favourable environment for the sort of reflexive CLA work that Clark, Ivanic and Simpson are engaged in: practices of academic writing which achieve a hybridization of traditional academic styles and colloquial, informal, spoken styles are now well positioned within the order of discourse. Personalized writing, space to project identities which academic writers feel comfortable with, are part of this evolution. This shift is often construed in terms of a suspect contrast between one's 'real self' and the artificial identities taken on in academic writing. What is I think actually at issue is pressure for specialized academic identities to give way to private domain or 'lifeworld' identities. It would be a mistake to overstate the hegemonic shift or underestimate the continuing power of traditional forms within certain types of institution and particular disciplines. Nevertheless, the shift is clear.

But this shift in educational discursive practices and orders of discourse needs to be explained, i.e. it needs to be situated within wider socio-cultural changes which it is a part of. I would like at this point to strike a cautionary note: it is often difficult to assess the full social and cultural import of a change in discursive practices, and therefore its effect upon power relations and power struggle in the institution concerned. This underlines for me the importance of avoiding directive, top-down interventions designed (perhaps by well-intentioned theorists like myself) to shift practices in a particular emancipatory direction: such decisions must be left to the people directly involved, 'on the ground', who are generally better able to weigh up the complex odds and interpret the sometimes ambivalent, complex, and contradictory values, risks and benefits.

Consider for instance the case in point, in the light of my comments in paper 7 on the ambivalence of the 'conversationalization' of public discourse. The impetus in educational organizations to break down barriers between academic discourse and the more informal and personal practices of the private sphere is not isolated: it is part of a general rejection in contemporary societies of elite, professional, bureaucratic, etc., practices, and a valorization of ordinariness, naturalness, 'being oneself' and so forth, in discourse and more generally. It is part of the conversationalization of public discourse, and it ties in with the informalization of contemporary society and its post-traditional properties. Seen in these terms, it can be interpreted positively as a democratizing development.

But the push for democracy is not the only source of attacks on tradition, and not the only impetus for the breaking down of barriers. Education like other institutions has been and is being marketized, incorporated into the consumer society and culture. This entails a standardization of practices across institutions on the model of the market. One obvious and indeed notorious surface example of this standardization is the generalization of the persona and vocabulary of the 'consumer' (or 'customer') across institutions, including the reconstruction of students as consumers. The difficulty is that it is not always easy to distinguish between attacks upon and attempts to reconstruct traditional academic practices which are democratically rooted and those which are rooted in marketization. How for instance might one decide whether a student who is resisting the impersonalness of academic writing is operating from a democratic rejection of elitism, or as someone who wishes to assert his or her authority as consumer? (On the 'authority of the consumer', see Keat, Whiteley and Abercrombie (1994) and Fairclough (1994).) One way of reading the difficulty in this case is in terms of appropriation: one could see the impetus towards marketization of education as having appropriated some of the themes and values, and discursive practices, of the historically earlier impetus towards anti-elitism. The 1960s being appropriated by the 1980s, so to speak.

The point is not in any way to retreat from reflexive critical language awareness work, still less to defend traditional practices. It is to highlight the difficulty in contemporary society in being entirely confident about the target, in the sense of what needs changing, and what it needs changing to. People on the ground must make up their minds about these complex issues, as they will whether critical language work is in progress or not. We need CLA work of a sensitive, non-dogmatic and non-directive sort. We also need, in support of it, critical discourse analysis research into the complex and ambivalent interdependencies between discursive practices and socio-cultural systems and transformations in education.

This example raises a more general issue. There have recently been proposals that CDA should partly shift its emphasis from critique of existing discursive practices to exploration of alternatives.[2] This is broadly welcome: the founding motivation for critical analysis is emancipation and the building of emancipated forms of social life, not critique *per se.* Such work must however proceed with caution. Critical analysis can be 'turned' and appropriated by dominant social forces, and critical interventions to build new practices can look uncomfortably similar to what I have called technologization of discourse. A more productive orientation on the part of CDA must, I believe, be framed within a profound commitment to democracy. CDA can contribute to the social imaginary, to the stock of feasible Utopias which can inform choices which people make individually and collectively, but the choices must be made by the people concerned and affected on their own behalf.

NOTES

1. The first and third sections of this paper will appear in a modified form as part of a paper with the same title in a book edited by D. Corson, *Language and Power in Education.* The second section ('Language awareness: critical and non-critical approaches') draws upon collective work with colleagues in Lancaster, reflected in Clark, Fairclough, Ivanic and Martin-Jones (1991).
2. Voiced for instance by Gunther Kress at a conference on Discourse and Ideology in Vienna, December 1993.

TEN

The appropriacy of 'appropriateness'

This paper deals with the concept of 'appropriateness' in language, and the commonplace view that varieties of a language differ in being appropriate for different purposes and different situations. I argue first that many important contributions to recent debate on language education and language awareness depend heavily upon a view of sociolinguistic variation that centres around the concept of appropriateness. The second part of the chapter is a critique of such theories of sociolinguistic variation. I argue that such themes are an ideological obstacle to the development of CLA.

The first part of the paper will show how central 'appropriateness' has been in recent rethinking of language education and language awareness in Britain. I shall refer mainly to the Cox Report on the teaching of English in schools (DES 1989), but also to language and communication elements in the Certificate of Pre-Vocational Education (FEU 1987). I shall be arguing that theories of appropriateness underpin controversial policies on the teaching of standard English, but also the development of a competence-based 'communication skills' view of language education with a new emphasis on 'oracy' and spoken language education. Indeed, 'appropriateness' is the linchpin of an attempted integration of the two.

The second part of the chapter is a critique of models of language variation based upon 'appropriateness'. I argue that such models incorporate profoundly misleading assumptions about sociolinguistic variation. I also argue that such models derive from a confusion between sociolinguistic realities and political aspirations. In no actual speech community do all members always behave in accordance with a shared sense of which language varieties are appropriate for which contexts and purposes. Yet such a perfectly ordered world is set up as an ideal by those who wish to impose their own social order upon society in the realm of language. So I suggest that appropriateness is an 'ideological' category, which is linked to particular partisan positions within a politics of language – within a struggle between social groups in a speech community for control of (or 'hegemony' over) its sociolinguistic order. And I argue that the critique of appropriateness and models of language variation based upon it, and the development of alternatives, is a central part of making the case for CLA.

'APPROPRIATENESS' IN LANGUAGE EDUCATION

The concept of 'appropriateness' has been prominent in recent discussion of the teaching of English in schools, and of prevocational education (DES 1988, DES 1989, FEU 1987), as well as in language awareness programmes and materials (Hawkins 1985). In this section of the chapter I want to focus upon two questions. First, how does appropriateness figure within dominant conceptions of language variation? And how in particular does it help to rationalize policies on the teaching of standard English? Second, what is the relationship between appropriateness and competence-based, skills-orientated views of language education? I refer mainly to the Cox Report (DES 1989) but also to prevocational education programmes (FEU 1987).

APPROPRIATENESS MODELS OF LANGUAGE VARIATION

The following extract is a particularly good example of how appropriateness figures in the Cox Report:

> Pupils working towards level 7 should consider the notion of appropriateness to situation, topic, purpose and language mode and the fact that inappropriate language use can be a source of humour (either intentional or unintentional) or may give the impression that the speaker or writer is pompous or inept or impertinent or rude. Pupils should learn that Standard English is the language of wide social communication and is particularly likely to be required in public, formal settings. Teaching should cover discussion of the situations in which and purposes for which people might choose to use non-standard varieties rather than Standard English, *e.g. in speech with friends, in a local team or group, in television advertising, folk songs, poetry, dialogue in novels or plays.* (6.29, original italics)

I shall discuss in turn three issues raised here: appropriateness and standard English, inappropriateness and normativeness, and appropriateness within language awareness. I shall also discuss a section of the Report which shows rather clearly the limitations of a model of variation based upon appropriateness.

Appropriateness and standard English

Appropriateness is the cornerstone of the Report's policy on the teaching of standard English. The Report argues that children have an 'entitlement' to standard English, and that 'many important opportunities are closed to them' if they do not have access to standard English (4.3, 4.5). The recommendation therefore is that schools should aim to develop pupils' ability to understand and produce both written and spoken standard English. But this recommendation should be understood in the context of the Report's view of the objectives of the English curriculum and the priority it gives to widening pupils' repertoires of varieties of English and, in the case of bilingual children, their multilingual repertoires (10.13). The 'overriding aim' of the English curriculum is, according to the Report, 'to enable all pupils to develop to the full their ability to use and understand English', in order to maximize the contribution of English to 'the personal development of the individual child' and 'preparation for the adult world' (2.13, 2.14). In pursuit of these objectives, 'teachers should aim to extend the range of varieties of English in which children are competent . . . to enable children to do more with their language' (2.15). The aim is therefore to 'add Standard English to the repertoire, not to replace other dialects or languages' (4.43), and to do so in a way which 'respects the language background of the pupils' (4.36).

But there is an apparent paradox. How is it possible to add without replacing? Is it possible to teach pupils a variety of English so much more prestigious and powerful than their own dialects or languages, without detriment to the latter? The Cox Report suggests that it is possible, and its argument rests upon the concept of appropriateness; different varieties of English, and different languages, are appropriate for different contexts and purposes, and all varieties have the legitimacy of being appropriate for *some* contexts and purposes. On the face of it, this resolves the paradox. But as soon as appropriate contexts and purposes for varieties other than standard English are listed (see the italicized part of the extract from 6.29 quoted above), it is clear just how fragile this resolution of the paradox is. For these are of course largely in the domain of the private and the quaint, and exclude those public, formal and written domains which have most social prestige.

Will children not get the unspoken message that their varieties *may* be 'appropriate', but are pretty marginal and irrelevant? Part of the argument in the second part of this chapter is that the impression of an orderly division of labour between standard English and other varieties cannot in any case be justified.

Inappropriateness and normativeness

Let me turn now to inappropriateness, and the issue of normativeness. Inappropriateness is portrayed in the above extract from the Report on the one hand as a source of humour, and on the other hand as possibly leading to adverse social judgements (that the speaker or writer is 'inept', 'rude', etc.). No good *serious* reasons are given for being inappropriate – it is either a slip-up or a joke. (The Report does not mention the racist or 'classist' nature of much of the humour deriving from inappropriacy.)

The normative and prescriptive nature of the concept of appropriateness becomes particularly clear in discussions of *in*appropriateness. The Report itself ties appropriateness to prescriptivism at one point: 'we need both accurate descriptions of language that are related to situation, purpose and mode (i.e. whether the language is spoken or written), and prescriptions that take account of context, appropriateness and the expression of meaning' (4.19). But the way in which description and prescription are linked together shows a special characteristic of appropriateness in comparison with other prescriptive concepts such as 'correctness': what is prescribed as appropriate is taken to be in line with descriptively established regularities in the practices of a speech community. This makes the suspect assumption, which I return to in the second part of the chapter, that speech communities are characterized by well-defined varieties clearly distributed among contexts and purposes, so that what is appropriate or inappropriate is a clear-cut matter for all of us. I referred earlier to a further characteristic which distinguishes appropriateness from other prescriptive concepts: it ascribes legitimacy to each and every variety as appropriate in some contexts.

But the theory and language of appropriateness coexists in the Report with a historically earlier theory and language of variation which is normative in a less liberal mode:

> Pupils need to be able to discuss the contexts in which Standard English is *obligatory* and those where its use is *preferable* for social reasons. By and

large, the pressures in favour of Standard English will be greater when the language is written, formal and public. Non-standard forms may be much more widely *tolerated* – and, in some cases, *preferred* – when the language is spoken, informal and private. (4.41, my italics)

The appearance of *tolerated* lifts the veil on a tradition of prescriptive bigotry towards non-standard varieties which is largely absent from the Report. The normativeness of this earlier tradition takes the form of prescriptive rules and regulations of a legislative character; *obligatory* and *preferable* belong here, as does *required* in the extract quoted earlier. This is in contrast with the normativeness of the appropriateness model, expressed as I have suggested in terms of descriptive rules and regularities. I suggest that the coexistence of these two overlapping normative languages ('discourses' in one sense of that much-used term) in the Report highlights one important role of appropriateness models of language variation: they help to endow prescriptivism with a relatively acceptable face.

Appropriateness with language awareness

The extract from paragraph 6.29 of the Cox Report quoted above refers to the teaching of knowledge about language – to language awareness. The Report proposes that understanding of how language variation is governed by principles of appropriateness should be developed in tandem with the capacity to speak and write appropriately, and to assess the speech or writing of others in terms of appropriateness. What I referred to above as the 'suspect assumption' of clear-cut and determinate appropriateness relations between varieties, contexts and purposes is here given the status of knowledge. Suspect (and as I argue later, partisan) assumptions treated as knowledge may reasonably be regarded as ideologies – interpretations and representations from a particular point of view corresponding to particular interests, which are projected as universal. The Cox Report's recommendations on language awareness can in this respect be seen as advocating the teaching of ideological doctrines of language variation in tandem with practices of appropriate use.

I want to conclude this part of the chapter by mentioning one section of the Report where the appropriateness model of language variation is stretched to breaking point: the discussion of relationships between culturally different varieties of interaction associated with different ethnic groups (differences which may be manifest in 'body posture, gesture, preferred distance between speakers, discursive styles, the ways in which politeness is marked or attention to other speakers is signalled'), and between female and male speech styles. The following extract is indicative of the difficulties:

> Whether these characteristic differences are judged positively or negatively will depend on the context and purpose of the task. For example, in some tasks, the more direct way of speaking that is more common to boys will be advantageous; in others, the more tentative approach more frequently found in girls will be more appropriate. (11.15)

Leaving aside the question of whether these characterizations of boys' and girls' speech styles are justifiable, this is an attempt to force these types of variation into an appropriateness model whose inability to accommodate them is thereby exposed. The relationships between the communicative styles of different cultural groups, and between the speech styles of women and the speech styles of men, are relationships of tension, contradiction, and power; the different styles belong to different, divergent and potentially antagonistic repertoires. In trying to accommodate these relationships within an appropriateness model, the Report misconstrues these different styles as alternatives in complementary distribution within a single repertoire. It is indeed the case, in a situation of fluid and shifting gender and ethnic relations such as ours, that these contradictory styles may come to coexist within the repertoires of particular groups and individuals. But such changes are partial and complex, and require a far more sophisticated theoretical framework than a model which flattens variation into a unitary and unidimensional set of complementary options. The need to go beyond an appropriateness model is manifest.

Let me summarize what I have said so far. I have suggested that appropriateness provides an apparent resolution of the paradox that use of standard English is to be taught, while use of other varieties is to be respected; that an appropriateness model of variation is the (relatively) acceptable face of prescriptivism; and that giving an appropriateness view of language variation the status of knowledge in language awareness teaching serves an ideological role. I have also suggested that the attempt to contain ethnicity- and gender-related variation within the appropriacy model overstretches the model and shows the need to go beyond it.

Appropriateness and skills

Competence-based views of language and language education dominate recent educational thinking – the Kingman Report, the Cox Report –

THE APPROPRIACY OF 'APPROPRIATENESS'   239

but also (and even more so) the whole range of the prevocational programmes (FEU 1987). But the impact of competence and skills models is much broader than that. There is a general shift towards seeing knowledge operationally, in terms of competence, what people can do; and towards seeing education as training in skills. Indeed the distinction between education and training is coming under increasing pressure, not least from government: according to the former Secretary of State for Trade and Industry Lord Young of Graffham, 'there is no room in a modern world for the old divide between "education" and "training"' (Young 1987). Language competence and skills, communicational competence and skills, come to be items in a list which includes scientific, technological, practical and social competence and skills (FEU 1987).

The development of prevocational education programmes has been a major feature of the 1980s, and these programmes have operated as a powerhouse in developing competence-based systems for many subject areas which have subsequently had a broader influence in primary, secondary and higher education. I shall refer specifically to the syllabus for the Certificate of Pre-Vocational Education (CPVE) to illustrate competence-based views of language education and the way in which they interact with appropriateness models of variation (FEU 1987).

The syllabus is set out as a series of core competences each of which is divided into more specific competences (glossed as 'skills, knowledge and attitudes'). Communication is one of the core competences, whose main aim is 'to develop communication skills as a way of structuring relationships between people in a changing and multicultural society'. It is divided into the five 'aims' of listening, speaking, reading, writing, and communication and interpretation, each of which is further broken down into more specific skills. For example, 'speaking' involves five skills, including: 'talking effectively in a variety of styles and range of contexts — one-to-one/group, familiar/unfamiliar, formal/informal'; 'formulating and conveying requests and instructions clearly and concisely'; 'initiating and sustaining conversations in a range of contexts' (FEU 1987: 30).

Appropriateness figures prominently. For example, 'listening' is glossed as 'to listen and respond appropriately to oral requests and presentations', 'speaking' as 'to talk appropriately in a range of situations'. It also figures under the aim of 'role identification' within the core competence 'social skills': 'distinguishing between appropriate and inappropriate behaviour in a range of personal and situational or organizational roles', 'selecting appropriate behaviour and procedures for achieving a specified goal'.

Competence-based models in education are associated with wider social and cultural tendencies and themes. They incorporate a particular vision of the social subject and of the educability of the subject. They are democratic in their view of subjects; they imply that everyone has the capacity to learn, dependent only upon training. They are simultaneously normalizing, and sometimes tightly programmed. They lay down common target behaviours, knowledges and understandings for all learners, sometimes in very precise terms (e.g. the CPVE skills referred to above, or the language skills specified in the Cox Report as attainment targets for ten different levels of attainment). They are at the same time individualizing: they focus upon each separate individual as housing a configuration of skills which can be worked upon and improved, and in this respect they connect out to contemporary tendencies for the 'self' to become more autonomous, more 'self-steering' (Rose 1989), and to the contemporary salience of individualism.

And competence-based models are spreading. They have been rapidly 'colonizing' many domains of social life in the past decade, perhaps because they seem to fit in well with the values of 'enterprise culture' (Keat and Abercrombie 1990). As the example of CPVE above has shown, competence-based models are certainly prominent in the educational and training initiatives of the 1980s which have been inspired by enterprise culture values. Their success seems to correspond to the changes in the nature of work and corresponding increase in demands upon the communicative and linguistic abilities of workers.

The generalization of competence models across the curriculum entails the generalization of assumptions about knowledge, behaviour and learning which make less sense in some parts of the syllabus than in others. For instance, that the domain of knowledge to be taught is well-defined and determinate, and componentially structured into broad competences or skills which are in turn made up of more specific competences and skills; that the relationship between competence and behaviour is a simple relationship of application, and that there is a transparent relationship between domains of behaviour and domains of competence; that competences and skills are freely transferable, so that a competence learnt in one context may be applied in others.

I do not believe that any of these assumptions is valid at least without major qualifications in the case of language, and I would in fact want to argue that the generalization of a competence model to language is misconceived. There is no space to argue that position in detail here, but what I shall be suggesting shortly is that competence models of language presuppose unacceptable appropriateness models of language variation. One thing which should be noted first, however, is that competence models are not just a recent imposition from outside, from fashions in education, but have their own history within linguistics. They can be traced back to the Chomskyan conception of *linguistic competence* (Chomsky 1965) via Hymes' notion of *communicative competence* (Hymes 1972), which was influential in bringing a competence perspective into language education in the so-called *communicative approach* to the teaching of language, especially English as a foreign language (Candlin 1975). The division of language into the main categories of *skills* (speaking, listening, reading, writing) for pedagogical purposes is a long-established practice in applied linguistics.

Let me turn to the relationship between a competence/skills model and appropriateness. An appropriateness model of language variation facilitates the application of the competence/skills model to language, because it offers a way of squaring the variability of language with the view of language as unitary, normative and determinate practices which people can be trained in. If it is indeed the case that members of a speech community have a shared and well-defined repertoire of language varieties, and if it is indeed the case that each variety can be matched with contexts it is appropriate to with minimal overlap or indeterminacy, then language education can be simply a matter of training people in skills and techniques, increasing their know-how, making them more skilled in language as one might make them more skilled in handling tools. If on the other hand as I suggest below repertoires are plural, variable and often ill-defined, and if the matching of language to context is characterized by indeterminacy, heterogeneity and struggle, how on earth can language education be reduced to skills training? So the rationality of applying the competence/skills model to language depends upon the appropriacy of an appropriateness model of variation, and the concept of appropriateness is therefore of considerable ideological and political significance.

Let me bring the discussion of appropriateness in language education, and the first part of the paper, to a conclusion. I have been suggesting that appropriateness is a vehicle for other things in recent documents on language education − for policies on the teaching of standard English, and for extending competence models to language. On the one hand, appropriateness helps rationalize a policy of teaching children to understand and produce spoken and written standard English while apparently respecting other dialects and languages. This policy is justified in terms of the 'entitlement' of children to the 'opportunity' which standard English opens up for them. But teaching the appropriate use of standard English inevitably has other effects which the Cox Report remains silent about: it uses the educational system to transmit shared language values (if not practices) based around the hegemony of a particular dialect, but in a way which overcomes on the surface the contemporary dilemma of how to do that while making the politically necessary concessions to liberalism and pluralism. This use of the educational system corresponds to a traditional establishment (or 'Old Right' as Barnes 1988 puts it) agenda. Language standardization after all is first a matter of hegemony – the hegemony of a particular class extended to the linguistic sector of the cultural domain, manifested as the hegemony of a dialect – and only consequentially a matter of opportunity.

On the other hand, appropriateness helps rationalize the extension to language of a competence-based model of education. Whereas the teaching of the standard is an Old Right priority, teaching language competences and skills is a priority of the modernizing New Right (Barnes 1988, Hewitt 1989). It is based upon a planning perspective and the anticipation of new requirements for employees and citizens. It is orientated to a new conception of citizenship, and a sense that modes of hegemony must change in a rapidly changing world. What appropriateness helps to do, in the Cox Report for example, is effect a compromise between these Old Right and New Right perspectives and priorities. It is the linchpin which holds them together in an uneasy, and no doubt temporary harmony.

CRITIQUE OF APPROPRIATENESS MODELS OF LANGUAGE VARIATION

What then are the objections to appropriateness models of language variation? There are I think two major lines of objection, which I shall discuss in turn: first, that appropriateness models are based upon presuppositions which misrepresent sociolinguistic variation; and second, that they are ideological in the sense that they portray a political objective as a sociolinguistic reality.

Presuppositions of appropriateness

What image of language variation do appropriateness models give? In one sentence, it is I think an image of clearly distinguished language varieties being used in clearly distinguished contexts, according to clear-cut conventions, which hold for all members of what is assumed to be a homogeneous speech community. Let me spell out more precisely some of the presuppositions about sociolinguistic variation which appropriateness models are based upon.

1. There is a 1:1, or at least a determinate and well-defined many-to-one, fit between varieties of a language and the contexts/purposes they are appropriate for.
2. This determinate fit characterizes all parts of the sociolinguistic order.
3. This fit holds for all members of a speech community.
4. The distinction between appropriate and inappropriate language use is clear-cut.
5. Varieties of a language, contexts, and purposes, are well-defined and clearly demarcated entities.

None of these presuppositions stands up to close scrutiny. In assessing them, it may be helpful to have specific areas of contemporary sociolinguistic variation in mind. I shall refer to two: cross-gender communication in organizations, and medical interviews.

How does a professional woman (in a university or in industry, say) talk appropriately to a senior male colleague, and vice-versa? One need only formulate the question to see that it is difficult to answer in any direct or simple way. A significant feature of the current climate of problematized gender relations is that women and men are often not sure how to talk to each other, and often find themselves in communicative dilemmas. There exist many divergent practices which correspond to some degree, for instance, to different levels of commitment to feminism. And the practices which exist are contested and struggled over, often explicitly, as when people argue for guidelines on non-sexist language use to be adopted by organizations. Any notion of unitary sets of appropriateness conventions for such cross-gender communication would therefore seem to be unsustainable.

Another example, which on the face of it looks more promising for the appropriateness model, is communication between doctors and their patients. But there are problems here too. There are traditional forms of medical interview which are tightly structured around question–answer sequences, with the doctor asking nearly all the questions and the patient being constrained by narrow criteria of medical relevance in answering questions, and with control of the topics raised and the overall course of the interview being firmly in the doctor's hands (Mishler 1984). No doubt one could use an appropriateness model here. The difficulty is that contemporary medical interviews are far more diverse than this suggests. Another form of doctor–patient interview is more like counselling: structured around patient accounts of problems, which are not tightly controlled in terms of medical relevance, but often show criteria of relevance and a communicative style typical of informal conversation. The doctor may exercise minimal control, ask few questions, but show a great deal of empathy with the patient (for examples see Mishler 1984, ten Have 1989, and paper 5). Such contrasting forms of interview are in a relationship of tension and conflict, and the choice a doctor makes tends to go along with her or his views of medicine, conception of patients, and so forth. There is no unitary set of appropriate behaviours in medical interviews either.

I now return to the set of presuppositions above. Presupposition (1) specifies a close fit between varieties of a language and contexts/purposes, yet these examples suggest that there may be considerable indeterminacy in that relationship. Moreover, the difference between the two examples suggests that, contrary to presupposition (2), there may be considerable unevenness between different parts of the sociolinguistic order as well as over time in the degree of (in)determinacy of the variety – context/purpose relation: I suspect that most women in organizations have experienced sociolinguistic dilemmas and indeterminacies, whereas traditional medical interview is probably a powerful model still for a great many patients. Presupposition (3) claims that a particular fit between variety and context/purpose will hold for all members of a speech community, but both examples cast doubt upon this in suggesting that different groups of people may have not only different senses of the variety/context/purpose relation but also practices which may come into conflict. Another important aspect of presupposition (3) is that it points to the marginalization in an appropriateness model of a central characteristic of the contemporary British sociolinguistic order: its multilingualism. There is a plurality of sociolinguistic resources in contemporary Britain, with widely divergent access to them; not a unitary set of resources used according to shared norms, as appropriacy models suggest. Given the complexity and non-consensual nature of the variety – context/purpose relation, it will evidently not be possible to differentiate appropriate and inappropriate behaviour in a clear-cut way in many instances, and so presupposition (4) becomes problematic.

The final presupposition, that varieties as well as contexts and purposes are well-defined and clearly demarcated, is also problematic, and there seems again to be unevenness between different parts of the sociolinguistic order. A job interview and an informal chat may for example appear on the face of it to be very different varieties, associated with quite different sorts of context and purpose, yet job interviews may sometimes resemble informal chats. We need to recognize that while boundaries between varieties are sometimes carefully policed, in some parts of the sociolinguistic order there are complex mergers and overlaps – interviews in conversational style, information which slides into advertising, written language which is full of features of colloquial speech, and so forth.

I referred in the first section of the chapter to the close relationship in the Cox Report of an appropriateness model of variation and policies on the teaching of standard English. These objections to the five presuppositions apply, of course, to the particular case of variation between standard English and other dialects and languages. Education itself for example is proof that, contra presupposition (1), there is no determinate fit between standard English and particular contexts and purposes: whether and where other varieties are to be used in educational contexts and for educational purposes is a constantly contested issue, a domain of sociolinguistic struggle. This implies that, contra presupposition (3), there are different conceptions in the speech community of where standard and other varieties are appropriate. It is also clear that, contra presupposition (2), the frontier between standard English and other varieties has been less stable and more contested in education than in, say, law or science. Consequently, the presupposition throughout the Cox Report that there is a clear-cut distinction between appropriate and inappropriate uses of standard and other varieties (presuppositon (4) above) is not justified.

In short, then, models of language variation based upon the concept of appropriateness project a misleading and unsustainable image of sociolinguistic practice and how sociolinguistic orders are structured.

Appropriateness as ideology

Levinson gives a critique of conceptions of pragmatics based upon the notion of appropriateness (1983: 24–7), which includes the following three criticisms of the notion itself. They overlap, of course, with the five presuppositions discussed above.

1. It implies a culturally homogeneous speech community, whereas real speech communities manifest cultural heterogeneity.
2. Speakers 'do not always comport themselves in the manner recommended by the prevailing mores – they can be outrageous, and otherwise "inappropriate"'.
3. 'In being grossly inappropriate, one can nevertheless be supremely appropriate', in the sense that speakers exploit (and violate) conventions to communicate particular meanings – ironic meanings, for example.

I think Levinson is right about (1) and (3), but that he misses a whole range of further and really more damaging criticisms of appropriateness which are partly but inadequately evoked by (2). Let me develop this by commenting first on (1).

What Levinson has in mind is illustrated by his example of a village in South India 'where there may be say twenty distinct castes' and 'a single honorific particle may have just one meaning (e.g. speaker is inferior to addressee) but have twenty distinct rules for its *appropriate* usage'. Levinson's example sees each caste as a separate and parallel (sub-) speech community within the wider speech community. Thus (1) deals with social *groups* coexisting but not interacting. By contrast (2) deals with *individuals* contesting appropriateness conventions. A very important omission from Levinson's account is *groups contesting conventions*.

What is at issue here is how one sees the relationship between a language and those who speak it in a highly complex modern society such as modern Britain; or rather between the totality of the linguistic resources of a society (which may include many languages) and those who draw upon them. A common view, which Levinson basically subscribes to, acknowledges that linguistic resources are divided – variable – in ways which correspond to the class and other divisions of the society, but sees these divisions in a static way, as a synchronic state. His is a more sophisticated view of variation than what I have been referring to as appropriateness models, but shares with it the property of synchronic idealisation. A different view, which I subscribe to, sees such divisions as constant processes of contestation and struggle between class and other groups, which are struggles over linguistic resources as well as other cultural resources. From this second point of view, seeing a speech community as a static synchronic entity is not only idealizing and simplifying, it is also falsifying: it has the effect of making contestation and struggle invisible. Yet contestation and struggle are, I would argue, the absolutely fundamental processes out of which speech communities are shaped and transformed. A 'synchronic state' from this point of view freezes a complex array of processes, and flattens out important distinctions in relative degrees of stability between different parts of such a 'state', distinctions which are connected to the multiplicity of different time-scales or 'periodicities' over which changes occur.

We may call the second perspective 'historical', not just because it is concerned with linguistic change, but more importantly because it sees language as embedded in social history. This in my view is the only properly social way of envisaging language. How then are appropriate-ness models to be regarded from a historical perspective? In summary, my view is that appropriateness models derive from a confusion between sociolinguistic realities and political projects in the domain of language: social order – e.g. a regulated sociolinguistic order correspond-ing to the notion of appropriateness in which each variety is neatly attached to its particular context and purpose – is the political objective of the dominant, 'hegemonic', sections of a society in the domain of language as in other domains, but it never has been sociolinguistic reality. Appropriateness models in sociolinguistics or in educational policy documents should therefore be seen as *ideologies*, by which I mean that they are projecting imaginary representations of sociolinguis-tic reality which correspond to the perspective and partisan interests of one section of society or one section of a particular social institution – its dominant section. Let me develop this view.

What I want to suggest is that the sociolinguistic order is a domain of hegemonic struggle, and that one dimension of the struggle of a group to establish its hegemony over a domain or institution is a struggle for sociolinguistic hegemony (see paper 5). Parts of the sociolinguistic order may at a given point in time be relatively stable, and may even approximate to the picture conveyed by appropriateness models – well-defined varieties in neat complementary relationships to contrasting functions and contexts, with most people using these varieties 'appropriately' most of the time. But the whole of the sociolinguistic order of a complex society like ours is never like that, and even points of stability become contested and destabilized. In many instances, there are alternative language practices – the example of a medical interview given above is a case in point. They may just coexist, but the issue of dominance relationships between them generally arises. And dominance commonly means not the elimination of all but one practice, but the relative marginalization of non-dominant practices, or the incorporation of non-dominant practices into dominant ones. Establishing sociolinguistic hegemony means establishing relations of domination and subordination among alternative language practices.

This view of the sociolinguistic order as one terrain of hegemonic struggle will perhaps be surprising to people whose conception of language had been influenced by modern linguistics – one is used to the idea that power relations are enacted within the sociolinguistic conventions of speech community, but these conventions themselves are seen as solid social facts, not as themselves stakes in and outcomes of struggle between social forces. There is an oppositional tradition within linguistics however (Volosinov 1973), as well as a tradition in social theory (Foucault 1984) which recognizes a power struggle to control language. According to Foucault, 'as history constantly teaches us, discourse is not simply that which translates struggles or systems of domination, but is the thing for which and by which there is struggle, discourse is the power which is to be seized' (1984: 110). Foucault adds that 'in every society the production of discourse is at once controlled, selected, organized and redistributed by a certain number of procedures whose role is to ward off its powers and its dangers, to gain mastery over its chance events, to evade its ponderous, formidable materiality'. The procedures include 'prohibition': 'we know quite well that we do not have the right to say everything, that we cannot speak of just anything in any circumstances whatsoever, and that not everyone has the right to speak of anything whatever' (1984: 109). What sociolinguists have generally seen – innocently – in terms of a speech community's rules (rules for 'who says what to whom, when and where') is here portrayed by Foucault as the taming and mastery of discourse.

Sociolinguistic hegemony, like other dimensions of hegemony, involves not just shaping practices directly, but also generating theories and doctrines of sociolinguistic practice. Thus one dimension of the developing hegemony of standard English over other varieties was the emergence from the late seventeenth century onwards of 'doctrines of correctness' (Leonard 1925). Doctrines and theories have a double role. First, they help to naturalize hegemonic practices. For example a formulation such as 'language variety x is (not) appropriate in contest y' metaphorically expresses a historically specific relationship between people – those who speak the language, those who struggle to impose hegemony and those who contest it – as a timeless relationship between things: between a variety, and a context. It is a case of 'grammatical metaphor' in Halliday's sense (Halliday 1985). It construes what is historical and contingent as natural and necessary. It is also a case of what one might call 'linguistic fetishism' on the model of Marx's famous 'commodity fetishism' (1974: 76–88): constraints which arise from particular social relations are fetishistically attributed to language itself.

Second, doctrines and theories incorporate political projects (in the sense of objectives), especially the 'hegemonic projects' of groups who aspire to hegemony in the domain of language. That is, they project upon the messy and contradictory realities of a sociolinguistic order an idealized and Utopian view of what the sociolinguistic order ought to be like from the partisan perspective of a dominant social group. Theories of appropriateness are a case in point. It is certainly not the case that all members of a speech community act in accordance with shared ideas of appropriateness, but it is a natural enough aspiration and project on the part of those trying to impose (their) order upon a society or a social institution. Sometimes the project takes the explicit form of institutional rules and regulations (in schools for example: no speaking in class without teacher's permission, no shouting in the corridors, and so forth), but often it does not.

Doctrines and theories take the common-sense form of language attitudes, and indeed a measure of their hegemony is the extent to which they come to be naturalized as attitudes. It is a strength of ethnographic approaches to linguistic research that the study of the language attitudes of members of a community is seen as an essential complement to and part of the study of their sociolinguistic practices. Practices and attitudes fuel each other. But at the same time there may be striking mismatches between what people do and what they think they (ought to) do, and it is important not to confuse the two in analysis.

'Appropriateness' belongs to the domain of language attitudes: it is one sort of judgement that is made by members of speech communities about language use (Hymes 1972). However, there has been a great deal of slippage between the analysis of language attitudes and the analysis of sociolinguistic practices, and 'appropriateness' has come to be widely used as an analytical concept within the description of the latter. It is common to find linguists writing about what 'is appropriate' in a speech community rather than what is 'judged to be appropriate' (by particular groups). Here are two quite typical examples:

> The development of awareness has a marked effect upon a pupil's ability to cope with the whole range of his work, because he comes to see that many problems are not so much problems in grasping the content of what he studies, but problems of handling the language appropriate to it.
> (Doughty *et al.* 1971: 10)

> The next short paragraph seems to be a summary statement of the line to be taken, or of the point at issue, and is generically more appropriate to the discourse convention of an editorial than to that of a newspaper report.
> (Carter 1988: 12)

Such wordings are also common in educational documents, such as the Cox Report cited earlier. They imply the image of a sociolinguistic order based around shared norms of appropriateness, a misrepresentation of sociolinguistic realities as I have argued above. But I have suggested that such an image embodies a hegemonic political project. That is why using 'appropriateness' in this way is ideological: it places the analyst inside the hegemonic project, so to speak; it puts linguistics (sociolinguistics, educational linguistics) in the position of helping to normalize and legitimize a politically partisan representation, and turns a social scientific discipline into a resource for hegemonic struggle. I hasten to add that there is no implication whatsoever of conscious connivance on the part of analysts: the processes whereby people come to be ideologically coopted are generally unconscious ones which none of us are immune from.

Let me now sum up the second part of this paper. I have criticized appropriateness models of language variation on two connected grounds. First, because they project an idealized image of the sociolinguistic order which is hopelessly at odds with the indeterminacies, unevennesses, diversity, tensions and struggle of real sociolinguistic orders, such as that of modern Britain. Second, because they are ideological. That is, in projecting this idealized image of the sociolinguistic order they are also projecting a hegemonic objective and ideal. This second criticism raises a more general issue: thinking and theorizing about language, as Crowley (1989) for example shows in the case of 'history of the language' as a linguistic subdiscipline in Britain, should be open to assessment in its political context – in terms of how it relates to, is shaped by, and helps shape, wider processes of hegemonic struggle.

CONCLUSION: APPROPRIATENESS AND CRITICAL LANGUAGE AWARENESS

Appropriateness models of language variation are widespread, and often have the status of common sense in the theory and practice of language education. They are a major obstacle to the spread of critical language awareness programmes of the sort advocated in this book, which is why the critique of appropriateness is an important issue here. The view of critical language awareness some of us have put forward (Clark *et al.* 1990, 1991) stresses the mutually reinforcing development of critical understanding of the sociolinguistic order, and practice, including the creative practice of probing and shifting existing conventions. Appropriateness models block a critical understanding by ideologically collapsing political projects and actual practices, and they block a creative and critical language practice by foregrounding normativity and training in appropriate behaviour. As we have argued elsewhere (Fairclough and Ivanic 1989), there is a tendency (e.g. in the Kingman and Cox Reports) for creativity in language practice to be ghettoized in parts of the English syllabus dealing with teaching of literature, while non-literary language practice is overwhelmingly construed in terms of appropriateness – 'getting it right'.

This does not mean that the concept of appropriateness has no place in a CLA programme. On the contrary, it is important for learners to scrutinize doctrines of and attitudes towards sociolinguistic practice: they are part of what such a programme should make learners aware of. Judgements on the basis of appropriateness can be assessed in the light of their own sociolinguistic experience, including experience of inequalities between language varieties and constraints upon some of them. Judgements on the basis of appropriateness can also be evaluated in terms of their social genesis and social functions – recall the account in terms of hegemony I gave above. It is also crucially important that learners' own linguistic practice should be informed by estimates of the possibilities, risks and costs of going against dominant judgements of appropriate usage. Learners should, for example, have a picture of dominant judgements of when standard English is appropriate, but also of how widely such judgements are shared and followed in practice. And they should be encouraged to develop the ability to use standard English in conventional ways when they judge it to be necessary to do so, because they will be disadvantaged if they do not develop that ability. At the same time, they should be encouraged to see their own relationships and struggles as members of various communities as continuous with the relationships and struggles out of which the sociolinguistic practices, doctrines and attitudes of their speech community have been generated. And to see that they contribute through their own practice to the shaping and reshaping of the sociolinguistic order – to reproducing it or transforming it. And to appreciate the possibility, advantages, and risks of critical, creative and emancipatory practice as speakers and writers, and as critical readers and listeners, using for example other languages and dialects for the prestigious purposes and contexts where standard English is generally said to be appropriate. Critical language awareness, in other words, should not push leaners into oppositional practices which condemn them to disadvantage and marginalization; it should equip them with the capacities and understanding which are preconditions for meaningful choice and effective citizenship in the domain of language.

ACKNOWLEDGEMENT

I would like to thank Romy Clark for her helpful comments on this paper.

Bibliography and references

Abercrombie, N., Hill, S. and Turner, B. (1980) *The Dominant Ideology Thesis.* London: Routledge.

Althusser, L. (1971) Ideology and ideological state apparatuses, *Lenin and Philosophy and other Essays.* New Left Books.

Argyle, M. (1978) *The psychology of interpersonal behaviour* (3rd edn). Harmondsworth: Penguin.

Atkinson, J. and Drew, P. (1979) *Order in court.* London: Macmillan.

Austin, J. (1962) *How to Do Things with Words.* London: Oxford University Press.

Bakhtin, M. (1981) *The Dialogical Imagination.* University of Texas Press.

Bakhtin, M. (1986) *Speech Genres and Other Late Essays.* University of Texas Press.

Barnes, D. (1988) The politics of oracy. In M. MacLure *et al.* (eds) *Oracy Matters.* Milton Keynes: Open University Press.

Barthes, R. (1977) Introduction to the Structural Analysis of Narratives, *Image, Music, Text.* Selected and trans. Stephen Heath. London: Fontana.

Beck, U. (1992) *The Risk Society: Towards a Different Modernity.* London: Sage.

Bell, A. (1991) *The Language of News Media.* Oxford: Blackwell.

Bell, D. (1976) *The Cultural Contradictions of Capitalism.* Heinemann.

Benson, D. and Hughes, J. A. (1983) *The perspective of ethnomethodology.* London/New York: Longman.

Bernstein, B. (1975) *Class, Codes and Control 3: Towards a Theory of Educational Transmissions.* London: Routledge.

Bernstein, B. (1982) Class, modalities and cultural reproduction: a model. In M. Apple (ed.) *Cultural and economic reproduction in education.* Routledge.

Bernstein, B. (1990) *The Structuring of Pedagogic Discourse.* London: Routledge.

Billig, M. (1990) Stacking the Cards of Ideology: The History of the *Sun Souvenir Royal Album, Discourse & Society* 1(1): 17–37.

Billig, M. and Condor, S. *et al.* (1988) *Ideological Dilemmas.* Sage Publications.

Birch, D. and O'Toole, M. (1988) *Functions of style.* London: Frances Pinter.

Boden, D. and Zimmerman, D. (1991) *Talk and Social Structure.* Cambridge: Polity Press.

Bourdieu, P. (1977) *Outline of a Theory of Practice.* Cambridge: CUP.

Bourdieu, P. (1984) *Distinction: a Social Critique of the Judgement of Taste.* Translated R. Nice. London: Routledge.

Bourdieu, P. (1991) *Language and Symbolic Power.* Cambridge: Polity Press.

Bourne, J. (1992) PhD Thesis University of Southampton.

Brown, G. and Yule, G. (1983) *Discourse analysis.* Cambridge/London/New York: Cambridge University Press.

Brown, P. and Levinson, S. (1978) Universals of language usage: politeness phenomena. In E. Goody (ed.) 1978, pp. 56–324.

Brunsdon, C. (1990) Television: aesthetics and audiences. In P. Melancamp (ed.) *Logics of Television.* Indiana University Press.

Buci-Glucksmann, C. (1980) *Gramsci and the state.* Lawrence & Wishart.

Callinicos, A. (1987) *Making History.* Cambridge: Polity Press.

Cameron, D. (1985) *Feminism and Linguistic Theory.* London: Macmillan.

Candlin, C. N. (1975) *The communicative teaching of English.* London: Longman.

Candlin, C. and Lucas, J. (1986) Interpretation and explanation in discourse: modes of 'advising' in family planning. In Ensink, T. (ed.) *Discourse Analysis and Public Life.* Foris Publications.

Cardiff, D. (1980) The serious and the popular: aspects of the evolution of style in radio talk 1928–1939, *Media Culture & Society* 2, (1).

Carter, R. (1988) Front pages: lexis, style, and newspaper reports. In M. Ghadessy (ed.) *Registers of written English.* London: Pinter Publications.

Chilton, P. (1990) Politeness, Politics and Diplomacy, *Discourse & Society* 1(2): 201–24.

Chomsky, N. (1965) *Aspects of the theory of grammar.* MIT Press.

Cicourel, A. V. (1976) *The social organisation of juvenile justice.* London: Heinemann [1968].

Clark, R. (1992) Principles and practice of CLA in the classroom. In Fairclough, N. (ed.) *Critical Language Awareness.* London: Longman.

Clark, R., Constantinou, C., Cottey, A. and Yeoh, O. C. (1990) Rights and obligations in student writing. In Clark, R *et al.* (eds) *Language and Power: Proceedings of the BAAL Annual Meeting, Lancaster 1989.* London: CILT.

Clark, R. and Ivanic, R. (1992) Consciousness-raising about the writing process. In Garrett, P. and James, C. (eds) *Language Awareness.* London: Longman.

Clark, R., Fairclough, N., Ivanic, R. and Martin-Jones, M. (1990) Critical Language Awareness Part I: A Critical Review of Three Current Approaches to Language Awareness, *Language and Education* 4: 249–60.

Clark, R., Fairclough, N. Ivanic, R. and Martin-Jones, M. (1991) Critical Language Awareness Part II: Towards Critical Alternatives, *Language and Education* 5: 41–54.

Cole, P. and Morgan, J. (eds) (1975) *Syntax and semantics 3: Speech acts.* New York: Academic Press.

Conein, B. *et al.* (1981) *Matérialités discursives.* Lille, France, Presses Universitaires de Lille.

Connerton, P. (ed.) (1976) *Critical sociology: selected readings.* Harmondsworth: Penguin Books.

Coulthard, M. and Montgomery, M. (eds) (1981) *Studies in discourse analysis.* London: Routledge and Kegan Paul.

Courtine, J-J. and Marandin, J-M. (1981) Quel objet pour l'analyse de discours? In Conein (1981).

Coward, R. and Ellis, J. (1977) *Language and materialism: developments in semiology and the theory of the subject.* London/Henley/Boston: Routledge and Kegan Paul.

Crowley, T. (1989) *The politics of language.* Macmillan.

Davis, K. (1988) *Power Under the Microscope: Toward a Grounded Theory of Gender Relations in Medical Encounters.* Dordrecht: Foris.

Department of Education and Science (DES) (1988) *Report of the Committee of Inquiry into the Teaching of English Language.* London: HMSO (Kingman Report).

Department of Education and Science (1989) *English for Ages 5 to 16* HMSO (Cox Report).

Dews, P. (1988) *Logics of Disintegration.* Verso.

Doughty, P., Pearce, J. and Thornton, G. (1971) *Language in Use.* London: Edward Arnold.

Downing, J. (1990) US Media Discourse in South Africa: The development of a Situation model, *Discourse & Society* 1(1): 39–60.

Drew, P. and Heritage, J. (1992) *Talk at Work.* Cambridge: Cambridge University Press.

Dreyfus, H. and Rabinow, P. (1982) *Michel Foucault: beyond structuralism and hermeneutics.* Harvester Press.

Eagleton, T. (1991) *Ideology.* Verso.

Edmondson, W. (1981) *Spoken discourse: a model for analysis.* London/New York: Longman.

Ellis, J. and Ure, J. (eds) (1982) *Register Range and Change: International Journal of the Sociology of Language* 35.

Engels, F. (1976) *Anti-Dühring.* Peking: Foreign Languages Press. [1877–1878]

Fairclough, N. L. (1982) Review of Bolinger, Language – the loaded weapon. *Language in Society* 11. 110–20.

Fairclough, N. L. (1985) Critical and descriptive goals in discourse analysis. *Journal of Pragmatics* 9, 739–63.

Fairclough, N. (1988) Register, power and sociosemantic change. In Birch and O'Toole, *Functions of style.* London: Francis Pinter.

Fairclough, N. (1989) *Language and Power.* London: Longman.

Fairclough, N. (1989a) Michel Foucault and the analysis of discourse, *Centre for Language in Social Life Research Paper* 10. Lancaster University.

Fairclough, N. (1989b) Language and ideology, *English Language Research Journal* 3: 9–27.

Fairclough, N. (1990) Critical Linguistics, 'New Times', and Language Education. In R. Clark *et al.* (eds) *Language and Power: Papers from 22nd Annual Meeting of the British Association of Applied Linguistics.* London: CILT.

Fairclough, N. (1992a) *Discourse and Social Change.* Cambridge: Polity Press.

Fairclough, N. (ed.) (1992b) *Critical Language Awareness.* London: Longman.

Fairclough, N. (1992c) Review of B. Torode (ed.) *Text and Talk as Social Practice Sociolinguistics,* 18, 144–50.

Fairclough, N. (1993) Critical discourse analysis and the marketisation of public discourse: the universities *Discourse & Society,* 4, 133–68.

Fairclough, N. (1994) Conversationalisation of public discourse and the authority of the consumer. In R. Keat, N. Whiteley and N. Abercrombie (eds) *The Authority of the Consumer.* Routledge, 253–68.

Fairclough, N. (forthcoming) *Media and Language.* Edward Arnold.

Fairclough, N. and Ivanic, R. (1989) Language education or language training? A critique of the Kingman Model of English language. In Bourne, J. and Bloor, T. (eds) *The Kingman Report.* Committee for Linguistics In Education (CLIE).

Featherstone, M. (1991) *Consumer Culture and Postmodernism.* Sage.

Firth, J. R. (1957) *Papers in Linguistics 1934–1951.* London/New York/Toronto: Oxford University Press.

Fisher, S. (1991) A Discourse of the Social: Medical Talk/Power Talk/Oppositional Talk?, *Discourse & Society* 2(2): 157–82.

Fishman, J. A. (1972) The relationship between micro- and macro-sociolinguistics in the study of who speaks what language to whom and when. In: J. B. Pride and J. Holmes (eds) *Sociolinguistics.* Harmondsworth: Penguin Books, pp. 15–34.

Forgacs, D. (1988) *A Gramsci Reader.* Lawrence & Wishart.

Foucault, M. (1971) *L'ordre du discours.* Paris, Gallimard.

Foucault, M. (1972) *Archaeology of Knowledge.* Tavistock Publications.

Foucault, M. (1979) *Discipline and punish: the birth of the prison.* Translated by A. Sheridan. Harmondsworth: Penguin Books. [1975]

Foucault, M. (1981) *History of sexuality,* Vol. 1, Penguin Books.

Foucault, M. (1984) The order of discourse. In Shapiro, M. (ed.) *Language and politics.* Blackwell.

Fowler, R. (1991) *Language in the News.* London: Routledge.

Fowler, R., Hodge, B., Kress, G. and Trew, T. (1979) *Language and control.* London/Boston/Henley: Routledge and Kegan Paul.

Fowler, R. and Kress, G. (1979) Rules and regulations. In Fowler *et al.* (eds) 1979.

Fraser, L. (1986) Where? What? and How? Awkward questions in the theory of ideology, Language and Politics Working Paper 1986. (Available from Language and Politics, Centre for Language in Social Life, Department of Linguistics, University of Lancaster).

Fraser, N. (1989) *Unruly Practices.* Cambridge: Polity Press.

Freire, P. (1985) *The Politics of Education.* London: Macmillan.

Frow, J. (1985) Discourse and power, *Economy and society,* 14.

Further Education Unit (1987) *Relevance flexibility and competence.* HMSO.

Giddens, A. (1976) *New rules of the sociological method: a positive critique of interpretative sociologies.* London: Hutchinson.

Giddens, A. (1981) Agency, institution, and time-space analysis. In: K. Knorr-Cetina and A. V. Cicourel (eds) *Advances in social theory and methodology: towards an integration of micro- and macro-sociologies.* Boston/London/Henley: Routledge and Kegan Paul, pp. 161–74.

Giddens, A. (1984) *The Constitution of Society.* Cambridge: Polity Press.

Giddens, A. (1991) *Modernity and Self-Identity.* Cambridge: Polity Press.

Giroux, H. (1983) *Theory and Resistance in Education: A Pedagogy for the Opposition.* New York: Heinemann.

Givón, T. (1979) *On Understanding Grammar.* New York: Academic Press.

Goffman, E. (1981) Footing. In *Forms of Talk.* Oxford: Blackwell.

Goody, E. (ed.) (1978) *Questions and politeness.* London/New York/Melbourne: Cambride University Press.

Gramsci, A. (1971) *Selections from the prison notebooks,* edited and translated Q.

Hoare and G. Nowell Smith, Lawrence & Wishart.

Gregory, M. and Carroll, S. (1978) *Language and Situation: Language Varieties and Their Social Contexts.* London: Routledge.

Grice, H. P. (1975) Logic and conversation. In P. Cole and J. Morgan (eds) 1975, pp. 41–58.

Haberland, H. and Mey, J. L. (1977) Editorial: Linguistics and pragmatics. *Journal of Pragmatics* 1: 1–12.

Habermas, J. (1984) *The theory of communicative action*, vol. 1. Heinemann.

Habermas, J. (1989) *The Structural Transformation of the Public Sphere.* Polity Press.

Hacker, K., Coste, T. G., Kamm, D. F. and Bybee, C. R. (1991) Oppositional Readings of Network Television News: Viewer Deconstruction, *Discourse & Society* 2(2): 183–202.

Hall, S. (1982) The rediscovery of 'ideology': return of the repressed in media studies. In M. Gurevitch, T. Bennet, J. Curran and J. Woollacott (eds) *Culture, society and the media.* London/New York: Methuen, pp. 56–90.

Hall, S. (1988) The toad in the garden: thatcherism among the theorists. In C. Nelson and L. Grossberg (eds), *Marxism and the interpretation of culture.* Macmillan Education.

Hall, S., Critcher, C., Jefferson, T., Clarke, J. and Roberts, B. (1978) *Policing the Crisis.* London: Macmillan.

Halliday, M. A. K. (1978) *Language as social semiotic: the social interpretation of language and meaning.* London: Edward Arnold.

Halliday, M. (1985) *An Introduction to Functional Grammar.* London: Edward Arnold.

Halliday, M. A. K. and Hasan, R. (1976) *Cohesion in English.* London: Longman.

Halliday, M. and Hasan, R. (1985) *Language, Context and Text.* Geelong, Victoria: Deakin University Press.

Halloran, J., Elliott, P. and Murdock, G. (1970) *Demonstrations and Communication.* Harmondsworth: Penguin Books.

Haroche, C., Henry, P. and Pecheux, M. (1971) 'La sémantique et la coupure saussurienne: langue, langage, discours', *Langages* 24.

Hartley, J. (1982) *Understanding News.* London: Methuen.

Hasan, R. (1973) Code, register and social dialect. In B. Bernstein (ed.) *Class, Codes and Control 2: Applied Studies Towards a Sociology of Language.* London: Routledge.

Hawkins, E. (1984) *Awareness of Language: An Introduction.* Cambridge University Press.

Hawkins, E. (ed.) (1985) *Awareness of language series.* Cambridge University Press.

Henriques, J. *et al.* (1984) *Changing the subject.* Methuen.

Heritage, J. C. and Watson, D. R. (1979) Formulations as conversational objects. In G. Psathas (ed.) *Everyday Language: Studies in Ethnomethodology.* New York: Irvington.

Herman, E. and Chomsky, N. (1988) *Manufacturing Consent: the Political Economy of the Mass Media.* Pantheon Books.

Hewitt, T. (1989) The new oracy: another critical glance. Paper delivered to the British Association for Applied Linguistics annual meeting, Lancaster.

HMSO (1985) Fifth Report From the Home Affairs Committee, London.

Hobsbawm, E. (1977) Gramsci and political theory, *Marxism Today*, July 1977.

Hochschild, A. R. (1983) *The Managed Heart*. Berkeley: University of California Press.

Hodge, R. (1984) Historical semantics and the meaning of 'discourse', *Australian Journal of Cultural Studies* 2: 124–30.

Hodge, R. and Kress, G. (1988) *Social Semiotics*. Cambridge: Polity Press.

Hymes, D. (1972) Models of the interaction of language and social life. In Gumperz, J. and Hymes, D. (eds) *Directions in sociolinguistics*. New York: Holt, Rinehart and Winston, pp. 35–71.

Hymes, D. (1972) On communicative competence. In Pride, J. and Holmes, J. *Sociolinguistics*. Harmondsworth: Penguin.

Ivanic, R. and Roach, D. (1990) Academic writing, power and disguise. In Clark, N. *et al.* (eds) 1990.

Ivanic, R. and Simpson, J. (1992) Who's who in academic writing? In Fairclough, N. (ed.) 1992b.

Jameson, F. (1984) Postmodernism, or the cultural logical of capitalism. *New left review* 146.

Janks, H. and Ivanic, R. (1992) Critical langue awareness and emancipatory discourse. In Fairclough, N. (ed.) 1992b.

Jordanidou, A. (1990) *Read me the old news: a study of discourse practice*. Lancaster University PhD Thesis.

Keat, R. and Abercrombie, N. (1990) *Enterprise Culture*. London: Routledge.

Keat, R., Whiteley, N. and Abercrombie, N. (1994) *The Authority of the Consumer*. London: Routledge.

Kress, G. (1988) *Linguistic Processes in Sociocultural Practice*. Oxford: Oxford University Press.

Kress, G. (1993) Cultural considerations in linguistic description. In D. Graddol *et al.* (eds) *Language and Culture*. (Papers from the 1991 Annual Meeting of the British Association of Applied Linguistics) Multilingual Matters.

Kress, G. and Hodge, B. (1979) *Language as ideology*. London/Boston/Henley: Routledge and Kegan Paul.

Kress, G. and Threadgold, T. (1988) Towards a social theory of genre, *Southern Review* 21, 215–43.

Kress, G. and van Leeuwen, T. (1990) *Reading Images*. Deakin University Press.

Kress, G. and van Leeuwen, T. (forthcoming) *Reading Images* (revised edition). London: Routledge.

Kristeva, J. (1980) Word, dialogue and novel. In Kristeva, J. *Desire in language*. Oxford: Blackwell.

Labov, W. and Fanshel, D. (1977) *Therapeutic Discourse*. New York: Academic Press.

Labov, W. and Waletzky, J. (1967) Narrative analysis: oral versions of personal experience. In J. Helms (ed.) *Essays on the Verbal and Visual Arts*. University of Washington Press.

Laclau, E. (1979) *Politics and Ideology in Marxist Theory*. London: Verso.

Laclau, E. and Mouffe, C. (1985) *Hegemony and socialist strategy*. London: Verso.

Larrain, J. (1979) *The concept of ideology*. Hutchinson.

Lash, S. (1990) *The Sociology of Postmodernism*. London: Routledge.

Leckie-Tarry, H. (forthcoming) *Register*. London: Pinter Publications.

Leech, G. N. (1974) *Semantics*. Harmondsworth: Harmondsworth: Penguin.

Leech, G. N. (1983) *Principles of pragmatics*. London/New York: Longman.

Leech, G. N. and Short, M. (1981) *Style in Fiction*. London: Longman.

Leonard, S. A. (1925) *The doctrine of correctness in English language and literature*. University of Wisconsin Press.

Levinson, S. (1979) Activity types and language, *Linguistics* 17: 365–99.

Levinson, S. (1983) *Pragmatics*. Cambridge/London/New York: Cambridge University Press.

Lyotard, J-F. (1988) *The Differed: Phrases in Dispute*. Manchester University Press.

Liebes, T. and Ribak, R. (1991) A Mother's Battle against TV News: a Case Study of Political Socialization, *Discourse & Society* 2(2): 203–22.

McHale, B. (1978) Free indirect speech: a survey of recent accounts, *Poetics and the Theory of Literature* 3, 249–87.

Maingueneau, D. (1987) *Nouvelles tendences en analyse du discours*. Hachette.

Maldidier, D. (1984) Michel Pêcheux: une tension passionnée entre la langue et l'histoire. In *Histoire et linguistique*, Éditions de la Maison des Sciences de l'Homme, Paris.

Malinowski, B. (1923) The Problem of Meaning in Primitive Languages. Supplement 1. In C. Ogden and I. A. Richards *The Meaning of Meaning*. New York: Harcourt Brace.

Mandel, E. (1978) *Late Capitalism*. London: New Left Books.

Margerison, C. (1987) *Conversation Control Skills for Managers*. London: Mercury Books.

Martin, J. (1989) *Factual Writing*. Oxford: Oxford University Press.

Marx, K. (1974) *Capital* v 1. Lawrence & Wishart.

Marx, K. and Engels, F. (1976) (1845–6) The German ideology, *Collected Works* v 5. Lawrence & Wishart.

Mehan, H., Nathanson, C. and Skelly, J. (1990) Nuclear Discourse in the 1980s: The Unravelling Conventions of the Cold War, *Discourse & Society* 1(2): 134–65.

Mey, J. (1985) *Whose language? a study in linguistic pragmatics*. John Benjamins.

Michael, M. (1991) Discourse of Danger and Dangerous Discourses: Patrolling the Borders of Science, Nature and Society, *Discourse & Society* 2(1): 5–28.

Mishler, E. (1984) *The Discourse of Medicine: Dialectics of Medical Interviews*. Norwood, NJ: Ablex.

Morley, D. (1980) *The 'Nationwide' Audience*. BFI.

Morley, D. (1983) Cultural transformations: the politics of resistance. In H. Davis and P. Walton (eds) *Language, image, media*. Blackwell.

National Congress on Language in Education (NCLE) (1985) *Language Awareness*. CILT.

Nietzsche, F. (1990) (1886) *Beyond Good and Evil*. Penguin.

Norris, C. (1992) *Uncritical Theory*. Lawrence & Wishart.

O'Barr, W. (1982) *Linguistic evidence: language, power and strategy in the courtroom*. New York: Academic Press.

Pêcheux, M. (1982) *Language, semantics and ideology: stating the obvious*. London and Basingstoke: Macmillan. (Translated by H. Nagpal.) [1975]

Pêcheux, M. (1988) Discourse: structure or event? In Nelson, C. and Grossberg, L. *Marxism and the Interpretation of Culture*. Macmillan.

Pilger, J. (1992) *Distant Voices*. Vintage

Poster, M. (ed.) (1988) *Jean Baudrillard: Selected Writings*. Polity Press.

Potter, J. and Wetherell, M. (1987) *Discourse and Social Psychology*. Sage.

Pratt, M. L. (1981) The ideology of speech act theory. *Centrum* (new series) 1: 5–18.

Quirk, R., Greenbaum, S., Leech, G. N. and Svartvik, J. (1972) *A Grammar of Contemporary English*. London: Longman.

Rose, N. (1989) Governing the enterprising self. Paper delivered at conference on Values of the Enterprise Culture, Centre for the Study of Cultural Values, Lancaster University.

Rose, N. and Miller, R. (1989) Rethinking the state: governing economic, social and personal life (MS).

Sacks, H., Schegloff, E. A. and Jefferson, G. (1978) A simplest systematics for the organisation of turn-taking in conversation. In J. Schenkein (ed.) (1978) pp. 7–55. [1974]

Saussure, F. de (1966) *Course in general linguistics*. New York/Toronto/London: McGraw Hill. (Translated by W. Baskin.) [1916]

Scannell, P. (1991) *Broadcast Talk*. Sage.

Scannell, P. (1992) Public service broadcasting and modern public life. In P. Scannell *et al.* (eds) *Culture and Power*. Sage.

Schank, R. and Abelson, H. (1977) *Scripts, plans, goals and understanding*. New York: Lawrence Erlbaum.

Schegloff, E. (1992) *On talk and its institutional occasions*. Drew and Heritage 101–34.

Schenkein, J. (ed.) (1978) *Studies in the organization of conversational interaction*. New York: Academic Press.

Seidel, G. (1990) 'Thank God I Said No to AIDS': On the Changing Discourse of AIDS in Uganda, *Discourse & Society* 1(1): 61–84.

Selden, R. (1991) The Rhetoric of Enterprise. In R. Keat and N. Abercrombie (eds), *Enterprise Culture*. London: Routledge.

Sinclair, J. McH. and Coulthard, R. M. (1975) *Towards an analysis of discourse: the English used by teachers and pupils*. London: Oxford University Press.

Slembrouck, S. (1992) *The Study of Language Use in its Societal Context: Pragmatics and the Representation of Parliamentary Debates in Newspaper Discourse*. PhD Thesis, Lancaster University.

Sorensen, J. (1991) Mass Media and Discourse on Famine in the Horn of Africa, *Discourse & Society* 2(2): 223–42.

Spencer, J. and Gregory, M. J. (1964) An approach to the study of style. In N. E. Enkvist *et al.*, *Linguistics and Style*. Oxford: Oxford University Press.

Stubbs, M. (1983) *Discourse analysis: the sociolinguistic analysis of natural language*. Oxford: Basil Blackwell.

Talbot, M. (1990) *Language, Intertextuality and Subjectivity: Voices and the Construction of Consumer Femininity*, PhD Thesis, Lancaster University.

Tannen, D. (1986) *That's Not What I Meant!: How Conversational Style Makes or Breaks Your Relationship with Others*. New York: William Morrow.

Tannen, D. (1991) *You Just Don't Understand: Women and Men in Conversation*. London: Virago.

Tannen, D. and Wallat, C. (1986) Medical professionals and parents: a linguistic analysis of communication across contexts, *Language in Society* 15: 295–312.

Taylor, C. (1986) Foucault on Discourse and Truth. In D. C. Hoy (ed.) *Foucault: A Critical Reader.* Oxford: Blackwell.

ten Have, P. (1989) The consultation as a genre. In B. Torode (ed.) *Talk and text as social practice.* Foris.

Therborn, G. (1980) *The ideology of power and the power of ideology.* London: Verso.

Thibault, P. (1991) *Social Semiotics as Praxis.* University of Minnesota Press.

Thompson, J. B. (1984) *Studies in the theory of ideology.* Cambridge: Polity Press.

Thompson, J. B. (1990) *Ideology and Modern Culture.* Cambridge: Polity Press.

Thorne, N., Kramarae, C. and Henley, N. (1983) *Language Gender and Society.* London: Newbury House.

Threadgold, T. (1989) Talking about genre: ideologies and incompatible discourses, *Cultural Studies* 3 (1) 1989.

Tolson, A. (1991) Televized Chat and the Synthetic Personality. In P. Scannell (ed.) *Broadcast Talk.* London: Sage.

Ullah, P. (1990) Rhetoric and Ideology in Social Identification: The Case of Second Generation Irish Youths, *Discourse & Society* 1(2): 167–88.

Ure, J. (1982) Introduction: approaches to the study of register range. In Ellis and Ure (eds) 1982.

van Dijk, T. (1987) *Handbook of Discourse Analysis,* 4 vols. New York: Academic Press.

van Dijk, T. (1988) *News as Discourse.* Erlbaum.

van Dijk, T. (1990) *Discourse & Society:* A New Journal for a New Research Focus, *Discourse & Society* 1(1): 5–16.

van Leeuwen, T. (1987) Generic strategies in press journalism, *Australian Review of Applied Linguistics* 10(2): 199–220.

van Leeuwen, T. (1993) Genre and field in critical discourse analysis, *Discourse & Society* 4(2): 193–223.

Volosinov, V. I. (1973) *Marxism and the Philosophy of Language.* New York: Seminar Press.

WAUDAG (1990) The Rhetorical Construction of a President, *Discourse & Society* 1(2): 189–200.

Wernick, A. (1991) *Promotional Culture.* London: Sage.

West, C. and Zimmerman, D. E. (1983) Small insults: a study of interruptions in cross-sex conversations between unacquainted persons. In Thorne *et al.* (eds) 1983.

West, C. (1990) Not Just 'Doctor's Orders': Directive-response Sequences in Patients' Visits to Women and Men Physicians, *Discourse & Society* 1(1): 83–112.

Williams, G. (forthcoming) *French Discourse Analysis.* Routledge.

Williams, R. (1976) *Keywords.* London: Fontana.

Williams, R. (1981) *Culture.* London: Fontana.

Winograd, T. (1982) *Language as a cognitive process,* Vol. 1. London: Addison-Wesley.

Wodak, R. (1991) Turning the Tables: Antisemitic Discourse in Post-war

Austria, *Discourse & Society* 2(1): 65–83.

Wodak, R. *et al.* (1990) *'Wir Sind Alle Unschuldige Tater'. Diskurshistorische Studien zum Nachkriegsantisemitismus.* Frankfurt-am-Main: Suhrkamp.

Wouters, C. (1986) Formalization and Informalization: Changing Tension Balances in Civilizing Processes, *Theory, Culture & Society* 3(2): 1–18.

Yankah, K. (1991) Oratory in Akan Society, *Discourse & Society* 2(1): 47–64.

Young, Lord (1987) People, enterprise and jobs. Speech to the National Economic Development Council on its 25th anniversary, 29 April.

Zima, P. (1981) Les mécanismes discursifs de l'idéologie, *Revue de l'institut de sociologie (Solvay)* 4.

Index